AN AMERICAN SCREAM

AN AMERICAN SCREAM

A Docu-Novel

LAIRD SMITH

To order additional copies of this book, contact:
Xlibris Corporation
1-888-795-4274
www.Xlibris.com
Orders@Xlibris.com
37885

Contents

Foreword 13

The Sessions 19

The Journal 169

Retrospective 203

DEDICATION

This book is dedicated to those people who, even though they suffer, try to do the right thing, those who don't fall prey to the seductions everywhere to give in: to the ones who will survive what is coming by a peaceful yet determined effort to make sure their presence on this earth reflects a life worth living.

An American Scream

A Docu-Novel

In the voice of a Senior citizen *An American Scream* analyzes a woman's life through psychotherapy sessions, a journal of her experiences after therapy, and an essay she writes about how the U.S. has changed. With clarity about how much she has been affected by the changes in sexual mores, the Vietnam war, technology, media accountability, consumerism, growing old, the recent loss of basic freedoms and the true cost of the standard of living in the U.S., there emerges a profile of America the Beautiful being slowly torn apart from its most basic and treasured qualities.

The protagonist, named Susan, is educated, well-spoken and piercingly honest about what has brought her to a therapist. After therapy she commits to righting a wrong in her family that her own denial made possible. Then Susan also stops denying negative changes in the U. S. and writes an essay about major historical events affecting the country and her life, the life of an American threatened by more change than has ever before been confronted by Mankind.

Serving as the Foreword to the book, the short story *Retribution* pinpoints the nexus of what is wrong with U.S. culture. On the edge of madness the narrator takes you through a surreal journey to cure the disease that infests the buzzing metropolis of Los Angeles where the dream is to have what your neighbor has with the means of obtaining it being the degradation of one's soul and values.

Scream reflects the American condition today where millions are living paycheck to paycheck while adjusting to an escalation of violence and lack of ethics, trying to find inner peace and safety for their families, confronting a consumer ethos getting harder to actualize, and not falling backward into the increasing gap between rich and poor in a society gone mad with greed and selfishness.

Lairdsmith@comcast.net
Jason1rader@yahoo.com

FOREWORD

In the next few pages is a short story that captures a sense of revulsion ending in a surreal warning about the disintegration of our society. Rader says in words what Salvador Dali said with brushes in "Soft Watch at the First Moment of Explosion".

Laird Smith
August 2007

RETRIBUTION

By Jason Rader

My mind begins to wander, stronger as I come closer to the woman on the traffic island. The questions come oozing in as they did the previous three days. How can she just sit there and endure the spilling mean streaks of the Los Angeles people? Sneering yuppies, degrading gang-bangers, the ridicules of children and the occasional tail pipes of jacked up trucks and SUVs spewing typical exhaust directly into the face of this thin, stringy, black-haired woman. Can it be that this woman stands up at a certain time of day and escapes to her domicile only to return the next day to sit in the same exact position, slightly hunched over in her chair, in the same purple dress? The first day I thought she was a mannequin, some elaborate hoax set up on the island between the waves of traffic to conjure the laughter of mobile passers-by. I saw her blink the second day.

I rise an hour earlier this morning for my instincts tell me the extra time might be needed. This morning is particularly turbulent as was the night. Last night three gun shots rang out and one this morning. The shot this morning was close and I hear a couple screaming a few doors down from me. I leave and lock my front door to start what I envision will be an adventurous day. Three doors down from me I see the reason for the parents' cries. I pass by the open door and hardly glance at the recipient of the city's aggression in the form of exploded lead. I step over his lifeless legs and walk on. Work is calling.

That noxious feeling comes to me again, just another day in the 90 degree heat, the same stench in the air and same people chasing the same elusive dream. You see, the dream in Los Angeles is to have what your neighbor has. To obtain this dream means the degradation of your soul and values. The people who realize this to the fullest are the richest.

13

I hop into my 1990 Civic and out to the aggressive asphalt. Traffic is horrendous today and the freeway is extra thick with angry drivers. My stock radio pumps the latest testament of control in the form of Hip-Hop and I exit onto one of the busier streets of this decrepit city. Few cars are over two years old. Few cars are worth under $70k. Looking up I can't help but wonder about the scattered souls looking down at us from the high-rise buildings above. Ants we must be to them and I am of the lowliest. I deliver the mail at the Merker building. I am alive because I deliver mail quickly. Today I will be late. Today I will be fired. This is my choice. In many peoples' lives there comes a time when they will make an irrational decision. They will choose to make a seemingly wrong choice that turns out not to be wrong at all. For me this is certainly one of those days.

I am two blocks away now and I can barely see her stringy strands of hair briefly flowing upwards in the wind of some moving traffic. I wait as a 7 series BMW passes and I jet over behind it. "You fucking asshole," I hear as a man in a Cadillac almost has a coronary behind me. Thank God he doesn't have a gun. Three more lanes and I am where I need to be. I turn left into a Burger King parking lot and turn off my ignition directly across from the placid lady in her folding chair. My gaze is unbroken as our purpose begins to unfold.

The traffic is inching by slowly and I see a 65 Impala housing four gang-bangers. Compton Crips I assume, with their blue rags and tattooed necks. They laugh and spit while they pass and as they stop I am riddled with fear for the woman on the island. She makes no move as if a statue placed for the amusement of evil. They move on. A short time later I see a mother and her son in a giant, black SUV. The boy scrutinizes the woman with intense anticipation that he will reach her soon. They are three car lengths away now. Knock knock! I am startled by a homeless man tapping on my window. "Got any change?" I shake my head no. "Fuck you then!" He mutters then kicks my door and stumbles off. I turn my attention back to the woman again only to see the boy empty his drink onto her dress. It soaks one side of her and drips down the island curb. "Jesse, what the fuck, you got the side of my car dirty you little shit", his mother screams. "Wait till we get home, I'm gonna beat your ass".

The time has come. I reach for the door handle and step outside to breathe in what seems to be strangely different, stale smog. Not bothering to lock my door, I slam it closed. The sound echoes through the high-rise buildings like some shock wave and from that moment on the world becomes surreal. My body and soul shift from reality to a peaceful pseudo-reality dream state. I pay no attention to anyone as I make my way through the cars to reach her. Stepping up onto her curb I hear the anger of the motorists being thrown at me and it is dull to my senses. I look down at her and wait for some kind of movement or acknowledgment. Three minutes seem to pass and after all this time, all the time in these three days she moves. She sits up, straightens and tilts her head upward. She looks at me but her dirty, stringy black hair obscures her gaze. Slowly but precisely she stands as if her bones were not fused by the three days of agony and her muscles had not been atrophied. Without a word she takes a step off the curb and then another towards the sidewalk. Somehow there is now a straight path between the traffic and as she walks she seems to be unnoticed by the souls in the metal polluters. I follow her into an office building and she walks through the lobby as if she had been there many times before. We are standing in front of the elevator and the doors open. When we step inside I hear a voice, "Wait . . . I'm going up!" A man in a business suit steps inside. Immediately his attention is drawn to the woman and his face crinkles at the smell of her degradation. "Hey lady . . . do you need some change or a condom or something?" The man giggles at his own condemning wit. At the twelfth floor the elevator stops, the doors open and the man steps out. He glances back at me and laughs, "Man get your bitch home . . . or to a clinic." The doors close and then open up at the thirteenth floor.

Time slows now, grinding to a paranormally slow rate. She turns her head toward me and brushes the hair from her eyes. Black and lifeless they are. Her crackled lips separate and one scratchy word is released. "Peace." She turns her head forward and takes a few steps out of the elevator. Business. Phones blaring, keyboard punching, papers shuffling, cubicle visiting and ants running back and forth to make various deadlines. A woman walks in front of us, "It's almost 10:30 Bill, we don't have ten minutes!!" I start to wonder why so few people have noticed us. Then a man in a black suit asks, "Can I help you? Are you alright?" Staring directly forward the woman opens her mouth wide extending her neck muscles as if she is trying to fit a whole apple into her mouth. A shriek blasts from her lips shattering the windows and computer screens of the thirteenth floor and the man drops to his knees clenching his ears in agony. She never takes a breath. Blood begins trickling slowly from the ears of the other inaudible screaming drones, and death is reaching them one by one. Activity and frantic business excitement gives way to lifelessness and stillness. By the third minute the room is completely still while her shriek continues. Black pours from her mouth unto the floor discoloring all it touches. Like paint, this blackness begins to envelope all I see. All is black now except the building across from us. Overcome by panic I turn around to the elevator but choose the stairs for fear of where the metal box might take me. I race down the flights as fast as I can and by the fourth floor I can see the blackness above me coming. On the lobby floor I burst through the stairwell doors. Frantically I race toward the large glass doors leading to the outside. I see a reflection of the woman in a marble pillar as I pass. Grasping the door handle I glance back to see the black come through the stair well, then the elevator. It's coming faster now. "RUN . . . RUN!!" I envision myself screaming though I utter not a word. Like a squirrel evading a starving hawk I dash and jump as fast as I can to reach the chair she was sitting in for so long. The chair grinds the asphalt as I plant myself in it. I grasp the handles with all my might. Like black ink spilled onto paper it comes fast, covering everything connected to the ground. I see it freezing everything it touches. Like Sodom and Gomorrah people stop, solidified: many statues. Everything is turning black and I shut my eyes tight with fear.

I hear screaming, traffic and the bustling energy of fear giving way to my breathing. The pounding in my chest becomes louder with every second that passes until all I hear is peace and I convince myself to unstrain my squinting eyes. They open to take in the silent aftermath. All is black as far as I can see except for the orange-brown sky and a single flying bird and I stand to get a better view.

THE SESSIONS

Transcribed Tapes

Therapist's Comments and Questions Are in Boldface Type

SESSION ONE

Taos, New Mexico, 1998

Hi Susan, come on in and have a seat. Please just call me Bob. I've already gone over the paperwork you filled out so now what I'd like to do is get really clear on why you've come to see me. No rush. I've booked an hour and a half for this first session.

Nice to meet you, Bob. I'll settle into this snug barrel chair if you don't mind. Decaf from the White Dove didn't quite take away my inner chill from the 17 degrees below zero in Questa last night. Nice room, I could just sit in here alone and meditate for a long time but I know I've got to allow you into my thoughts to get the help that I apparently need.

Sometimes people aren't too sure why they want some therapy but you mentioned on the phone you needed help to decide whether or not to get a divorce after 10 years of legal separation. So, is that a correct statement of your goal in therapy?

Well, yes, that's one concrete goal but there are other ones too. To help explain why I'm thinking seriously about divorce, I've brought something I wrote with me today that pretty much gives a feel for what our marriage has been like and I wonder if you'd let me read it to you to get the ball rolling? His name is John by the way. It'll take about 15 minutes to read this.

Yeah, that's fine. Let's hear it.

I call this piece *Shades*. (Clearing her throat she begins to read.)

"If you leave him, I'll give you what you want," he said.

"What do I want?" I ask.

"Love," he replies.

My husband is sitting on the floor in front of me at 2 in the morning, cross-legged just one foot away, telling me to leave him, but in the third person.

He is absolutely someone else right now. A drunk someone. He won't remember this conversation tomorrow and he'll be as perplexed as I am now when he hears about it.

I'm sober.

All I can do is chuckle quietly at the quandary this exchange leaves me in, a frequent feeling since I fell in love with him. But this is new, this third person thing. So, is he two personalities in one skin? Is he gone and a demon is here now? Is he playing one of what he calls his "mind fuck" games? At least he's friendly. Often he can lapse into violence or totally unpredictable and outrageous behavior instantly.

I generally tip-toe very carefully when he's been drinking but suddenly I laugh out loud when a memory flashes through my mind of one of his past drunken behaviors. At the end of a night of partying, he had jumped onto a car in the bar parking lot and proceeded to mimic a monkey for an extensive period of time, quite well in fact. That memory folds into another one of him pretending to be a very vocal bull across the fence from a real one. After awhile the bull talked back to him without rancor.

My sudden laugh has caused him to finally take off his mirror shades, a frequent prop when he's been drinking. He's got a very skeptical and annoyed look on his face but he doesn't ask me why I laughed. He knows it's something he did. He's got that same look he had when he opened the passenger door as we traveled down a freeway one of the rare times I was driving and then said, "If I jump out will you jump out too?" He was obviously thinking about how Viking wives would immolate themselves on their dead husband's fiery biers. I didn't answer his question then. If I had said "Yes" it would've been a lie and to say "No" would've enraged him. I don't say anything now either.

Almost jumping out of that car was not long before he put a shotgun in his mouth at a friend's house and the cops were called. They took him to a locked psychiatric ward. By the time I could get in to see him he had worked one hand free from the restraints they had him in on a gurney in a small locked room with a barred window which his eyes ran over wildly seeking escape.

He's just looking at me in that way he has that makes me feel like a mouse being watched ravenously by a snake. Then he takes another big gulp of tequila which changes his face into a mask of stone. There's more tequila, in fact the worm is still in there.

Our eyes are locked but I'm thinking about one time when he missed the off-ramp to get onto another freeway to go home, even though I told him it was coming up, then he recognized his mistake and going at least 70 miles per hour he did a quick U turn on the freeway, bumping over the concrete median in order to go up the other side's on-ramp to proceed in exactly the right direction. That was one of the many times I had to close my eyes because I didn't want to see the inevitable wreck that somehow never happened. He only drove like this with me in the car when he was drunk.

Just have to wait this out. Leaving the room or even standing up would not be advisable actions right now. So, instead of worrying about what might happen, I search my mind for memories when I didn't have to close my eyes. What pops up is the night I wanted to eat at the Crab Cooker in Balboa. There was no left hand turn lane across from the eatery. Or rather, none for our side of the road. There was one lined with curbing on the other side of the road which he drove up the reverse of how it was supposed to be used, turned left, crossed over and parked. There was no opposing traffic. Illegal but not scary. Later, in line for the ferry he got bored and flipped a U suddenly. Have no idea how he did that with no room in front or behind us. Back then if you asked him what he was first he'd say "a driver" and then "an actor." That is, if he chose to answer you at all.

That night at Balboa we danced with total strangers on the promenade leading to the pier. We were on foot and they were on skates with a boom box. He always knew how long something like that could last and would exit us in time to prevent any trouble. I'm never in danger from anyone else but him when I'm with him.

He's touching me. The usual gentle tweak of a nipple because I'm facing him and sitting down or else he would have goosed me. He's not mad, well not angry anyway. The really hard part is that we are one. Went for physicals together one day and we had exactly the same heart rate and blood pressure readings. Now that's something. Symbiosis. Often called co-dependence now but maybe how a marriage is supposed to be really.

If only he didn't drink. I tried pouring it all out or hiding it in the dryer once. It's not all the time but sometimes his drinking is bad, very bad. When he goes out alone I can usually tell when it's going to be bad so I leave with the kids before he gets back. One night, when he found us gone, he pretty much destroyed the interior of our home. We all refer to that night as "the tornado". He shot a TV, shot a dresser, tore an antique secretary limb from limb, destroyed one of my grandmother's paintings, turned all the furniture upside down, broke the front room plate glass window, emptied the frig unceremoniously, and pulled an enormous plant out of its pot, among other things. He didn't remember it the next day but the destruction gave even him pause for thought.

It's interesting though that he didn't break even one mirror tile on a wall covered with them. Never known him to break a mirror on purpose and after accidentally breaking one during a move he announced we would have seven years of bad luck. He'll punch through glass though. Once he punched out most of the windows in a French door. As far as I'm concerned it's better than hitting me which has happened upon occasion too.

Now he's decided to recline on the floor but even though he's closed his eyes I know he won't pass out or go to sleep yet, that takes hours, maybe days. It may be a ruse anyway, he may be looking at me through eyelid slits. So, I just sit still and go on thinking about "the tornado". While we were all cleaning up after it, a fire started in a junk pile in the back yard. After putting it out before it spread to the neighborhood or our house, he told me, "I know how to do that, set a timed fire," the implication being he might have done so during "the tornado" but he couldn't remember. Always wondered what else might have happened during his blackouts because he generally insists on winning a pissing contest.

He had one such contest with his bookie Papa Bear. They went at it sitting across from one another at our glass top dining room table. Their tough guy exchanges got to the point that Papa Bear announced he could kill both of us if he wanted to before anyone could stop him. My husband quickly upended his wine glass, pushed it into the table so it broke leaving a jagged stem which he held by the base and, while pointing it at Papa Bear, said very quietly, "Think so?" That ended that and the bookie announced to me that my husband had balls the size of cantaloupes. He loved him for that. No one was drunk that time. When it was for real, I wasn't around but I might hear about it later from someone else, not him.

Once I secretly followed him but when he finally saw me, he ended it, came over to get me and we left. Just like that. He stopped the confrontation just by turning his back and walking slowly away from two guys who were screaming at him, "You can't leave!" while they stood apparently cemented to their assigned spots. Just before he saw me I had seen him bump into the rear of what looked like a circa 1930's cherry red Mercedes Sport Cabriolet with exterior chrome pipes on the body—don't remember what it was now but he pushed it into a wall, gently, on purpose. Then he sat there and waited. This hood guy and his bodyguard came running out, the latter sucker punching my husband before he could even get out of his car. Once out he just stood there and let them rave on. I heard him say, "Hey, you broke my glasses." As usual he had his shades on even though it was well after midnight. He loves cars and wouldn't really damage one like that. He was making a statement. Why is a long story that involves him being disenchanted with Ronald Reagan because of a fact he had heard from the car's owner that night and because the guy's woman had rudely driven that red car onto our front lawn earlier.

He's sitting up slowly. He always moves slowly until he moves fast and then it's so fast you can't see the motion, just feel the effects of it. He's more like a Doberman than a Pit Bull. He attacks quickly and doesn't hang on. He only sat up to take another swig of tequila out of a bottle that could hold milk for all the difference you can see on his face when he drinks. He listens and looks around carefully.

He's a Vietnam era vet. Worse, a pre-declared-war Vietnam era vet who operated out of Guam after being recruited at the age of 17. Not sure what he did but a Marine Sergeant who counseled us once told me, while my husband was in the bathroom, that he was probably a spook, maybe a "tunnel rat" and might be able to speak Laotian. He's a small guy physically but hard as a rock all over, except his testicles which are the normal size and firmness. Those are his only Achilles Heel so far as I know. He went to that counseling opportunity with me exactly one time. He was wearing his slippers. For years he wore them everywhere.

Always vigilant, pretty much always bored, never at peace, unable to relax while doing nothing physical most of the time except breathing, completely domineering, and he's absolutely unmanageable but nonetheless he makes me laugh a lot. That, the sex, his ability to really listen and cut to the chase, and his granite jaw are what keep me with him. And, of course, his blue, fathomless eyes.

He's already gotten what this third person of his told me he wanted tonight, more than once. But I come back. Maybe I won't some day but I'll always feel married to him. My mind's eye sees him as a burning oak tree and I'm the moth fatally attracted to the flames. Not sure how he sees me but one of the things he has said to me is, "You're my Tao."

He's also told me repeatedly that he makes people leave him before they finally abandon him. So far he hasn't succeeded in driving me away. Guess we're in a competition to see who can hold out the longest. Or to put it another way:

> *He and she set out one day*
> *to join forces,*
> *To help each other determine*
> *future courses.*
> *He was very hard and stern*
> *and judging;*
> *She was very soft, but firm*
> *and loving.*
> *Their lives once crossed could*
> *never be the same*
> *Because the Chess Master had them*
> *together in the game.*

When did you write that?

Recently, but all of it happened a long time ago, more than 25 years ago. There's more, much more.

You were right when you said it would give me a good picture of what you were faced with in your marriage to John. This is a first for me. No one has ever come in here before and read me something about their life. I am left wondering what is so different about right now that you're considering

finally getting a divorce, especially given the poem you recited which I'm assuming you also wrote.

I wrote the poem the year after we fell in love along with about 80 other ones. They just fell out of me. What's different now has to do with the fact I'm having trouble coping with the reality that our son is a recovering drug addict who, we just found out, has a mental illness that turns out to be the real problem. The drug stuff is actually self-medication we've been told. He was basically kicked out of a rehab and told, in my presence, that he's not a drug addict but needs psychiatric help. The drug stuff was not youthful rebellion or depravity but caused by illness. Legal medication trials are underway now so, hopefully, that'll help with a lifestyle change for him but I'm left feeling guilt about why I didn't advocate for medical help years ago. Getting back to his dad, I know he's done hard drugs with our son and I'm furious about that.

Hence, you're finally thinking about divorce?

Oh yes, but not without assessing my role in this whole thing and that may take a lot of back tracking because I was in denial about our son's mental illness for a decade! I refused to see it. Seems so obvious now. I should have known. Why didn't I see it? And what else might I be in denial about? Additionally, I need help figuring out how to help repair my son's life.

Well, these are all ambitious goals but about the last one, the reality is you can't fix someone else's life. They have to do that themselves. You probably can figure out why you were in denial about his illness and that might explain some other stuff for you, too. All of this might get you closer to making a decision about divorcing or not. It's already clear to me that you're a pretty reserved person. You speak like an educated woman and I can tell you're not going to get really emotional in my presence if you can help it. Am I right?

Yes, not that I haven't been a raving maniac in my time but not any more, age helps with some stuff. I'm also content in my spiritual life which comforts me and that keeps me from losing it like I used to sometimes.

That being the case we might really get some work done together. Strong emotions can short circuit progress during therapy and make it difficult for me to ask pointed questions. Nonetheless, it'll take a couple of sessions before I know enough about you to ask the right questions.

Finding something in me that can explain such a big mistake, a missing puzzle piece, sounds like a tall order. Now that I've read *Shades* to you I'm not sure how to continue. It's weird to talk with you about all this stuff because I don't even know you and I'm a very private person. I know what you are of course, a psychotherapist, but I don't know you and here I am starting to tell you about my most personal stuff. I'm also not sure how to begin reviewing my life to anyone and make sense of it.

Try starting with some basics, Susan.

Okay. First of all I'm 58 and on Social Security Disability. They decided I couldn't really work since '96, wasn't really employable any more. Thought I'd last a lot longer than that! Didn't even snap to it and apply for disability until October of '97 and by that time I was living on $75 a month and food stamps. Had a housing voucher and that's the only thing that kept me from being homeless. I think not working made me more aware that my son had a very big problem with drugs. Any parent who has gone through this knows the scope of what I mean when I say it was thoroughly horrid.

Yeah. I do substance abuse counseling too and dealing with a full blown drug addiction whether self-medication or not in a loved one is incredibly difficult for family members who actually engage the problem rather than pretty much writing the person off and calling it "tough love." Personally, I think total disengagement is throwing a person away but many disagree with me. To face it and try to do something about it is very hard. That's really tough love.

Hardest thing I ever dealt with. When they gave him a diagnosis and said medication would help there was a ray of hope. That rehab observed him in close quarters for two days and came to the conclusion he wasn't a drug addict at all but mentally ill. Only took them two days and I didn't see it for a decade! Not long after his diagnosis and treatment was started my Social Security back payment came. It was over $14,000, the most money I'd ever had at one time in my life! That probably sounds pitiful to some people but to me it was a small fortune. I had a list of how to spend it. One of the things I was able to do was help relocate my disabled son to get away from old associations. His doctor says it might take as long as two years to get the right medications and dosages figured out.

So, do you have any ideas about anything that might be going on inside you that could cause you not to recognize your son's mental illness until someone else pointed it out?

Well, according to Social Security I have some sort of affective disorder along with my medical problems. Personally I think I have PTSD. Sometimes I just way over react inside myself even if I don't lose it. If I can process some of the trauma in my life, maybe I won't do that any more. That's another goal actually. Mostly though I want to decide about divorcing or not and I want to know how a college graduate with a major in sociology and a minor in psychology, that's me, could be so stupid as to deny all the symptoms that point to mental illness in her own son? I don't think PTSD is the answer to that question.

Maybe PTSD played a role, maybe not. It would depend on the past trauma. But I can tell you that denial of mental illness in a family member is very common. Most people don't really know how to detect mental illness anyway, it takes a doctor. Can't see the forest for the trees type of thing.

Funny, with all our desires and acquisitions it's that space between our ears where we really live, that drives us. Our minds interpret all we encounter to weave our idiosyncratic point of view about reality to which we uniquely react. A view full of holes made by our defenses apparently.

Do you think in words or images?

What? Uh, I would have to say I think mostly in images. The words come to describe the pictures. Why did you ask that?

Seeing pictures in my mind is hard for me. An author has to be really good to paint a mental image for me, 'cuz I've always thought in words although they don't flow as easily through my skull or off my tongue now that I'm getting old. I dream in images, though, with a teeny bit of dialogue thrown in.

The reason I brought this up is that my mentally ill son thought in numbers from birth to about 10-years-old when I learned about it. I knew he had verbal communication difficulties but never guessed that was why. I was amazed when I learned about the numbers! He told me back then that I was the number two. Is thinking in numbers a sign of mental illness or just a style of thinking?

I'm not sure. Have to do some research on that. Who is the number one by the way?

Yahweh, the father. That's the name of God or Lord God as the King James Bible puts it.

Oh.

Susan, I can't help but notice that you said you were in denial about your son's illness for 10 years and that's the same amount of time you told me you and his father have been legally separated. Do you think there's a connection? Recent research suggests that while an individual might have a propensity for mental illness, it often takes trauma to activate it.

In this case there was plenty of trauma all right and way before the legal separation but my son's recently revealed a symptom he's had since the age of five! Because it was in his head, he assumed it was like that for everyone but gradually he began to wonder about it and was ashamed to mention it before now.

Did you know about this symptom?

In a way. He would allude to some stuff but I thought of it as dreams or imagination. Never suspected it was mental illness and he didn't mention much, maybe two or three things. I suppose that puts the denial back much further.

Okay, so we're trying to figure out what the source of the denial was. How do you think we should start?

Guess I'll go clear back to high school. I think that's where it began, where I must have got off track enough not to see what was wrong with one of my very own children. I think this is when it started because of my choice of a first husband which also suggests denial.

That's a provocative statement. Care to expand on this first husband thing?

His name is Chris and I will eventually get into that but what I just realized is that when I think back to being a teenager the first thing I remember is the day we were told in our classrooms that the Russians had put something called Sputnik into orbit. It was exciting because it'd never been done before! A synthetic satellite was up there now circling the earth along with the natural one. You know, the moon. Then someone mentioned that it meant the Russians were ahead of us scientifically. Even my-then-Pollyanna self could deduce they might now have a better way to deliver THE BOMB.

Ahhh, THE BOMB.

The advent of Sputnik was one of the times when everything changed for humanity I think. What they call a quantum shift now. There was another one 12 years earlier, August of '45 actually, when our government dropped atom bombs on Hiroshima and Nagasaki. I was only five-years-old when Japan surrendered. There was another quantum shift when President Kennedy was assassinated. I had just turned 23 and adored him. I know it had a profound effect on me.

You know what? I never realized there were years until I was eight-years-old in 1948. Up 'til then it was day to day and season to season for me. Even though I had birthdays and grew older I didn't understand about years until I was eight. I remember when I snapped to it. That strikes me as weird.

Not sure what to make of that. So, you were talking about Sputnik and living under the threat of THE BOMB. How did that affect you?

By irrevocable, underlying terror from then on. I know I often wished we had a bomb shelter. Sputnik made nuclear annihilation an even bigger threat.

My father worked with computers so I was familiar with this thing we now call "technology". I'd seen his company's big computer that filled a room at Holloman Air Force Base. It was a mess of boards filled with crossed and colored wires. They talked to it with key punched cards. Today they keep Stealth bombers at Holloman but back then it's where they sent monkeys up in rockets among other things they dreamed up like the manned rocket sled, remember? Always felt bad for those monkeys. Or are you too young to know about these things?

Probably I am because I was born in '73 and I don't recall that stuff. Of course I know about Sputnik and I've always had a theory that fear of the bomb was the underlying cause of the cultural revolution of the 60's. What do you think?

Seems likely to me because parents have always been hypocrites so why all of a sudden in the 60's did youth throw out all the conventions? There was definitely a sense of "live now for tomorrow you may die." The slogan was "Make love, not war." So fear of war and repudiation of war was definitely an element. Of course as the Hippie movement grew the vehicle for this attitude was the Vietnam War which we always worried might set off Russia.

Knew a former special ops guy a few years ago who said that the whole reason we got into Vietnam was because of the friendship between Presidents Eisenhower and France's de Gaulle. This guy also claims that during the Vietnam era he busted up a drug op by the CIA at Chicago's O'Hare airport among other things. I typed up his memoir manuscript for him and that's what he said.

How did you personally feel about the Vietnam War?

I didn't know enough about it at the time to have an opinion but I was very aware of the demonstrations against it. My main thought was, "Why are we there?" No one I knew at the time went there to fight.

I also wasn't affected much by the hippie movement. I was the right age, but in the wrong situation. I got married in '59 and had four kids by '69 and I was stuck in conventionality before the movement got into full swing. Had so many kids so quickly because we didn't have the pill until after my second child. When I did start taking it the dosage was so strong it gave me terrific headaches when I went off it for the five days so I didn't use it much. I also had a part time research job around that time where I had to interview numerous doctors using a prepared question and answer form and they commented there had been a lot of depressions in women who took the pill and also more divorces among those patients than was usual. Those types of research studies forced lowering the dosage more and more until such symptoms went away while the birth control was still effective.

Getting back to your youth, do you want to talk about that first marriage now or go back again to right after Sputnik?

Going back seemed to be leading somewhere so I want to keep going from there. I guess in the 50's our country was trying to do what Russia did with Sputnik but focusing more on getting a human being up there, or at least a monkey to begin with. The Russians just put the thing into orbit and worked on the human being part later. Eventually, though, they also put the first man in space, Yuri Gagarin in '61, and the first woman in space too. Three weeks after Yuri, John Glenn went up there to circle the globe three times I think it was. Back then we actually called it "going into space."

By the way, I went to high school with the German rocket scientists' kids. They all got A's and the rest of us hated that because they ruined the grading curve! But they were sweet and we liked them, or at least I did. It wasn't until I read Michener's "Space" about 10 years ago that I began to realize who those German kids were and what a unique experience that had been for us to go to school with them. They had very odd handwriting and studied all the time. The result is that I had a very good high school education in most subjects. Imagine those German kids having to learn English fast and going on to make A's in an American high school! They were all industrious to the max. According to Michener, the U.S. sent rescuers into Germany to get these rocket scientists and their families out, to bring them over here so we could have their knowledge about rockets. There was even an Act of Congress to make them citizens! The bunch of scientists the Soviets got must have been a little further ahead.

So what does all this have to do with why you were able to be in denial about your son's mental illness do you think?

Maybe I do something in my head without being aware of it in order to ignore the threat of annihilation and it slops over onto other things? Or maybe I'm just rambling around amidst the junk in my mental closet because it's an activity that comes with old age. Or maybe it's insanity. Seriously, though, I do believe that thinking about the past has value which is mostly being wasted because old age isn't respected in this country. Maybe that will change when the baby boomers hit their Senior years. I'm a little ahead of that curve.

You're 58 right? That really isn't old nowadays.

It feels old to me. I guess that's because too much stuff has passed under my bridge and eroded the superstructure of my life. Sounds a little poetic but it's really just fragility. You're right of course, 58 isn't that old really, but it's old enough to start that very tiring and disturbing peering backwards and I already need a break from it right now.

When it gets a bit sticky in the cranium I try really hard to unglue my fascination with the past, to return to today. Okay, let's see, today, August 20th, 1998. As I recall from the news, we bombed the terrorists who apparently bombed our two embassies 13 days ago, a President with dubious sexual morality and who really knows how to "parse" words is running the country, and a teenager admitted giving birth in secret and putting the baby in the trash to die. It's also my oldest son's birthday by the way. Then, conversely, sometimes when it gets a bit sticky in the present I go back to what's in my head: the past.

So let's go back again, it's OK. Probably you need to go back to get anywhere with this. I was just curious how you thought this technology stuff might have caused you to be able to enter a denial mode. The 50's brought nuclear proliferation and Sputnik which are maybe the reasons for the 60's phenomena of "Make love, not war." It had to affect you and everyone else in your generation deeply I'm sure.

Bob! I hope you aren't suggesting that all of us old people are in a generalized state of denial! Hey, maybe we are. Maybe that's why we haven't really gotten up in arms about the state of affairs in our country, in the world in fact. I think you're right, though, the recent past is full of some really scary stuff and it had to affect everyone.

In my lifetime there was Hitler and World War II first which all ended with us dropping atom bombs on Japan, then came even bigger bombs and an arms race, then the "police action" in Korea, then Sputnik, then came Vietnam, then they killed Jack Kennedy for starters. Actually I think he died before we really understood that we had "advisers" in Vietnam. The Korean War seems to have been when our military decided to police the world. Other pervasive changes included personal computers, Faxes and cell phones, numerous undeclared wars and police actions, a growing and incredible standard of living, which was nice it seemed, and now we have the internet just to mention a few of the changes I've lived through.

The end of the so-called Cold War was great and everyone celebrated for several years until it started to be clear the nukes were still around and in some cases they were not under good control. What had actually happened was we just stopped being enemies with the Soviet Union of Socialist Republics which proceeded to break up, creating a whole bunch of other problems.

In my own past life there's a closet homosexual for a first husband, a mad and passionate love for a bi-polar second husband, and then trying to undo the damage to my five children from these two marriages to say nothing of all the mundane stuff like jobs and now adjusting to growing old. A lot to live through and my son's mental illness is a challenge I want to be able to live through well. First, though, I have to know why I hid it from myself!

Your private past sounds pretty intense.

Listening to myself talk to you, complaining even, makes me almost nauseous because whatever has gone on in my life has still been easier than about 90% of the rest of the people in the world have had it! We are so spoiled in the U.S. Our expectations are way higher. Have to remind myself how good I have it.

Did you notice I didn't mention putting a man on the moon as a major past event? I think that Jack, we all called him Jack, wanted to push us technologically far beyond the Soviet Union's capacities in order to quell fear and panic even. Who knows, we might suddenly have nukes raining down on us from that Sputnik thing. He would have to plan something astounding that says we beat them technologically for us to feel a little safe from them. But I don't believe now that we went to the moon. Sure believed it then though. I looked at the moon through that telescope along with millions doing likewise on that night in '69 and marveled that we'd actually accomplished that. Russia needed to believe it too, it was a matter of national security. I was very pregnant with my fourth child on that day I tried to imagine us on the moon. It was probably the most amazing hoax in modern history! Maybe I'm wrong but then why don't we have a settlement there almost three decades later? Or maybe we do and we just don't know it. Who knows what's going on any more? Not me, that's for sure.

Do you think the missing piece in you, as you call it, is gone because you've been lied to and you feel insecure about what's real?

Maybe. I know from experience that information is managed and it's a little crazy-making to know so much but not know if it's really true! When you get old, you reflect, you start pigeon holing everything and where do you put stuff you don't know for sure is true? It just sticks in your head bothering you. Just wait, it'll happen to you too. It's hard to sort it out and a bit irresponsible to ignore it, don't you think?

You said you had experience with information management. How so?

Basically, I have a gift for hearing the most recent stuff that's going on. I walk into big news stories all the time. I'm what they call "hot" in the news business. The disillusionment at the end of a particular news story I wrote had to do with information management.

You wrote news?

In my early 40's I was a journalist for awhile. I stopped writing news when I found out the degree it's controlled even at the local level. What's the point of being a good news hound if you can't really get the best stories published in the mainstream media? That was a serious loss of innocence. Back then we didn't realize it was managed. Everyone knows it now, and if the powers that be can't manage it away completely they "spin it".

Another disillusionment happened when I was 33 and was arrested the only time in my life, so far anyway. I hadn't done anything wrong. To say it was a big shock is mild. I pled not guilty and was acquitted by a jury of my peers. The advice my public defender gave me was to plead guilty and pay a $50 fine. But I wasn't guilty! The specter of having to leave my five children to spend a year in jail if I demanded a trial and was found guilty was brought up repeatedly. Talk about pressure to fold. Oh, the complete loss of justice occasioned by the plea bargain! It's a helpful process if you're guilty but really stupid and dangerous if you're innocent.

I wanted to sue the cops who arrested me wrongly but the legal aide lawyer wouldn't take the case. His exact words were, "I can't get a hard on for it." I still can't believe he said that! A polite "no" would have sufficed. I have a newspaper article somewhere that says over one fourth of U.S. citizens will be put in jail at one time or another! Holy cow! I just know that most convicts are in prison for victimless crimes too. What a waste. Why can't we figure out how to help people who aren't violent and don't hurt others instead of throwing them in prison? And why is it that people of color are the most numerous in jails and that rich people get off easy?

Being arrested must have been terrible.

It was absolutely humiliating to be handcuffed before being put in the back of the police car right in front of my house, taken to the county jail, searched, mug shots taken and then put in a holding cell to wait to be bailed out, hopefully. I was in there with a lady who had been arrested for drunk driving. She was still tipsy and bawled the whole time. I fumed. I had been employed once at a prison camp and knew the ropes so to speak. That job taught me what a really terrible two-sided system of crap the penal system is. Finding myself wrongly incarcerated was very traumatic because I knew the games they play in there.

You worked in a prison camp? What was your job?

Yeah, it was a minimum security conservation camp just outside Chino Men's Prison. I was supposed to keep the central files up to date and to type the parole board reports. I was also supposed to take notes at the morning camp meeting but was only allowed to go to it once. The Superintendent just couldn't stand the idea that I might hear bad words. He was a Southern gentleman. He was gone one day and the counselors invited me into the morning group meeting for some reason. They probably wanted to see what the 80 odd men would do in my presence and, no doubt, how I would react to the meeting. No one in there said anything bad at all. Not one curse word or untoward reference. It would probably have been good for me to be there every day to keep it civil which I think was the administration's point in hiring me seeing it was a therapeutic community. The recidivism rate at that time was about 85% in regular prisons and in this camp it had gone down to about 35% as I recall. Don't get me wrong, some people deserve to be in prison and there was one guy in particular I was very glad was no longer on the streets and I'd never have wanted to be alone with him but most of the others were there for really small matters in my opinion. One young guy was in there for possession of one joint of marijuana. Then you had the career guys. One of 'em told me it was home, three squares a day and he knew the rules. He was a burglar and when I asked him why he kept coming back he told me he just loved playing the game of trying to beat the cops by being a successful burglar and that when he got caught it was OK because prison was his home. While I was there a young inmate who did the carpentry work for the camp befriended me and told me he'd read his central file, which was forbidden. He was busted back to the maximum security prison because I stupidly told a guard about it. As per the therapeutic policies of the camp, which relied on peer pressure, I assumed this information would be taken to daily group and felt terrible about what happened. I just told the wrong person; should have told a counselor. I pretty much quit over that. The camp was supposed to run on Glasser's reality therapy model but more and more custody type staff got into it and that was ruining the whole thing. I'd heard about the job in my sociology class.

I was about 24 and that job happened because my first husband and I went into counseling and it was suggested I get a part time job while he worked on his "latent homosexuality". While I worked there the prison psychiatrist held sensitivity training for the staff and the reactions they had to my presence at the camp were very interesting. It went all the way from, "It's great to have a woman around to have coffee with," to "I'm afraid she'll get raped and it'll go on my record." Then a counselor said, "I think she's a castrating female." That very last comment was a total shock to all the rest of the people in the room and came from a guy who'd made a pass at me at a party which I'd ignored. The psychiatrist immediately stated that this guy knew exactly what that meant. That counselor dropped his head and admitted such an attitude was in the eye of the beholder, his eye. The Superintendent from the Department of Forestry side of the camp was the one who had coffee with me every morning and his reaction to that comment was immediate anger and disbelief.

I think the employees at the camp learned a lot about each other during that particular session of the training. Another guard said he worried about me being raped too adding indignantly that it wasn't because he had a concern for his record but that he just didn't want that to happen to me. When the comments about rape came up, I mentioned that if they had that worry it was odd where they had placed my office. The camp's corrections staff was housed in a shotgun-style barracks building with an unlocked front and back door at each end of a long hallway with my office near the back door among storage rooms. The next time I went to work after that session my desk and stuff had been moved to the large office in the front of the building with lots of windows and my desk was where the Superintendent could see it along with the central files.

Some of the staff's attitudes about the presence of a female at the camp were a big problem. The idea was that in reality men and women are around each other all the time and that duplicating that particular reality within the incarceration setting was part of training convicts to go back outside successfully. I actually got a call a year after I quit that job from a super-custody guard who wanted to know if I'd seen a guy who'd been at the camp when I was there and who'd just recently walked away. He clearly wasn't warning me but interrogating me. Imagine that creep thinking I had something to do with that! I didn't even recall the missing guy. That guard's mind set was horrible.

I am so glad that DNA testing is setting innocent people free nowadays because what a hellish existence full of complete injustice those people have endured. Do they get a massive monetary award to make amends I wonder? Nothing could ever make up for being innocently in prison but having some money to start over with would be nice.

You've really developed all of this into a rant. Why so much emotion? It was a time long ago.

Why? Because I hate injustice and it's clearly still around. Innocent people suffer all the time from many scenarios not of their making and it makes me incredibly sad, especially when it involves children. People like to say life isn't fair, well DUH! But you know what, that little phrase is often a big cop out for the bad behavior that causes innocents to suffer.

Well, now I'm getting really close to spiritual matters. Suffice it to say that I can accept injustice now and not go on a crusade, unless it involves me or mine directly, because its part of the plan which gets the Creator's purpose accomplished and more important it's out of our control anyway. But I still hate injustice. Makes me see red. A lot of what drives a journalist is the possibility of coming across hidden information that indicates injustice or its first cousin, inequity. The point of being an investigative reporter is to tell the truth about stuff that goes on that should be corrected, hopefully, by the exposure. Right?

I don't know, I thought it was just to tell the news in an unbiased fashion.

Of course being unbiased is essential but what really drives a true journalist is the search for a wrongness to expose. Lots of plain old news gets reported but when wrongness is located the story takes on a new life that encourages social action. It's the way citizens in a democracy can keep informed about problems requiring their attention.

Actually I never thought of it that way but I guess that's why freedom of the press is so important, so that the voters can know when something's not right and then do something about it before it gets too far off track.

Yes, but the only problem now is that instead of getting news from the printed media most people get their news from TV which is often biased, inexact, very truncated, overtly "managed" and often sensationalistic rather than informative. But even the printed media news is managed carefully it turns out.

When I was in high school, information management was called propaganda and censorship. We were taught it was something only the Russians did but the U.S. only told the truth. At the age of 42 I suddenly learned the reality of information management right here in our country. Add to that the massive desensitization that is going on, propelled by the media, and you have a real problem. Because of it even if some news gets through the management no one cares much unless it involves children or imminent destruction.

People today wouldn't even particularly care if they found out for sure that the moon landings really were a hoax! On the other hand, even if the majority of people don't care a lot about past and present truths, especially if it doesn't affect them, sometimes they do and boy, howdy, watch out if Americans *en masse* finally get fed up with something really wrong. Classically we take our anger to the polling booth to oust the no-gooders. And if change doesn't happen, then oh well. Like that old saw says, "People get the government they deserve." I think de Tocqueville said that but not sure now. I don't even want to talk about the Electoral College, disillusionment number three.

What do you mean by desensitization? Does it affect you too?

Yes, it's affected us Senior citizens too. Because of your youth, do you even realize how desensitized we have become? Are you too young to remember the old movies and TV shows where only married couples fully clothed in PJs and separated in twin beds were allowed and that was considered rather scandalous? When stories all had a good ending and there were no anti-heroes? When lying was considered abysmal and certainly never a source of comedy? When rare violence in entertainment was only alluded to, seldom portrayed, and if acted out there was no blood? When divorce and a child out of wedlock were scandalous circumstances? When as far as most regular people knew the only illicit drug was heroin and it wasn't available everywhere for troubled people to take except for in the slums of very large cities? Except for cocaine of course, which early on was in Coca Cola. When I was a child I knew a younger child who had to have Coca Cola every day! That child was addicted to cocaine! That drug problem slipped through the cracks, no pun intended.

So much sensitivity has gone by the wayside. Now we're even to the point that the immeasurable value of one, single life is really not recognized that much any more, unless it's someone we know or a family member, or it's a celebrity, a very rich person, or some very compelling event as in the case of violence against children. One life, any life, lost unnaturally used to be terribly shocking to all of us, including fatal car accidents. I remember how it was 50 years ago. Barely.

Oh it's still considered valuable to be honest by most people even up to admitting what's really going on that's wrong. The problem is we don't seem to care enough about the erosion of values to do anything about it. I think this is probably because we've been too busy buying stuff *ad infinitum*. We have all these things that seem really great, but there is an underlying decay. And the media dreams up more violence than hopefully exists just for entertainment, all the while playing down old values and morals by pandering to the lowest and basest in human nature especially in comedic themes. Anyway, that's my opinion.

You're very upset about some contemporary stuff that's certainly clear, but does anything make you happy?

Mostly what makes me happy is the sanctuary of the elderly, "the grandkids". But, that brings up thoughts of the world they have been born into. So many changes, so much wrong, and it escalates all the time. Will they be snatched by a pervert? What else will they be facing? And are they being prepared, really? They get a lot of material goodies and get to do a lot of fun things, but facing the future requires seriously developed stuff in the head and I don't often see them getting what is necessary for the resolve and determination life demands.

How can they get what they need in their heads when most parents are working all the time to buy more stuff? In most families no one is paying exclusive attention to them and their heads. Wonder what they'll call the generation behind the Gen-Xer's? The Headless Generation maybe? This is our future I'm talking about. Education sure as heck isn't hacking it either. Most kids think of school beyond the 4th grade as jail.

"Oh to hell with it all!" my mind often trumpets. Unfortunately, that's not an option for me. There was someone around to put stuff in my head and it didn't include running away from reality although I did about my son's mental illness, didn't I? Worse than running away, I refused to see it.

Is that a singular event, this one denial? Oh, wait. You did mention something about your first husband so I guess that's another. Are there any more denials you've identified?

Not that I can think of right now. Obviously when you are denying something you are actively refusing to think about it at all. Some young people today will be in a lot worse shape than me though when they get old because a lot of children really aren't being prepared at a fundamental level to be responsible adults and they're being fed terrible stuff to have in their brains for their whole lives. They might be able to deny that stuff but I suspect it festers in there.

So what exactly is going into young people's brains that you don't like?

What they see and hear regularly on TV and in the movies is horrific but admittedly sometimes true. The true stuff's bad enough but there are all these horror films and stupid stuff like vampires! In my opinion it's not even OK to put some of those images in an adult's head let alone a child's head. Once in the head, always in the head in some fashion. It doesn't just go away. Sometimes it festers and there is a really horrendous result from a cancer of the mind.

It is true that there are horrific things going on with school shootings, serial killings and so on. Maybe it's always been this way, though, but it's just more apparent because of TV news.

I don't believe that. We don't even hear half of what's going on. Knew a cop once who said multiple gang drive by shootings happened every day in a fairly big city and only one now and then is reported. It's definitely worse. If you had lived in the 50's you'd know it's worse by far. Having all these images of violence in our heads must derail some people. James Joyce knew about this head problem. Stream of consciousness. He's mostly remembered for the sex in his novels which is tame by today's standards. But what he really did was try to show how a person's mind works, the flow of consciousness, in his case the male mind. Guess what, I know a guy who said he thought about sex 85% of the time! Surely that's aberrant?!

That's excessive but we guys do spend a lot of time thinking about sex. Getting back to youngsters, like you said, some of this bad stuff that kids see is real and isn't it important for them to know of its existence?

Yes, I suppose so. That's the rub isn't it? We are no longer able to be sure nothing really damaging gets into our children's heads. It's got to have an affect and probably not a good one. Studies show viewing violence on TV increases the incidences of children acting violently. So, if this stuff is in their memories, what do they think about? That awful stuff? Or do they even ponder at all because they usually seem to be thinking about what to do, where to go, what to buy, and so on rather than anything philosophical for instance.

It's beginning to be the case that young and old alike can only enjoy stream of consciousness at great risk because they have to pay very close attention to what's going on around them. Stay focused on right now, right here. Everyday life now requires constant monitoring. I know that psychologists call it hyper-attentiveness but not sure they realize that we all have to be that way now because it is a very busy and dangerous world out there. Or, we can just stumble along and hope nothing bad happens which I think is irresponsible. Lots of people just opt for alternative drug-induced realities, all too frequently. Ever read Brave New World and 1984? We're almost there! Maybe it's just because I see the drug trap my son fell into but I really think there are many more insidious traps out there for kids today than there used to be. To counter it, to help a kid refuse to participate in drugs, for instance, and the crime that often follows it, is really hard. I've noticed too that big cities have areas where there really isn't much being done about the massive drug stuff going on there, drug ghettos that are often called "war zones". It's like all the people there could just die so far as the establishment is concerned. A lot do die, from drug overdoses and by killing each other or themselves. It's beginning to feel like population control in a way.

It's probably just gotten too big for them to really handle.

If so, that's pretty scary. Well, I'm certainly revved up. Hey, maybe I'm here to let my stream of consciousness go because it's gotten to the point someone needs an appointed time and place to do that and I need to do it really bad. It's just that our young people can't just let their minds go and they should be able to do that. They should be able to think experientially, not be afraid to try something new and idealistic. But if they're not careful they can get trapped quickly into something horrible that they'll have difficulty emerging from intact.

Don't you think it's always been hard for youngsters when they leave the nest? Wasn't it hard for you?

No I don't and no it wasn't. In the 50's and 60's it was much easier to get a start into adult life without getting seriously side tracked. This really bothers me. Young people don't have much of a chance any more. In addition to all the negative input they experience, in order to get a decent job today requires a college degree. Kids who are poor and a little messed up won't be able to do that at all. Lots of kids fall into this category. The pace of life is so fast now too. I read someone calculated that the average business person now has 176 one to one points of contact every day with other people! And they wonder why people take drugs.

But we're in a time when people can get close to self-actualization if they plan well and while that's very challenging it's also very exciting isn't it?

Self-actualization. And just what is that anyway? Psychobabble for the complete development of an individual's potential? I'm sure all the corporations would like to see all their wage slaves be able to do more and more and more and more. Did you know in the U.S. people take way fewer vacations than in Europe? Americans are already working and informing themselves to death. Or, they can't get good enough employment to support themselves and then their egos suffer terribly. Any more self-actualization or failure and lots of people will end up malfunctioning in some serious way.

This country has always believed in work, it builds self esteem to work and it pays the bills and I think self-actualizing means getting closer and closer to working at something you like to do and are good at doing.

Work is good but down through history a few people have profited by the back-breaking work of the majority of people and I don't think that's right. I also don't think work builds self esteem either although there is great dignity in doing what you have to do to get by without succumbing to doing easy and bad things to get money. Can you tell I'm a socialist, because I am. Always have been. As far as I'm concerned everyone should get a livable wage, free health care, an acre of land to grow food on, and the materials to build their own home. Those who are able to will also work, at things they like to do and, as you said, are good at doing. Why should a few have so much and 98% of the rest have so little? It's just not right.

Self-actualization. On another level I also think that's a fantasy. My belief is that each person's life is preordained to a certain end to which we all inexorably proceed while actually making radical decisions as we go along. How's that for a dichotomy of enormous proportions? Furthermore, the many stresses of living acting on the genetic proclivities of any individual creates a uniqueness while also precluding full actualization of any positive genetic potential for any of us. How completely egocentric, unrealistic, and tragic that we could begin to think we can decide where we're going and by assiduous self-actualization get there. We don't exist in a spiritual or a physical vacuum.

That may be your very well expressed point of view but a lot of people believe in free will, that they can decide how their lives will be. It's a treasured American tenant.

They can decide all right, that's why it's a dichotomy. As far as I'm concerned today's state of affairs makes me want to drop out and get out of town, go to the hills with a 20 gallon trash can of beans and rice. An acre of land with a year round spring would do, and a cabin with two rooms, no phone, no TV, maybe a radio, and an outhouse. Course I'm past menopause and such a life would be much harder for a younger woman, to be perfectly blunt about it. But there would be time for contemplation then. Men always seem to want weapons in that type of setting, for good reasons I suppose, but I just want peace and quiet, time to think, to contemplate.

If you divorce John you'd be there alone since it appears you don't feel you can love another man because you still feel married to him regardless of legal status. Wouldn't you be lonely?

Maybe alone, maybe not, but no I wouldn't be lonely. Of course you would ask that because nowadays someone who can be alone to contemplate is considered antisocial, depressed, unproductive, a flake, a nut, in orbit, etc. Thinking about something other than your job skills, how you're going to pay the bills, and what fun to engage in next is just not encouraged any more. The great minds of our past contemplated in order to come up with inventions, ideas, and creative expression even when they were poor.

Used to be "Tote that bale," now it's, "Get that money and go buy some stuff!" Not much else is thought about now. This makes the vast majority of us wage slaves during our earning years. The national minimum wage would be laughable if it weren't so sad. Absolutely no one could actually live on that and still stay clean, healthy, fed, and sheltered and we all know it. Politicians pat themselves on the back for that pittance.

We're not actually getting close to anything really personal here are we?

No, guess not. (long pause) I have a confession. It's genetic, the mental illness, and I knew something was wrong with John, my second husband, but I was afraid to really face it, call it by a name: mental illness. And I remember thinking, more than once, "Our son won't be like that." I held that faulty premise so willfully that I refused to see the truth. I really had no idea what mental illness was or what could be done about it and I no doubt feared innately that nothing could help.

Never thought I was prejudiced about anything, but I was about mental illness. So maybe the denial was just that I couldn't deal with it and I just stayed in denial until forced to face it. But why the prejudice to begin with? Wait! I just snapped to the answer, it's a residue of my intellectual snobbery. Thought I conquered that long ago. Pains me there was still some left in me, it's so sophomoric. And that last comment just proves there's more in there doesn't it? Wouldn't want to be thought of as sophomoric for heavens sake, no deep thinking intellectualism in that is there?

I also fear that another motivation for this willful position of denial was due to how I felt about the man I loved rather than the child I loved not enough, until now. I wanted something precious, something untainted from the strangeness of our tragic relationship, our son. Had to have him be OK to finally go on without my other half I think. Guess I'm giving you the apologia for my lapse in duty but it doesn't quell the guilt. Seems everywhere I look now I see my guilt. That's what having your eyes opened will do for you though and you just have to weather it, but I can use some help figuring it out because all I've said still doesn't explain the denial really. There's something more. How am I even able to do that, deny stuff?

We all have our reasons you know. Time's about up, we'll continue next week if you want. OK? You want to come back, same day, same time?

Yes, definitely, I hate to stop!

See you next week. Maybe spring will finally have sprung by then.

SESSION TWO

One Week Later

Hi, Susan. How would you like to start today's session?

I'm beginning to suspect what I need more than anything else is for someone to really listen to this stuff and help me to just let it go, finally, once and for all. No one in my family wants to hear any of it. It's too hard to hear. And friends are relentlessly optimistic and focused on what I should do, giving advice. Have you ever been trapped by something, someone, or a circumstance that you want to be free of but you just can't let go of it for some reason?

I think everyone can relate to that state of affairs.

That's how I feel about John. I seem to be sure that I should just try to forget him but it's actually impossible because there are so many positive and negative vivid memories associated with our relationship.

Tell me some of the good ones please.

OK. Well actually maybe the right words are compelling experiences rather than good ones. Let's see. One time we went into an East Indian store that sold incense, brass stuff, and so on, and the clerk took one look at John and said, "Thanks for doing your power walk in our town." That kind of thing sticks in my mind.

Another time we visited a place in Landers, California where there's a huge boulder called Giant Rock. It's several stories tall. This precise location was once a meeting place for Northern and Southern tribes and more recently for UFO enthusiasts. There was a door on the Southwest side with stairs going down. Someone had literally carved out under the rock making a little room. John photographed me half way down the stairs with the jagged base of the rock just above my head one month before over a thousand earthquakes, so the paper said, collapsed the entrance. He also took a photograph of the sky in Landers with many sun rays coming down to the ground on the day before the earthquakes which was published in the local paper. Landers was interesting for another reason too. That's where the Integraton building is located. A guy named Van Tassel built it supposedly at the instruction of aliens. It was to be a time and rejuvenation machine and is supposedly acoustically perfect. We met his widow who called me one day and said something like, "It's beginning! A volcano went off and now others will too." I asked her what was beginning and she was cryptic. About a month later Mount St. Helens blew. You gotta admit that's interesting!

Another time John initiated involvement for what turned into many months with an 80-year-old teacher named Ruth who was Sufi and wanted us to travel around the world with her to different Sufi enclaves to introduce them to us. She was immensely impressed by him and by us as a unit. She also took us to the archives of Meditation Mount in Ojai one night. Oddly, as interesting as it was I couldn't stay awake there and had to go to sleep as soon as they showed us to our room. At the same time Ruth was in our life, Mustafa came into it too. He told us he was the heir apparent to the Ottoman throne of Turkey and was in hiding while his ancestral property was in probate. Mustafa conducted a rite one evening which supposedly inducted us into one of the Sufi movements. John got the title Hazari and I got the title Mevlana, according to their beliefs. Can't recall exactly what these titles mean but John's had something to do with enormous and violent change, like a raging fire. This Sufi stuff happened coincidentally with the time I began a search for the TRUTH and it impeded my progress somewhat. Ultimately, though, I didn't give credence to any of this and said no to the worldwide traveling because of my children. Couldn't leave them. Furthermore, I had a spiritual experience one day while I was contemplating the very bad state of the world which pointed me toward the path of finding out about the Savior. I don't know if John would have gone to the Sufi enclaves or not if I had said yes. He pretty much just watched and listened to all of it and let me make the decision.

Then there was the time we lived in a round house directly behind Medicine Hill which was named by the local Native Americans who had lived there before this remote area was sold to a land trust. Medicine Hill was said to bring out the very worst or the very best in people. This is not a positive story at all but it's interesting. We were there about a month. It hung on a hill and overlooked mountainous scenery. I could see Medicine

Hill from the kitchen window. It was a superbly designed house with a windowed kiva in reverse on the roof and a rock bathroom. John hurt me so bad emotionally there that my agonized screams brought vultures to circle the house. I walked away one morning with our son, down the one mile dirt road to get to a phone in order to leave him again.

Well, OK, I can see all that was really, really interesting and seductive especially since you were then on a dedicated search for THE TRUTH. You're not putting me on here are you? It sounds unbelievable.

I don't lie, really. I know these things are beyond usual experience and that's why they were so seductive as you call it. There was much more that would be too hard to explain and take too long but that gives you an idea of the memories I have. What's even more interesting is that none of this fazed John really. It's as though he was used to this type of stuff happening to him. There are other intangible but more mundane things too. Things he taught me. For instance, he knew everything about dogs and he taught me to never pick up something they were intent upon because they would often grab it from your hand. So, the day I saw my three-year-old daughter being circled on the beach by a pack of six dogs I knew not to pick her up but instead walked into the circle, ignoring the dogs, and took her by the hand and just walked out with her. My instinct was to snatch her up and I had to fight it. I was seven months pregnant by the way with John's child. Those dogs were quiet behind us as we walked away and when I felt I could turn to look at them, they suddenly ran off. That piece of knowledge quite possibly saved my youngest daughter's life that day.

OK, I just got a new respect for John. But I have a question. Do any of these types of things happen to you when you are not with him?

Yes, but on a minor scale because I don't go odd places or seek them out. I'm a home body and rather circumspect in what I do. It's how I was trained in order to be safe. So, that's some of why it's hard to forget him and it's clear to me you can love someone and wish you could be with them at the same time you can also know you really should not be with them. Like my mother said, "Love can be either heaven or hell." She has some deep wisdom she passed on to me like: "Don't go to bed angry at a loved one because they or you might not be alive the next day and that would be really terrible," or "There's a time for everything, don't try to rush into it all at once." She doesn't even remember telling me these things now, but they are wise.

Your mother. Can some of your denial have to do with your mother and father?

Partly no doubt, but basically they were good to me and, besides, there's nothing to be done about any of that now so why belabor it? They're both in their late 70's. He's getting pretty tired and doesn't get around very well any more. She's doing fine. In fact she's in better health than I am. She's still very pretty and my father adores her. She had strawberry blond hair and blue eyes. Now her hair is a soft grayish white and she still has those eyes. As you can see I have brown eyes and now-graying dark hair and would not be considered very pretty although I'm not ugly. So, I never even tried to emulate her. Just don't have the equipment. Why bother with going back so far?

You minored in psych, remember? You know there's a very good reason to look at your childhood.

OK. Let' go there. That's where it all began. My life, my child life. First there was genetic structure and then there was life pushed onto it for good or ill. I know this is true and I even know some of the problems but why would that cause me to deny my son's mental illness and not be able to divorce John when we clearly can't live together in peace?

I'll bite. Why?

Shall I proceed by assorted theories to examine it or what?

However you want to do it is fine with me, just go ahead and start.

OK, let's start with Freud. Are you really ready for this?

Yes. Are you?

Who knows? I'm going to pretend I'm a student giving a discourse to a psychology professor about psychoanalyzing myself. That'll depersonalize it a bit and help me get it out.

Using the Freudian ideas of id, ego, and superego it seems clear to me that I have a fairly well developed superego and ego which regulate most of my needs or id pleasure seeking behaviors, keeping them under fair control, because throughout 58 years of life I have not committed any acts that are completely against the societal norms of the time. On the other hand, I have a fairly rigid ethical structure from an earlier time which takes exception to some of my life decisions. Some of them were actually inappropriate in my opinion even though society accepted them then and they are even more acceptable now. Such as having sex outside of marriage. The one area about which I have never had good pleasure seeking control is eating. It is also really clear to me that eating is a sublimation of my sex drive or libido. I think Freud's idea about the great importance of the sex drive to people's behavior is correct.

It also seems clear that during my life I can see a set of instincts or motivations which often take me by surprise while I yet still control them: such as the fact that I don't live with John because he is narcissistic, bi-polar, and extremely domineering but I still miss him because of the great sex life and the degree of intimate communication and interesting times we had. Even given the negative aspects of our relationship, I would say we were deeply compatible, really, in our value structures. He just can't live by his sexual values for assorted reasons. He does live by a very particular code of ethics though. While I was with him on a day to day basis my need to eat was much diminished and when I was afraid I would lose him I became thin for many years and now that I'm not with him I am fat again, although a part of that has to do with a particular medication I have to take now and again.

Wait, when and why were you afraid of losing him?

When he had a very public affair with a woman 10 years younger than me with bigger boobs, smaller hips, long red-blond hair and blue eyes. He even callously got me to sew four flags he designed for the town we lived in one of which was raised at the Mayor's home by her on videotape! He took it out of my hands and gave it to her to raise.

So that's what ripped it? You apparently got back together, you lost weight and tried to go on, but how was your relationship after that?

The thing burst into the open when he left with her one night after coming home drunk and telling me he was in love with her. Then he came back the next day and said he didn't want to leave with her, he wanted his family and home. I agreed but it was never the same for me. This literally made me crazy for over two years. I continued working but worried all the time when I was at work that he was seeing her and I would try to catch them. It was a terrible, crazy time for me. "Hell hath no fury," etc. And I never loved him again like I had before, which had been with complete abandon and devotion.

47

Did he do much to assuage your fears?

Not at all, after he was safely back home he began to act as though he thought I was funny and said repeatedly that I needed to "grow up". He also claimed I was selfish to be that way! He was actually a part of the sexual revolution of the 60's. I never was nor have I ever changed in that way. I believe in monogamy which I can do and in a way I think he believed in it too but he had crossed too many lines to be able to stop. Maybe he wouldn't have minded if I were unfaithful too, in fact sometimes I think he encouraged it so he would feel better about himself. I could never do that to him, it hurt me too much and I couldn't hurt him the same way. I hurt him though by leaving him, over and over, because I just couldn't deal with his drinking and anger.

What was his excuse for the affair?

At the time he said it was because the kids were too much, I was too difficult, there was too much stress. He even set it up for her to call the house to volunteer for a program he was running so he could blame me for his getting involved with her because I answered the phone and gave her the information about the program! Later he told me he just wanted to "fuck her" as he put it.

Do you think you and he were compatible sexually?

Yes, because sex is more than lust, it involves the whole gestalt of the relationship. Our gestalt was great but then it got off and he liked variety even though he didn't believe a married man should be unfaithful. Later, I also learned that promiscuity is a common bi-polar trait and one of the reasons marriage was hard for him. He tried though, really hard, to be OK that way.

I remember three, what I later realized were tepid orgasms in 10 years and four pregnancies in my first marriage. On the other hand sex with John was always so completely mind blowing that I felt I couldn't live without it and our very close relationship when I finally had to leave him for the sake of my children. I had four children from the first marriage and one with him. My sexual experience with John makes me sure that sex is a very dominant need that probably drives a person most of his or her life just as Freud speculated. Rigid control by the ego is required to keep a person's life from becoming totally chaotic just to appease the libido which comes out of the id.

The woman John had an affair with sounds a little like what your mother looked like. That must have been a terrific jolt.

Let's just say it unhinged me. As he puts it, his hormones got the best of him. He knows himself very well but rather than having really good insight as to why he is as he is, his basic conceit makes him develop an entire rationale for everything he does wrong. It's odd, he accepts the responsibility simply because he is a man and men do that, but his rationalizations about how and why he does what he does are not transparent to him.

At least he knows himself, what to expect from himself. A lot of people don't even know that let alone the reasons for it.

Back to Freud and the first man in my life, my father.

So we're back to Freud? OK.

An odd thing happened when I began to express my intellect in conversations with my father. My intellect is how I tried to impress him seeing as how my looks weren't that great. He and I disagreed frequently and it always ended with him hurting my feelings to get the upper hand because then I would cry. This was a cyclical thing that I never understood then and hurt me deeply. He would never allow me to think differently from him. He insisted that I must accept his point of view which my sense of integrity would not allow me to do unless I were convinced it were true. John did the same thing which I recognize now as that old term "mental cruelty". My early experience with my father probably set me up for this type of relationship.

My first husband, Chris, on the other hand, was very intellectual and we could talk about impersonal stuff without getting into a fight. He didn't hurt me with words but he turned out to be homosexual and came "out of the closet" in the 60's, after we already had three children and a fourth on the way. I eventually learned from him that he had had a meaningful homosexual relationship during his early high school years along with some other homosexual affairs while we were married. No doubt I married him trying to escape a continuation of the emotional trauma that happened between me and my father. So I feel I was actually set up for both of my marriages by my relationship with my father and by the psychological trauma of having Chris prefer men to me! But such is life, no doubt, just different setups for different people.

Are you actually able to relate to this as you go along or is it just an intellectual exercise?

I don't know for sure but it's the only way I know how to do it. As for Freud's so-called penis envy, I don't remember ever seeing a penis until I got married! I did feel powerlessness as a child but don't ever remember being concerned about wanting a penis. If that's true of me then it's definitely an unconscious aspect. I was an only child until I was 10 when my sister arrived and I was never in a position to see family friends' sons nude although there was fooling around in the dark with both a male and a female at about the age of 10. And my father was always modest and although I saw him from time to time in his boxer shorts I didn't see anything or even try to see anything.

You never saw a real penis before you got married? Really?

Really. Unless there was something that happened to me I don't recall. I do remember something odd. I used to walk home on a short cut from school at about the age of six. I would cross the side yard of a house which was not fenced that backed up to the school play yard. I remember a very bright light one day and after that I wouldn't go that way anymore. Feared it actually and went clear around the block instead to get home. What happened there anyway I wonder? I don't remember.

So you fear that you may have been molested sexually?

Maybe, and I know for sure I was molested twice by my grandfather, actually my step-grandfather. Is that a word? When I was about five I kicked him and was scolded for it by my grandmother and I thought to myself that he had done something wrong to me and that I'd kick him again if he did it again. I have no actual memory about what exactly he did but I knew even at that age it was wrong. Then when I was 14 he shoved his hand down my top from behind me in the kitchen when I was seated at the table. Right then my father walked in. He had us leave immediately and asked me in the car why I let that happen! Think I responded that I couldn't help it, didn't see it coming, and was in shock when he walked in. The hand was pulled out as soon as my father was in the doorway. I loved the blouse I was wearing. It had a boat neck and a gorgeous violin print on it and I was a violinist. I don't think I ever wore it again.

Your father's was a common parental reaction when the molester is a family member and the child is a teenager. Wrong but common. That you remember what you were wearing this many years later testifies to the fact of how shocked you actually were even though it was a very brief encounter. Maybe some of the shock was because your father tended to blame you.

Most of my strongest memories are about times when there was an injustice dealt to me. That's a big thing with me, injustice. OK. Back to not seeing penises, so far as I know, before my first marriage.

(Laughs)

I was very interested to learn what one looked like when I got married. Seems so very odd nowadays I know with all the free and early sex going on.

I have to admit this is very interesting on a clinical and historical level because it speaks about the sexual mores of a time long gone.

Boy ain't that the truth! I just flashed on something else that I never understood. When I was in the fifth grade there was a conversation going on after school about someone's sister being "raped". I had no idea what that meant but from what was said I immediately stated, "I was raped too." I don't think I've made you aware of it yet but I hate liars. I have only told two conscious lies in my life that I remember so I wonder why I said that? So far as I can remember I was never raped.

Actually I told one lie and was prepared for the benefit of someone else to tell a lie but it was never necessary. The actual lie I told was to tell my parents. I said that John and I were married when in fact we had not gotten legally married yet at all but were living together and had a son. Worse yet, I told them that because we needed $200 for rent and I knew they wouldn't give it to me if they knew we weren't legally married yet. They knew I had our child out of wedlock. My mother wouldn't even speak to me for a long time after she heard I was pregnant and she didn't come to help me after the baby was born like she had with my other four children. At that point I didn't care whether we were married legally or not because I had been married for life, I thought, which had ended in divorce and the whole getting married idea didn't seem too good to me anymore.

Are you aware you blithely segued away from telling me about your memories that indicate you might have been molested more than you know for sure? You closed the topic and started in on how you felt about marriage when you and John got together. Why did you do that do you think?

Freud would say it was a defense mechanism to keep me from remembering more. I didn't realize I did it until you pointed it out. Again, though, even if I were molested in a way I don't remember how would that cause me to deny my son's mental illness? I can see it leading to some disturbances in my sex life and setting up a pattern of denial but why deny that in particular? I just managed to go away from remembering the molestations again didn't I? In reality I have tried to remember more but I just don't. There's probably a good reason not to remember. Whatever, I just can't remember.

Sometimes we need to remember something to set it aside so it doesn't disturb us any more, but if you can't then you can't. Let me know if you do remember more though, OK?

I remember innocent kid stuff. At about the age of five I remember a boy my age wanting to "see" me and then I could "see" him but my parents heard this begin through a window and stopped it so it never happened. There was also some "doctor" play in the neighborhood but I don't recall any actual observation of privates by anyone. But you know what? It was as if we all knew there was something very exciting and naughty about playing doctor.

I knew about the penis of course because it was explained to me in my "birds and the bees" talk. Actually this talk was given to me by my father. I was about 10-years-old and an only child. My sister came along several months later and was my only sibling. Probably my mother's pregnancy prompted my question. My father discussed sex with me using an anatomy textbook and I think I do recall some drawings in it. This was in about 1950. The whole thing was very clinical and to the point. He told me about the sexual act that produced a baby and told me not to have sex unless I got married. He called it sexual intercourse. Absolutely nothing was said about what a compelling experience it would be. I just never saw an actual penis that I remember until I got married and like I said, I was very curious about it! So, don't know how I could have envied it like Freud thought women do. I was aware, though, that men ruled everything. I knew I would probably grow up to marry and have children but it wasn't a cherished dream of mine like I hear some women recount.

So you were not hell bent on getting married and having children?

No, but I knew that's what would happen to me eventually and I accepted it more or less. In high school, though, I decided that first I wanted to go to college as a journalism major. This was encouraged by my father who talked me out of accepting a music scholarship because he didn't think I could make money with a music education. He wanted me to be able to support myself if necessary. One time my dad told me I was unlovable. Maybe that's why he thought I should get trained for a profession. Now that I think about it, he probably thought no one would want to marry me. He also, in fact, had me read Emerson's "Self Reliance" when I was 8-years-old.

The year you first understood about years changing?

Good memory! Yes, and that's pretty interesting isn't it? I never tied those things together myself. That's exactly the kind of thing getting therapy is good for. During a short course of therapy I had some time ago the therapist speculated that because I was a first and only child until I was 10 my father may have tried to make me his son while still demanding that I be subservient because I was a female. Thus a lot of my attitudes, which predated the women's movement, were already in place with me feeling free intellectually although recognizing the power men obviously had, that they ran everything.

What did you think about the idea that he raised you like a son except demanded you to be subservient to him?

I think it has merit but there are other possible reasons he may have wanted me to be ready to be responsible for myself. Whatever his reasons, it made me a certain way but I don't think I could ever be sure about exactly why he might have done that, giving me a deeper sense of responsibility for my own care than most girls were given in that day and age. It's not something we can talk about at all. In fact we never talk about anything but mundane stuff and he picks the topics. I go along with that to avoid conflict because he's old now and I don't want to upset him. In fact, I let him get away with weird things like telling me during a visit, while we were all having dinner, to never use the word "yummy" around him again! No explanation, he just announced it after I had said that word during dinner. About 15 years before that he also told me to never call him "Daddy" again. That one hurt but I obeyed that "decree" and switched to "Dad". I asked him about a year later if telling me not to say "yummy" was just to get me to do something he told me to do and he said, "Yes." Again, no explanation.

Before he got so old did you still engage him meaningfully on topics he didn't choose?

Oh yes, and we fought as usual. Same bad experience as when I was young. In fact, he once said he'd call the cops on me if I didn't cease and leave immediately when I tried to point out the truth of a situation that had just occurred.

Wow. He's given you very little slack from day one it appears.

I think I can say that is definitely true and in addition he's not at all pleased with my life. Maybe it started because I was a special project, being an only child until I was 10. When I was in high school, though, he did a lot of really nice things for me like getting me a faux fur coat when he went to New York on a business trip. It was gorgeous. He also lugged a sound system down to the Scout Hut repeatedly for dances after football games. I just remembered that once when I was 13 he tried to spank me for something but my mother interceded telling him I was too old to spank. Now I'm thinking about how once he even took me shopping to get my formal and heels for a prom. I have a photo of he and I sitting on a love seat where I'm all dressed up in that formal and he's looking at me lovingly. So, I know he loves me. He's just disappointed in my life.

Now he's old he's told me a story at least three times that I think may account for his being what I would call obsessive/compulsive. At about the age of nine or ten, I think, he was in charge of taking nails out of cast off lumber and straightening them to be used in a cottage his step-father was building for the family. Imagine straightening bent nails so they could actually be used again! That had to have some kind of deep affect on him. It gives me the jitters to even think about trying to do that. Now what he does, for instance, is to keep all the cans organized in the cupboard, turned face out and right side up, and gets upset if my mother doesn't put them away like that. When I was a kid, he used to tell me, "If you don't remember to take the trash out every night now, you won't remember to do something important later."

Sounds to me like you have figured out the difficulties of your relationship with your dad and it no longer really hurts you like it once did.

I do know he can't hurt me anymore like that simply because I don't engage him on that level any more. I seldom take exception to anything he is saying and I let him pick the topics we discuss. It's not close but it's OK.

Going back to Freud's stages, as far as the latency period is expressed in my life I actually remember "liking" a boy very much in the 3rd and 4th grades. I even remember his name, Richard. There was another boy who obviously liked me and walked back and forth in front of our house all the time but I couldn't stand him because he made rude noises. Actually, I remember his name too, Paul. I think children have sexual feelings which are generalized rather than being specific before adolescence and this would fit with Freud's idea that sexual energies are still present but channeled into friendship and learning during the school years. But they also spill over into

---

54

"liking" and "not liking" certain persons of the opposite sex, at least in my case they did.

The idea that men were superior and women inferior and that women were actually masochistic, which Freud taught, doesn't seem valid to me. I never felt subservient or subordinate even though my father often told me I had to learn to subordinate myself. It was something I really didn't understand given his encouragement for me to go to college and so on.

Ok let's stop this right there. I don't think analyzing Freud's theories, even by using your own experiences is going to help you in any real fashion. Besides, it's clear you have addressed all this and know what your childhood did or did not do to you.

It's true that I've figured out a lot of it, but I still don't know why I was in such rigid denial about my son's mental illness beyond what I mentioned last week. Denial is basically a lie and I hate liars. So to keep from hating myself I have to understand what caused this, I just have to know. So would you humor me as I go through this and, better yet, tell me where I might be going astray, please?

All right, but you have to know that modern psychotherapy doesn't even use Freud's psychoanalysis theories. We are more concerned with helping you change whatever hurts you than we are in what made it be that way to begin with. It's clear though that you recall being molested twice for sure, but not what was actually done when you were about five. That is something your mind did to protect you, a denial of a kind. Maybe that's one of the reasons you are able to deny things.

Since I knew what my step-grandfather did was wrong and would kick him again but I don't recall exactly what he actually did, maybe I didn't want to tell my grandmother so I forgot it? Since I knew it was really wrong, I know it would have hurt her terribly because she loved me very much.

Maybe you thought she wouldn't love you any more if you told her and that's why you forgot it?

I don't know, but I do know that I have to find a reason for my denials in order to make the effort to change, to watch out I don't deny stuff, or I won't try to change, plain and simple. I am generally not a prejudiced person and finding a secret prejudice in me against mental illness, if that's the only reason I denied it, is an affront to my sensibilities. I'm motivated to change this denial stuff. But I need to know if it was simple prejudice about mental illness or something more. I need to get past the guilt so I can help my son.

Everyone denies stuff and I don't know if we can ever find out exactly why you did it in regard to the mental illness.

I think we can. I think I can with your help. It's probably more than one thing anyway, but there's more, I know there's more than what we've uncovered so far.

Tell me this, do you know where this Freudian thing is going?

Sort of, but right now it's only in my head as you already surmised and I need to get it to my heart to deal with it. Can I continue?

OK, sure, go ahead if you think it helps. You were talking about not feeling inferior even though you're a woman who was born in 1940 when that was generally accepted in practice and in theory, especially by men.

I really never felt subordinate even when I experienced the anger of a man who thought it should be that way, up to and including being hit. But I don't think I was ever masochistic like Freud theorized women are because I don't like pain at all and am shocked when dealt it. About the age of 30 I learned that some men can and do hurt women physically and it's wise for a woman to understand and heed this to avoid being hit. I already knew about the emotional hitting part from my father but I thought my reaction was a weakness in my character not that I was just more emotional because I'm a female. Now I think that men actually feel superior to women and, in fact, the Bible even says they are the stronger vessel. I think it's because we women are more emotional than men that we are weaker. Not that we lack intellect. Everywhere I look in my own life and what I know of other women's lives makes me believe this is a truism. More recently it's been said that "Men are from Mars and women are from Venus."

I think I agree with you about women being more emotional.

No doubt, you're a man. It's more like I agree with you. Getting back to Freud, as far as defense mechanisms go, when I was a teenager I worked pretty hard to repress my sexual urges, not always succeeding completely but finally actually being a virgin when I got married. Back then, girls who engaged in petting but who wouldn't go all the way were called "goody two shoes" and I was certainly called that. Since I was a "goody two shoes" while knowing deep down I had very strong sexual urges, I think this "goodiness" was a defense technique, which is OK. But I also remember being very holier-than-thou about girls who had sex and pitied the one or two girls I knew who had become pregnant and left town for awhile. This was before any birth control other than condoms, abstinence or withdrawal. I think my attitude about those girls who "got in trouble" was an expression of Freud's idea of reaction. He would say that I used such attitudes toward those girls to assure myself I had no problem in that regard.

Wait a minute. You might actually have just been trying to be a virgin when you married and succeeded in that, you know. You were obeying your father. Just because you were chided by some for it doesn't make you a fraud.

OK but this denial thing still got me off track. I knew all along something was different about Chris but I loved him and felt comfortable with him because we didn't have horrible verbal fights about ideas. On the other hand I was very ignorant and didn't know what homosexuality was or what they did until years later. But I know I wondered what was wrong with him and just tossed it off as the fact that he was young and thought that as he grew older he would gain self confidence and our relationship would mature. He didn't push me to go all the way either but back then I just thought he respected me and I really felt it was the girl's job to make sure intercourse didn't happen. Later, I had no idea about how sex should have been with Chris so I didn't know our married sex life wasn't right. I had no orgasms at all until after our second child. I had never even been told about orgasms but I enjoyed sex anyway. So, I'm not sure if marrying him was really denial or ignorance. I know for a fact that in my second marriage I was definitely in denial about John's mental illness and after that about our son's mental illness.

Did your mom finally talk to you about sex before you were married?

She told me she hoped I would marry a gentle man and that it would all come naturally.

Not very specific though was it? Since girls usually role model themselves after their mothers which you probably did in some ways even though you felt you could not be like her because you were so different, was there anything about how she was that could have contributed to this denial thing?

Well, that's a very interesting question because my mom was in almost total denial about anything negative, except political stuff for some reason, for most of my life. She was the proverbial "Pollyanna" so maybe I did learn that from her. John used to accuse me of that, being a Pollyanna. Pollyannaism is a form of denial isn't it?

For sure, but unless it reaches unreal levels it can be a good way to live life. It's a lot nicer to see the glass half full than to see it half empty.

Well I have never ceased to be an optimist but I wouldn't say I was a Pollyanna any more. So, I think being able to deny stuff is more than that.

About my mother. She is a good one, a really good mother. She always encouraged me in addition to taking very good care of me. She made my clothes and my dolly Rosalie's clothes. I don't recall her ever hitting me although she would sometimes yell at me. When I was a teenager and was worried about how attractive I was, maybe even worrying that I wasn't sexy enough, she said, "You are sexy in a nice way." As my adult life got harder, it got harder for her to relate to it. She told me about 10 years ago, "If I had been through what you've been through, I would have gone crazy."

So, on with Freud. I don't think I project at all and I hate that particular defense mechanism which has definitely been employed against me. Personally I'd rather confront a person directly than project my crap onto them as a way to attack them. It's a very hurtful form of lying. I also don't actually think I'm guilty of displacement much and hate it too when it is directed at me but that one's hard to pin down. It's so unfair and unjust and unconscious. I think the hydraulic displacement model that theorists talk about exists because I know great anger has been directed at me sometimes that was really meant for someone else and what they did. John was very angry at his mother because she didn't raise him much of the time but left him with her mother. I have no doubt at all that he took this anger out on me just because I was a woman too. All I can say about Chris is that during the 50's homosexuality wasn't accepted at all. Some people like me didn't even know about it really. So, I see his marrying me more as an escape from being discovered or an attempt to be "normal", rather than an attack on me *per se* because he hated his mom or something. I think he actually loved me as a person, but not as a woman.

You haven't hit on Freud's idea of sublimation yet.

There's lots of sublimation in my life of my basic arrogance about my intellect. I supposedly have an IQ of 140 so I see things, infer things, know about underlying stuff that some people just don't even notice. I'd always been very careful not to act arrogant about my intelligence but then I figured out that such an effort just meant I was exactly that, arrogant. Didn't understand that until someone I really admired said to me, "There's more to life than intelligence you know!" He also told me I was "narrow in my broadmindedness."

Ah, there it is, at least a partial answer for why the denial. I've been sublimating my extreme fear of anything intellectually debilitating, such as mental illness for instance, by excessive efforts to act as though it were not there, ergo: denial. He was MY son and therefore had to be OK intellectually! Period. Now that I've been educated about mental illness, I know that it has nothing to do with intellect but everything to do with chemical imbalances. My own self esteem needs would not allow me to have a mentally ill child. So there it is, what I needed psychologically kept me from recognizing the illness in my child, my flesh and blood. Bingo!

So I hear you saying that you've been an intellectual snob and conceited about your intellect and because of that and your ignorance about mental illness you refused to see or deal with it in your son. Further, tying it together with your Freudian analysis, the conceit came from a need to impress your father by using your intellect. A totally human predicament.

But not very nice is it?

Nice, smice. You know you had a real need to believe in your intellect to impress your father, so it's not at all unexpected that you took this part of your makeup to an extreme by defending it from anything that could endanger it and having a mentally ill child might do that. Maybe you could be mentally ill too. In fact you mentioned you were crazy for two years over John's infidelity and that must have scared you a lot.

So the mental illness prejudice was because my major self esteem crutch, my intelligence, might be in doubt if I actually saw this disability in my son. Further that this basic fear combined with my actual ignorance about what mental illness is: a disease, which often can be treated successfully. Many people still have this prejudice, maybe for different reasons though.

John was very interesting but scary and I was afraid of what he was, wouldn't call it what it was even though he'd had diagnoses before meeting me. From what he told me, first they said he was a hysterical personality and then later a manic depressive. Now his diagnosis is bi-polar. Different names for the same thing, a type of mental illness. He always acted as though the diagnoses were wrong. It appeared that he was just hiding out from trouble the couple of times he was in the VA mental hospital. Almost as though he fooled them to stay there. He certainly never went for psychiatric help on his own but he'd go to the VA for his own reasons when he wanted less visibility. So, he was in denial and, although I wondered about it, I pretty much tried to believe he wasn't mentally ill either. But I do remember thinking, "Our son won't be like him." Actually, there is more that I remember. I thought, "He'll be like me." Like me mentally, but he isn't although he has some of my other traits.

John is very intelligent, brilliant in fact, but something's missing, some element of practicality. I must have thought that he couldn't really be mentally ill since he was so intelligent. Ignorance again. Since I've been dealing with this I've noticed that a lot of people equate mental illness with mental retardation and I did too in an inverse sort of way. Quite the reverse is actually true.

So, are we through with Freud? I have to say you did a pretty good job and it actually got you somewhere. Let's stop for the day and resume next week so we can get closer to whether or not you want to divorce John.

OK by me. See you then.

SESSION THREE

One Week Later

Seems we've covered the denial thing pretty well. Are you satisfied with what you discovered?

Yes, I think we can give that a rest. There's something that really bugs me about my life I'd like to talk about. The death of my big dream. This doesn't have anything to do with the denial thing but it gets into the difficulty I have divorcing John. We've touched on this before. My disillusionment about being a journalist. Did you know about the management of news 15 years ago?

Seems like I did, but now I think of it, maybe I didn't really.

Back in the early 80's I really thought a good journalist could reveal the truth easily. It was a rude awakening to find out different. Please keep in mind that of all the possible vocations in the world, I had wanted to be a journalist since I was a little girl. This was probably because my father worked in a print shop for a long time and wrote house organs for different companies and organizations. I loved going to that print shop.

Just what exactly is a house organ?

You'd call them newsletters today I guess. Informational publications regarding an organization or business which are delivered regularly to members or employees.

OK, so this was a cherished dream and a vocation you really wanted, journalism, right? And somehow it involves John too?

61

Yes, and I got to do it a little after John found out I had this dream and he encouraged me to go for it, part time at least. Then along came this story I was writing for a bi-weekly newspaper about a local man who had recently died from cancer. According to a local doctor, this cancer was created by his patient's exposure to Agent Orange while the man had served in Vietnam. This was in 1982, before Agent Orange was recognized as causing disabilities and/or death and no benefits were being paid by the VA to veterans who were exposed to it. They wouldn't even fork over the money to bury this particular victim of Agent Orange. Seems they're doing the same thing today to Gulf War veterans.

My editor didn't want to run the Agent Orange story but it did involve a local man and a local doctor who went on the record, so she let it in the paper. I was tipped to the story by John. All of a sudden the story started to mushroom. The Veterans of Foreign Wars decided to lobby Congress openly and vociferously to get Agent Orange benefits for Vietnam vets and the local chapter was having a meeting about this new development which I covered as part of the story I was writing. The thing kept growing and it took four weeks to finally bring the story to a spot it could be published. Then, the morning after I gave the story to my editor who was planning to use it on the front page, the radio announced two Congressmen's names who were introducing federal legislation to give Agent Orange exposure benefits to vets. John heard the report and told me. I called the radio station and they gave me the 800 number for UPI, the wire the story came over. I called UPI. The correspondent immediately went into the broadcast media database and found the story but he told me it was now being "withheld" and it would not go out again. He got all excited and quickly went to the print media database to see if it had been "withheld" there yet. After commenting that "they" hadn't got to that database yet he gave me the names and pertinent facts. I called the Editor and gave her a new lead for my story. She weirded out and bumped the story to the editorial page and didn't include that new legislation was pending nor the names of the Congressmen who introduced it. Took me awhile to fully comprehend what this meant about the news business and today it's much worse I am sure.

Got another jolt when about six years later I was offered a job to be the editor of a small weekly paper and oh I would have loved to have that job BUT the managing editor told me the conglomerate that owned the paper would tell me what I could write and how I should write it, through him, on the editorial page. I couldn't do that.

So this dream was crushed and, in fact, re-crushed later?

Yep. There's more too. Not only is information controlled but before the Agent Orange story I was fired by a big city daily partly because of a favorable story I wrote about a political figure the paper didn't support. John set it up for me to follow a County Supervisor around all day and write a story about it. I wrote what I saw and it was positive. I was new and didn't even know the paper's management didn't support this guy. It wasn't enough to not print that story, they fired me! Turns out they fired me for another reason too. Everyone in my bureau was up in arms because I kept getting lead stories and I was just a contract part timer and they were "staff". It was accidental but they were furious. The County Editor called me up and said he had to fire me. I was abashed.

The first story I wrote for that paper appeared in all the County Editions because it was the only local reaction to the Jonestown mass deaths in '78, which event was easily the biggest story of the decade. I had decided on the spur of the moment to interview someone in the Rajneesh Ashram in Lucerne Valley when I was passing by it coming home from my regular job. When I arrived they told me no one was the leader in that community but they brought someone out to be interviewed. The Jonestown event had only happened two days before I got there. I said, "Jonestown," and he said, "Oh, that's that group in Guyana, right?"

I said, "Yes, what do you think about what happened?"

He said, "What happened?"

Being isolated without radio, TV, or newspapers they didn't know! So, I got his unmitigated reaction to hearing that over 900 people had died in Jonestown. Further, the ashram was considering relocating to India, to another country, just as the Jones followers had done by going to Guyana. We discussed the strange things that could happen if citizenship protections were removed. That story went county wide and that was how the bureau staff got to know and hate me.

A week later I went, on assignment, to cover a fire station opening and on the way I happened on a semi-truck wreck with a dead person. Additionally someone who was not supposed to be in the truck was involved and he was the son of the trucking company owner. The truck was hauling cattle which were now loose. The location was a famous death trap highway curve. Response to the accident included the Department of Forestry, the Sheriff's Search and Rescue team on horseback and their helicopter, and the State Police. Further, someone had taken color photos and the paper had just published color photos for the first time the week before that and I got the film. After getting that story and going on to the fire station opening, I went to the newspaper's main plant, heading for a computer, only to be accosted by a staffer from my bureau who was there that day to cover the "cops" desk.

Apparently, when he got there he had called the cops for info and they told him there'd been a wreck in which someone had died, which in newspeak is called a "fatality", but they wouldn't give him the information because "someone from the paper already had it." Me. He greeted me with, "I hear you got the fatality! I'm on cops today!" Boy was he mad. Bothered me that he was so excited about a fatality. Like it was something to be desired almost. That guy was also the bureau photographer and the day after I was fired one of my photos appeared in the paper. It showed the town sign on the freeway hanging upside down in disrepair. He must have had a fit.

Another thing happened while I was in the main plant. Writing stories was computerized then but I didn't really know the software or even understand computers because it was 1978. I had used a manual at the bureau to compose stories and send them over the phone wire but this was different. So I asked a news writer for help and she assisted me to begin with but when I got done writing she told me to hit a certain button to send it wherever it went in order to get into the paper and the screen went blank! She caused me to delete it! I rewrote it and asked someone else for help. It appeared in the treasured Metro edition.

So, not only did you find out that information is managed and that media supports political figures but also that there was strong competition in the field which apparently you had not expected?

Competitive is a very mild word for how career journalists are. A few days after the Jonestown story, I got another lead story published. I had interviewed residents in a mountain town who were in the path of a giant mudslide should an earthquake happen on a fault which the town straddled. The mudslide warning had just been published by a state agency that had been investigating the potential problem in this particular canyon that was full of housing. I just called up residents who lived in the endangered location and asked for their reactions. Got some good quotes. So, it was the lead story the next day but I had no idea that would happen. That's when the Bureau Chief called me up and said, "Why didn't you tell me you had the lead story?" I said I didn't know it would be the lead, I just submitted it.

After I was fired, I continued to write for some small papers part time or freelance. Once I interviewed a Supervisor at Three Mile Island Nuclear Power Plant who escorted President Jimmy Carter and his wife through the reactor that had not malfunctioned, explaining what had happened to the one that had the problem. Funny how the release of the movie "China

Syndrome" came near this accident. He told me stuff that sounded to me that the Three Mile problem may have been sabotage.

Probably the most exciting story I wrote actually got into two publications, one in Southern California and one in Northern California. There were seven concurrent forest fires in the San Gabriel and San Bernardino mountains. I accidentally found out the first one was started by arson on the hill behind a housing development full of police officers' and firemen's homes. Six months later arson at that location was proved. That was a scoop. There's more to this story though. John was with me because we were in town for personal business and on the way home one of the fires was jumping the freeway. We were the last car to go North up the East side of the freeway through the pass to go home before they closed the highway. The flames were licking the road. John suddenly went down an off-ramp, crossed over and went back South down the same, closed, section of freeway, now on the West side, all the time shouting at me, "Get pictures!!" The flames were already jumping the freeway and there were fires on the other side now too. He loved it, I mostly closed my eyes like I always did when he was doing something crazy and I happened to be with him.

Stories pop out at me. Once I was just having coffee with my mom when I looked up and saw a big TV camera pointed at us through the window. I ran outside to find out what was going on. It was a reporter from Channel 2 in LA, a CBS station. They were interviewing people on the street about the fact this town's economic base was the yearly marijuana harvest. I let 'em know I was a local reporter and they wanted to interview me. After that I interviewed them and wrote a story about it for the town paper. Then I relocated back down South a week or two later and when I was in the grocery store the clerk suddenly looked up at me and said, "I saw you last night on Channel Two news!" She was confused about why I was introduced by a different name than she knew. I explained I was writing a story about the Channel 2 news team in that town up North and that I used a pen name for all that.

I've been letting you ventilate and enjoying the stories too by the way but not sure yet how this gets us back to John and whether or not to divorce him.

There's more. I learned another disillusioning thing about the news media from when John was a radio news editor for all of three weeks before he got fired. Advertisers drive the media who need their money. You don't see many negative stories about big advertisers unless they go national. John had a great story about several companies that were advertisers on that station. The station manager could not afford to let the story be aired. A similar but bigger, national story broke six months later on *60 Minutes* and it was about how foreign interests are buying up our land and companies. This was in '79.

I see. Sounds as though John was involved with your journalistic experience and big dream a lot and, in fact, you often did it together.

True. He is hot too, even more than me but he doesn't write and I do. He continued to do investigative news and went on radio talk shows causing him a lot of trouble. Like when he suggested that the Sheriff's helicopter made drug runs. He went to jail before the fall out from that was over.

You miss that? Working together that way?

Yeah but he goes so far it's dangerous to life and limb. I would never go that far because I had five children. I have a really, really good nose for news and have good investigative skills that I learned when I worked in a welfare fraud department. I was taught how to ask hard questions without anyone getting very upset. John is abrasive, belligerent, and confrontive. So, it was also uncomfortable working with him. The newspaper jobs were my jobs, but he went places with me probably to protect me if I needed it.

He was ready to protect me any time. I was threatened once when I was an AFDC intake worker and John found out where the man lived, not from me by the way, and he went over there to tell the man that if anything happened to me he would be dead within an hour. Neither threat was carried out. The guy had a valid complaint by the way. Two of us quit the department over that and I went on to write a grant proposal to produce a TV documentary about welfare situations. Got the grant and got it in the can but it was never edited.

Tell me the very most interesting thing about all this news stuff please.

I guess it would have to be that I insisted the big city daily use my pen name and the managing editor of the daily said, "No." My husband paid him a visit. After first noting that Ann Landers is a pen name, he asked him why it's OK for her but not for me. The answer was still, "No." Then John told the managing editor that maybe he would chain himself to a pole in the main plant news room in protest if I weren't allowed to use my pen name! They let me use it. Maybe that's why I was fired too, although it wasn't mentioned.

You had a gleam in your eye when you told that story, in fact you chuckled. You get a kick out of his shenanigans don't you?

Yeah, so long as my kids aren't in danger. And there was danger sometimes. For awhile I'd pick up the phone and be treated to what sounded like someone being garroted. I think it was the nasty guy with the fancy car I wrote about in "Shades" but it might have been John's bookie's bosses when he owed them over $1,000 for about six months. Who knows? About that time is when it became too much for me although the impulse to leave was over an actual household fight.

Did you stay gone that time?

No. Left about four more times before it stuck.

So you don't do news anymore but you still see stories. You just won't write them? Even if you and John stay married you wouldn't write news anymore then would you?

He's tried on occasion to get me interested to do it but I won't do it any more. I might write a book though, maybe about phone companies. Here's just one, recent story about the stuff they do. My local phone company, a couple of year's ago when I still had a business, put $400 too much over a period of time on my bill which took me hours to figure out. I worked for eight months to get the money back. During this time they sent the bill to the wrong city for six months even though I called them repeatedly about not receiving it. Subsequently they told me I was wrong to say there was a substantial balance due on that same phone service because they could not locate the account, and then they misapplied my closing payment to the new possessor of my old phone number. They had trouble with my bill because I moved about four times in a year and also put the phone on call forwarding to another state once for a month. The phone company did all that but had some trouble keeping it straight. There's more to that story but it's too involved to tell you now.

That's a lot of moves. Lots of change. Going back to John for awhile, is he good with information technology?

Oh yeah. We always had two phone lines in our home and when answering machines came out he got one right away. I know he taught me a lot about communications and survival for that matter. He also had a CB radio. Almost never saw him for a month when he first got that and was learning it. His handle is Moondance. When we were together he always had a radio on listening to music or the news. It drove me crazy because I like it to be quiet sometimes, especially when I'm trying to go to sleep. Now he has CNN on most of the day but he's more involved with the local scene than the global one because he is very territorial. He wants to know his territory and works hard to understand it completely and have influence within it of an informal nature.

That was kind of a mouthful. Is he a godfather type or what?

You could say that, but he's Irish to the core. No, actually he's Irish most of the time and then when he's really drunk he's Apache. An interesting combination don't you think?

Not too sure about stereotyping.

Well, contrary to what's taught, there are traits based on past cultural and family experience, there just are. I've seen it too much. I think stereotyping is bad if you use it for negative and narrow minded reasons but let's face it Irish men are charming, full of blarney, tell great stories, and love to drink, fight, and make love. And Scots, which I am at least a quarter of, when they finally get angry nearly go crazy and bounce off walls. The English are reserved to a fault it seems to me and the Latinos are hot blooded or passionate to be more exact. Orientals are quiet and inscrutable but very practical. I'm old, have known a lot of people and interacted with many cultural groups and these things are often very true. All people have feelings, all people have similar needs but culturally they are very different.

What else is in your ethnic background?

Choctaw and what else I don't know. People have often thought I was Italian, Portuguese, Native American, Mexican or Jewish. All of that may also be true, but I'm pretty sure I am third generation out of Scotland on my mother's side and about the same amount of Choctaw on my father's side.

So, I'm getting here that you actually enjoyed being with John but it was too hard with kids, right?

That and the fact he's been known to hit me. There's also the problem that my folks and most of my kids hate him and don't want me around him. He was very strict, quite terrifying as a parent, and got drunk often enough and nasty enough to make them really dislike him. He did some other bad stuff too, like something really beyond the pale once. He put a gun in my mouth once.

Was it in anger?

No, he came home drunk but he wasn't angry and when he did it the safety was on. It was very frightening and something could have gone wrong. The safety could have come off or something. In fact his excuse is that he was trying to give me the experience of being raped which he thought I wanted. That must have been some other woman in his past that wanted that experience, and we didn't have sex after the gun thing either. He is rash and too sure of himself and that can be deadly. I don't think I have ever processed that event completely, it seems unreal but I know it happened.

So, now that the kids are gone more or less is it really possible to be around him much given the gun thing?

I actually don't think about the gun thing. Mostly I think I want to be free legally because I'm mad at him about how he has treated our son, about his lack of fathering after our separation and in fact being a very bad role model for our son by doing drugs with him. He always said, "Do what I say not what I do." That is pure hogwash. They are going to do what you do. Role modeling is so much more powerful than I ever knew or even suspected. I actually thought that people just grew up to be themselves. I had no idea they copied their like sex parent, hopefully. Turns out role modeling is very much where it's at in regard to parenting.

I'd like to go back to the denial problem again. Are you aware that something as frightening as having a gun put in your mouth might cause your ability to deny to really strengthen?

Never gave that much thought at all, I mean about the gun. It was so big that I just accepted it had happened, I was still alive and forgot it. Forgot it, same thing as denying it isn't it? Anything really difficult from that point on may have been easier to deny in order to keep my mind closed to the reality that the gun thing happened. Is that what you mean?

Possibility. How old was your son when that happened?

Not sure, I think he was about six.

Maybe five even?

Maybe.

Did he know about the gun thing at that time?

I don't know. He knows now. I think all my kids do but not sure when they found out about it.

If he did, that would constitute major trauma, to think his father could have caused the death of his mother. His mind might have done something to protect itself right then and there. I'm not sure but it's something to think about.

Yes it is but even as I say that I know my mind is searching to find something else to talk about, to go to another topic and it will try to keep me from really thinking about it much when I'm alone.

Let's just see shall we?

Ok, I feel relief that we aren't going to talk about it any more because there's a question forming about it. Could he really have ever loved me and have done that, taken such a chance, even if he were drunk?

It has nothing to do with love. It has to do with his illness and his background. But it was very, very wrong and dangerous. You're lucky you're here to talk with me about it.

There but for the grace of Yahweh I could have died and all my children been motherless. It just wasn't time for me to die I guess. Thanks for helping me to get this far into this matter.

But your son is grown now and although he is vulnerable and struggling with his illness he is his own man, yes? Is he a lot like his father?

No. He's much kinder but he has an edge sometimes like his father. He can also "think out of the box" like his father. He loves his father, seems to understand him somewhat, and basically takes everything he says with a grain of salt which is good. I just hate it that he didn't have a good father experience, that I had to leave in fact and that I couldn't provide him with another, better, father because I couldn't stomach the idea of being intimate with any other man. Like I said, I will apparently always feel married to John. Just no way anyone could ever be that interesting to me to say nothing of love. At least that's how I have felt for these 10 years.

So, then if you divorce him, you give up male companionship I guess.

Well, we could still be companions when possible even though we're not married couldn't we?

Could you?

He might be able to but I might not.

Kind of a pickle isn't it?

Yeah, so that's why I'm here.

So how were things financially with him?

Terrible. He gambled. He didn't work but did things like buy stuff and sell it and whatever else I don't know to come up with some money now and then. Once he bought a car covered with blue tile for $1000. A tile company had done it for advertising and donated the car to a fund raising auction. I was furious he bid on it and won but you know what, that car was a lot of fun. It was like a tank because it was so heavy. The top had been cut off. Looked like a convertible but there was no top. We lived in the desert so it was OK. It was actually beautifully done, a real show stopper.

You drove around in a car covered in blue tile?

Yeah it was a 1969 Dodge Polara. For awhile it was the only car that actually ran in our household.

Back to the finances and how it went with him.

We lost two houses ultimately. The first house was a starter and we rented it out when we moved to the bigger one. Apparently our entire financial thing was based on the fact that I had a steady job. Then I had to go to war with my employers over their corrupt deeds. Took that to the county level, then to the state level, then to the national level before it was over. The program in question was the Comprehensive Employment and Training Act better known as CETA, one of the very best programs that the feds ever developed. BUT corrupt people locally found it very easy to steal from it or at the very least to use it for political gain, and to take over entire county personnel departments with it. That was a very costly battle and our whole thing came tumbling down like a house of cards after that. He fought that one along side of me, first from within and then from without. It started because I kept doing corrective actions and writing memos about my cleanups. Then the Director called me into headquarters and wanted to know why I kept doing that. I told him that I just opened doors and bodies fell out so to speak and I cleaned up the mess and let them know it was fixed. Assumed that's what they would want.

Later I began to see that programs were not developing as they should, didn't have contract numbers like they should and so on. Additionally, literally millions went back every year because the target population was not really reached like it could have been. I was actually told by my supervisor that I should ask for my car to be overhauled before I signed an on-the-job-training contract with a mechanic shop for instance. I refused to operate that way and put about 400 people to work or in training as fast as I could. It was a wonderful program. Even put a blind man into diesel mechanic training and he succeeded, got a job, and that was on the front page of the CETA magazine eventually although nothing was said about my involvement. Only found out about the article by accident.

One time my supervisor came up and handed me several enrollment documents and told me to sign them. I'd never seen, let alone interviewed the applicants or checked out the worksites so I told him I wouldn't sign them. There was a law that if one signed such a document without really knowing who the applicant was, if they were eligible and if the worksite was a good one, there was a mandatory $10,000 fine and imprisonment.

Then one time my supervisor told me that the director was "lonely" and wanted to see me. I said, "He's married isn't he, so he shouldn't be lonely!" I was so shocked. I gave them all one hell of a time before it was over. This was way before the sexual harassment laws. I didn't need those laws. I just wouldn't go along with that at all, ever. John called me at work one day shortly after I told him about the director being "lonely". He told me to take a coffee break right now, told me where to go and said to invite my supervisor to go with me. I didn't think this guy would go to coffee with me what with me refusing to do the illegal things he told me to do but he jumped on it and we went to have coffee. When we got seated in a booth, suddenly John appeared and sat next to me. Then a friend of our's who was a red rag from the barrios sat next to my supervisor who was also Hispanic. Immediately my supervisor got very nervous. I forget what was said but I remember the looks. Our friend told me later this guy was a "Gabacho" which roughly means he was a sellout to Anglos. My supervisor never asked me to do anything weird again and stayed pretty much away from me altogether after that. In fact, I actually got transferred to another supervisor who was over an hour away. When the departmental powers that be saw the handwriting on the wall, that I was going to continue to operate legally and effectively, they said I had to come down and do my job at headquarters. My district was huge, some of the territory being over three hours away. I went there for awhile but one morning John got me up very early. He had a plan. We showed up at headquarters and had me moved out of there before anyone else came to work. I was very visible there, complete with a ballet shoes painting, a special lamp and fancy book ends on my desk in the bull pit and then I was gone.

From there on I worked out of a home office. They refused to give me materials, clients, or anything I needed but when they gave me assignments that were impossible somehow I got them done. Actually I think there was definitely Divine intervention involved. It was an amazing thing to be part of. By that time they literally ran county personnel and I got a check stub suddenly that had two extra weeks of vacation on it. I called up and told them it was wrong. What a trap. They got their just desserts when the entire program was scrapped nationwide and a new one that closed loopholes was put into place. But closing the loopholes made it more difficult to help people who needed jobs and training. CETA was scrapped because of greedy administrators. No doubt a lot of people like me complained.

That was the biggest, most important battle I fought in my life and as they say, the battle was won because the corruption was squelched, but the patient, meaning my family structure, died. I remember the day I came home and said I had resigned under protest. It's the only time I saw real tears hidden in John's eyes even though he had told me to carry a pre-written resignation in my purse. He knew what it meant to us when I resigned. I didn't. Naively I went on a rampage to right the wrongs, starting with the civil service commission, then the state employment department, then the department of labor and then-President Ronald Reagan. Sent them all the same nine pages, single spaced document about what I had encountered in that corrupt department.

That's the big one in your life and a turning point apparently.

One after another the kids peeled off rather than suffer a welfare existence as well as the escalating fights between me and John because of the financial stress. Because of his "phone" reporting on radio talk shows we were anathema in the area and there was no way I could get work again. He went into a mattresses kind of mode, staying at our foreclosed house for more than a year after it had been auctioned off on the courthouse steps. He has a saying, "I never give up."

So, then, he probably continues to encourage you if you show the least sign of keeping him in your life I would imagine.

———

You're pretty smart. He's actually proposed to me again by the way.

So you have to fight yourself and him to not be with him and he's wanting to put it back together.

Yes, but I need to let you know there are some things I haven't mentioned that make it hard to be around him and still have all the rest of my family in my life. They're big things too.

Torn.

Always. Prioritizing always and our son is the priority now because of his illness.

And now you're thinking of divorcing this man you love and enjoy?

I suppose so yes. And, I'm getting old. Don't think I could deal with all that again. Like the house for instance. He refused to sell it and only let me try to sell it in the last five weeks before the foreclosure auction. I almost did it too. It was only costing $375 a month. The rent for my two room efficiency apartment now is $450 a month. What a tragedy, and it would almost be paid for now too and worth about $300,000 at least. I found it but he put the deal together and made money doing it.

But he lost it, slowly and wouldn't give up there either.

It was excruciating. We were also into large credit card debt. Twice in my life I got involved in the credit card syndrome. Once, in the end of my marriage to Chris it developed into a bankruptcy filing. The second time I was involved in credit card debt was with John who refused to work regular, or as I now know he couldn't work steady because of his illness. Chris' stopped paying child support which had been lowered to $75 per child of whom there were now two still at home from the first marriage. I had worked full time and John used credit cards and other loans to keep things going for several years. He insisted on controlling the family finances, not because I couldn't do it but because he wanted to spend money the way he wanted. Like get drunk weekly at least, like gamble, like buy cars or whatever else he felt like spending money on. I must say his deals were good ones but the gambling was terrifying.

What he did in regard to our home was not to pay the mortgage payments until the house was in foreclosure and then he would get an equity loan and bring the mortgage up to date at the last minute. He could only do this two or three times to bring it out of foreclosure. Eventually this ended with the house being auctioned off on the courthouse steps which he insisted on watching.

What did you do then?

He insisted on living there. After awhile we were told to move out of the house, so we lived in the breezeway. Good thing it was in the desert. I was a basket case, can't even remember how we ate or if we did but three of the kids stuck it out for awhile in this situation with one living mostly at her friend's house across the street. Then my oldest son moved out but came back for awhile. The youngest two finally moved into John's mother's house with me. John refused to leave though and continued to stay at our old house in a broken down bread truck we had until the sheriffs came several times to tell him to leave. We called that truck "Pokey" and he was supposed to fix it and we were going to travel, live like gypsies. Never happened. He traded the gun, the one he put in my mouth once, to a friend in exchange for fixing Pokey but he never did it. Eventually I left the area with the kids because my mother-in-law's crazy Doberman hated and growled at our son in addition to everything else and I was afraid that dog would kill him.

This sounds absolutely crazy-making. Did you try counseling when all this was going on?

Yes, I went to see a guy once. It blew him away just hearing a little of this and he had nothing to offer. Never went back. Of course John wouldn't go. Later, one of the times I came back after leaving him, I talked him into going to a Vietnam vet family counselor that one time. It was actually a group and the focus was what the war had done to the men not on all this other stuff which was moot at that point anyway us having lost everything by then.

So, then you were on your own with the remaining kids. Trying to survive.

Fortunately I had learned a lot from him about survival but I never did resort to using what little money I got the way he often did which was to gamble with it. I've never even bought a lottery ticket. When he and I went to Vegas I would play the nickel slots. He won $5,000 in a poker tournament once he was fond of saying but didn't mention he promptly lost half back. He had managed to get a couple of casinos in Vegas to allow him to cash checks. Once he wrote $400 in checks and lost it all. There was nothing in the bank to cover those checks. That night I cried and cried. He couldn't seem to stop doing that type of thing. It's how he tried to keep the thing going I guess. He had managed to get a real estate license but seldom used it except to help us or others, not to make real money.

Somehow he covered that check stuff though because I don't hear about him going to prison for writing bad checks.

Yep, somehow he did. Not even sure how he did it. The worst was when football season came around. He won $1000 on Super Bowl XIII and I was so relieved I sent the Pittsburgh Stealers quarterback, Terry Bradshaw, a thank you letter. All during the football season John's "work" was to figure out which teams would win by which spread and to bet them in groups of bets. I don't know what they call that except illegal. Never did understand it and couldn't believe a grown man would do that, but a lot do.

Needless to say we fought and fought about all this stuff and more. What terrible battles we had. When I finally left for more than a night, I had two of my five children to support at first and then just one because the other one went to live with her married sister first and then with my parents which was a lot nicer than living with me financially speaking. She was in high school and had a good career there too. My eldest two girls had gone to live with their libertine father much earlier who had been living openly with another man for a long time. All those bills that had accumulated in the marriage just stood out there in bad credit land. John would never consider bankruptcy. It practically took an act of Congress to get him to allow me to apply for welfare finally while we were still together. Somehow he got the bookie to lay off.

Sounds like you're mad at him about a lot of things, real things.

Yes, but I forgive him for some reason, maybe because he's mentally ill. But there are some things that can't be overlooked because they had consequences that are still ongoing even though I have forgiven him. Sometimes it seemed like he'd deliberately mess everything up. Everything just goes wrong if he is around. Don't know if I could cope with loss of family and that too. He always said he had approach/avoidance syndrome that caused him to sabotage everything.

Sounds like the bottom line is to decide what you can cope with now you're getting older. Did you finally get situated?

Not really. Had many jobs and situations that required many moves. Did get a new car once but had to have a co-signer, my eldest daughter. That went bad four years into paying it off because it was stolen about two weeks after I had a $900 new transmission put in it for which I was still paying. I reported it to the police and filed a claim with my insurance company. They paid for part of a rental car for two months. Then the adjustor told me to go to where I bought the car and ask them to find me a comparable car for what the insurance will pay, which has not been decided as yet. He told me he will do a "local market study" to find out what the car is worth. I did my own study and found that it would cost $5000 to replace my car. The car dealer proceeded to offer me cars that were three to five years older than my car. A deal was attempted at one point and the adjustor announced they will pay only $3200. I told him to go buy a comparable car for that price and give it to me then. He said, "We don't do that!" and I explained to him that's because it's not possible. During negotiations, the seller talked the adjustor up to $3700 and he never budged off that.

This was a long nightmare wasn't it?

It was really bad. The finance company said that there was still $1700 owing on the note for the stolen car! That was a total of some $15,000 that $8,000 car, which I no longer had, actually cost me being paid off a year early mind you. Back in the day, say the 50's and 60's, when a car was stolen or totaled they bought you another one just like it, period.

I wound up with a car that was three years older than my stolen car but it had some nicer features, mainly air conditioning. I drove it home on a very hot day thankful for the AC and half way there it broke down. I called the dealer and they came to take me home and tow the car away. They fixed it. I got it. It broke down again. They got it. They fixed it. I got it. It broke down again. They got it. They fixed it. I got it. It broke down again. All the breakdowns happened within two weeks of my taking ownership of the car.

The last time it broke down, I drove it slowly, making a terrible noise, into the dealer. I parked the car, gave the keys to the secretary and told her I didn't want this car and I sat down. Before it was over the Sales Manager had to deal with me. His comment on this car, which I overheard when he called a subordinate, was, "Take that piece of shit car off my lot and send it to Mexico." That was an interesting revelation. I worried about the Mexicans while I waited. Then the Sales Manager decides to sell me a new car, a model that currently has a $700 rebate on it. He said he went "clear to the top" of the lending agency, which made this new car and made my stolen car, and got approval to do this. They added the $1700 I "owed" on the stolen car to the price of the new car which sells for $10,000. Then they subtracted $700, calling it a down payment in lieu of a trade-in. In reality I traded in "the piece of shit" car my insurance check bought for $3700 and which they sent to Mexico, but that escaped me at the time and they got away with it. They wore me down. They also gave me 21% interest on this car and my payment was an additional $100 a month to what I'd been paying on the car that was stolen which they and I both knew I couldn't afford. You know how it is. I was working in a big city and I HAD TO HAVE A CAR. I paid the transmission place too.

Wow, you lost $3700 and didn't even know it for awhile?

I'm not too bright at that stuff. Intelligent I am but common sense I don't always have. Later I took this new car in, still under warranty, because it was making a noise. They found nothing wrong and tried to charge me $59 to diagnose it. I refused to pay the $59 and during a heated discussion about it, the mechanic told me the model was discontinued the year I bought it because it was a "piece of shit" car. Of course. One way or another they were going to give me a piece of shit car it seems.

After struggling for two years to pay $303 per month I simply couldn't do it any longer. I called them up repeatedly and asked them to redo my loan so I could make a $203 payment, which is what my original payment was and what I could afford. They could start the five years over too I told them. They declined, over and over, to make any adjustment. So, finally, I returned the car to them. Regardless of my taking it to them, it is called an "unwilling repossession" on my credit report! Then, they proceeded to auction the car off for who knows what and now I'm getting repeated bills for $8,351.95 even though I don't have the car! If I became a millionaire I wouldn't pay them another cent.

They fix it now so you are "upside down" on your note and the insurance company never pays as much as you owe if the car is stolen or wrecked, and the lender makes you pay the difference to them. Everyone wins except the buyer. The kicker in all this is that the feds conducted a sting on a car stealing ring and found a warehouse full of stolen cars, among which was mine. It was five months after the theft. The insurance company called to see if I still had the $3700 check because they would trade it for my old car although they said "it has obviously been very mistreated." The whole thing gets laughable. I only buy old cars now. They just have to run, be legal and have a heater. No one steals them. When they get dints I don't care. Generation X buys junkers too unless they have parents who can afford to get them really good cars. They can't buy new cars on their own because they never have enough money or credit capacities.

Credit is a trap. My children range from living beyond their means on credit and under terrific stress to one child opting out of the establishment and for awhile he lived on a small piece of green land, away from town, in a small cabin he built with cast off scraps to avoid such a rat race. The latter child is part of Generation X and he's the one who is mentally ill too.

What is green land?

In this case the green land was in a remote area in Taos County, New Mexico. It's called green land because the taxes are not being paid on it and they don't actually have a record any more of who owns the land if anyone ever did. Why they don't have the records I don't know. Maybe there was a fire or something. Such land will eventually get sold at a tax lien auction but before that happens if someone puts a structure on it and lives in it for five years and meanwhile pays the property tax for it, which in my son's case was $5 a year, they can get possession of a deed on the land. Similar to homesteading land I think.

Talking about this particular land reminds of a really good story. A Japanese company bought up a lot of land that rims the West side of the Taos Gorge probably for a really low price because there are no public services there. The speculation was that they were going to ultimately put hotels up there. So far nothing has happened in terms of development though. Would be very expensive to actually raise functional buildings there but what a spectacular view they would have. If I were doing news still I would follow up that story.

About credit and living on it, if you and your husbands had managed the credit better, you might feel differently now about the whole mechanism but I have to admit it's a trap we all seem to fall into at least once.

What really gets me is that rich people, who have solid gold credit, get very low interest rates and lots of freebies! That's backwards or at least unequal. About all the unpaid debts John used to say, "I'd rather owe you for the rest of my life than cheat you out of it," because he wouldn't declare bankruptcy.

He has a bunch of sayings doesn't he?

Actually he makes up a lot of words, phrases, or sayings that make their way into the public vernacular. He's a trend setter. The only trend I ever remember setting was to wear argyle knee socks in high school. I am actually Miss Conventionality in many respects. He does unusual things like buy that car covered with tile.

As far as cars went, he loved classics. We had two suicide door Lincolns, '65s I think. They both worked for awhile but then they broke down. John never got them fixed, not enough money and although I think he might have been able to do it himself, he wouldn't. Boy, cars are a pain in the neck and just try to get a mechanic to do right by you if you're my age and sex! When I find a good one I treasure him! There's a great and honest, also kind and generous, mechanic in Questa. People come from all over to this man.

Let's break off on that note because we've gone over time but could you write the mechanic's name and number down for me? Even though I'm a man and younger it's still always good to know about a mechanic you can trust. Want to come again next week on the same day and at the same time?

Yes, and hang on a minute and I'll get his info for you. (Writes on paper). Here you go. See you next week. This was mostly ventilation but it felt good. Thanks.

SESSION FOUR

One Week Later

Do you think you would be comfortable enough now to talk about the circumstances surrounding your first marriage?

Sure, in fact I've written a piece giving the basic facts about that marriage. I'd like to read it to you. One thing that isn't in there, though, is about the ex-boyfriend of one of my closest friends who came back to town from college once and asked me out. He was, probably, the most attractive young man I've ever seen. My grandmother saw his photo and declared immediately that I should marry him! But, he wanted to make out on the first date and when I wouldn't he informed me I would have to change my attitude when I got to college. I disagreed and that was the end of that. Don't think I could have got past his having been my friend's steady anyway, even though she had left the area. By my last year in high school I was in love with my first husband. He was and still is a charming man, very talented in many ways, and very easy to be around. Sounds great, right! A friend had told me he didn't have "backbone" and I stood up for him. I thought he was simply not self confident yet and I was sure that would come.

What appealed to you about him?

He was in the Honor Society, had a disc jockey position at the local station, worked on the school newspaper with me and he played the piano, by ear, beautifully. No lessons, just raw talent. He was not a jock. His physique back then was called skinny which is called healthy and good looking nowadays. He aged fairly well by the way. Of course, Miss Virgin had no idea about certain sexual matters, later revealed.

81

When I graduated and my folks moved to another state, I missed him terribly. We wrote and wrote and I kept those letters for many years. I went back to his state to start college. I was a year older than he and after he graduated we planned to marry and we did. It was okay at first, but after a while I could tell something was wrong, something was between us. He was distant. At first I thought maybe it was because he was working full time at a mental hospital as an attendant and going to college full time. I was working too. His stories from the mental hospital no doubt fueled my fear of mental illness now that I think about it. Funny how life works. My dad had worked at the same hospital 20 years before and I think he suggested this job to Chris. So, can I read this to you? Probably take about 15 minutes.

Ok. When did you write it?

About three weeks ago. I call it *Have Compassion for the Closet*. (She begins reading.)

It was 1956. I was 16. My steady boyfriend of two years went out with a girl who would go all the way while I was two states away with my family on vacation. He was the school super jock so I guess she wanted him and she snagged him that way. Didn't last long and we tried to get back together but I was so mad at him I could never stop being snide if we were near each other.

I had also been molested while I was on that vacation by my grandfather who came up behind me and shoved his hand down the front of my boat-necked blouse while I was sitting at the kitchen table. My father walked in right then and wanted to know after we left why I let my grandfather do that! Then I come home to no boyfriend any more. He was a step-grandfather by the way. I lost 20 pounds in about a month over losing my boyfriend and my innocence.

So, during the next school year when I got to know a fairly new boy at school who was talented, intellectual, didn't insist on going all the way, wrote for the school newspaper like I did, and was actually a DJ on the radio while in high school I was pretty much ready to settle into a relationship that would be fun, interesting, romantic, and not traumatic. He could and still can sit down and play the piano without ever having had any lessons.

He was behind me a grade and after I graduated my family moved far away. I was devastated. We sent love letters back and forth all summer and I returned to his state for my Freshman year in college. I didn't date anyone else and we got married when he graduated like we planned. Now I know he married me because he wanted to get away from his home life which was horrible for him and because that's what a homosexual did back in the late 50's. That was the proverbial closet they got into: marriage. Many homosexuals lived a lie and imposed on women who unknowingly loved them in order to protect themselves from conventional society's ill will about homosexuality. Having two kids within four years kept him out of the service too and Vietnam was raging by then.

Ultimately, it wasn't until much later, 1969 in fact, when someone my husband had confided in told me about the many homosexual affairs my husband indulged in while being married to me, which I didn't believe and went to my husband to ask about and he confirmed it all, that I realized I couldn't spend my life with him. I had known something was wrong between us not long after we were married. I would badger him sometimes to "let me in." He had finally told me he had a "latent homosexual" problem because he was so thin and he admired well built men. There was, however, never any mention of sexual activity, which at that time I didn't even know existed in the world anyway. I thought homosexual meant someone who loved someone else of the same sex, not that they did anything sexual with them. That concept simply wasn't in my mind at all.

Sometime in 1963 my husband made known to me while I was getting ready for an old friend of his and his wife to visit, that there had been a physical, sexual relationship between my husband and this guy in another town before they both came to my high school. My husband said he had a real crush on him and maybe loved him still! We had two little girls then and today I am surprised I didn't drop over dead at that news. I can't even recall if his friend and wife ever came to our house. My memory is blank for awhile after he said that. I do remember later telling him to leave and when he didn't I found him an apartment that I wanted him to move into right away. I wasn't religious at that time but I was totally disgusted, shocked and ashamed to be married to him. Even then though, I didn't think about what they actually could do sexually, only faced those facts years later when my second husband forced me to understand what homosexual activity was in all its glory. He literally had to use crass language, repeatedly, to get me to see it and believe it. Until then all that I knew about sex was foreplay and the missionary position.

When I wanted my husband to leave, he wouldn't go. A friend who knew I was trying to get him to leave suggested counseling. So we went. I was told to get a part time job and stop thinking about it which I did. He was put into weekly individual and group therapy. After a year he seemed OK, better, like he really wanted me. We seemed, finally, to be close. We agreed to have another child. Then after our son arrived everything changed. He just stopped acting. He admitted that was what he'd been doing. I think maybe back then the psychological community thought that if a homosexual or bisexual acted the part of a heterosexual, it would create behavior modification or something. Not sure really. Just know it changed back to the way it had been and I was one miserable woman, except I had three beautiful children. Thinking back I assume now that maybe he didn't have any homosexual activity for that year he was only acting, probably doing what they suggested because he wanted a son. Then as soon as our son was born he stop going to counseling and he probably just went back to his old ways because there was clearly this distance again between us. It never occurred to me at the time that he was doing anything behind my back, living a second life. That's what a lie does to people. It creates distance and then betrayal of trust when the lie is discovered.

I figured whatever this distance was between us I would have to live with it because I got married for life and so far as I knew then he was faithful to me. Then we joined a community theater. We both had roles in some plays. One day while I was dusting the piano I came across a piece of paper right there on the cover to the keyboard. I read it because I wanted to know if it should be thrown out or was important. Turned out it was a love note from my husband to a man we both knew from the theater group. I was now eight months pregnant with our fourth child which situation was fine with me but had been unplanned. So you can see we still had sex from time to time even though there was a distance, probably because I initiated it.

That tore it. He left to follow this man to another town. He also gave up his teaching job and went to work as well for another theater person. I asked my folks to help me and the kids without telling them the problem, just saying that we were separating. My father came and got us. We lived with them about six weeks and by the time the baby was delivered my husband had already come back to say he wanted his family. He lost the job and he lost the man apparently. I was stupid enough to think he'd come to his senses and thought if we both agreed not to be involved with the theater that he could be all right. He got another job but that one didn't work out either. Finally he got a teaching job near the school he'd taught in before and then we left my parents house to set up our own home again. Within about two months he got a call from a theater person who wanted to do a play with him. I told him not to do it because we had agreed not to be involved with theater people. He did it anyway, a one act by Albee entitled "Zoo Story". Next thing I know this man who he's doing the play with comes on strong to me and tells me about all my husband's homosexual affairs. Not believing it but wanting to know the truth I go to my husband who confirms all these affairs and something even worse. I decide I can't let my husband raise our son and at the same time I fall in love with the one who told me the truth, finally.

This time I leave the whole situation including the man I fell in love with and go back to my parents for a short time and then get my own place in a nearby town. Right after that separation from my first husband and before my second husband and I lived together, I actually went out with and had sex with a man where I lived. I cried all night and knew I could never do that again. For me love and sex are inexorably tied together. So, at the age of 30, with four kids and no job skills, I was on my own and in great psychological disarray. Lots of things happened after that including a short stint of being with my first husband again that was based on another set of his lies and my great need at the time. That ended badly but eventually my kids and I lived with the man I loved and we had a son. We married within two years.

My first husband declared bankruptcy and got out of all the bills from our marriage. I signed it because I couldn't pay those bills by myself. We agreed he was to pay $460 child support a month. He actually paid that amount for several years, then he stopped paying any support at all for two years because my new husband and I heard something very scary from our elder son after he had visited his biological dad one weekend and we decided to keep visits as few as possible and always in a public location. Ultimately, when the court heard a request from my ex-husband for lowered child support it granted the petition and it went down to $75 a month per child and he never had to make up the two years he failed to pay either.

It was very difficult to keep five children housed, fed, healthy, and happy. I took any job I could get realizing that into this marriage I had brought four children who needed to be supported and the child support just wouldn't do it. My second husband went to get an AA on the GI Bill and he had also managed to get a real estate license. He tried to work from time to time but couldn't keep a job. Later I realized that was because he was mentally ill and untreated. He also drank too much, self-medicating, after which he sometimes became violent. Finally, I got a job with the county that also paid for me to go to college and that's how I got my BA.

Then my ex-husband tried to get custody of our four children and there was a week long court case into which he brought a woman who said she was his fiancée. He had also bought a house. I had begged him to buy us a house, over and over looking at model homes and he never would and the first thing my second husband did was to buy a house, even before we were married. This supposed fiancé was the same old lie. As soon as he lost the custody case they no longer were a couple but just off and on friends. During this court case our four children were interviewed privately by the judge. My father sided with my ex because he was furious I hadn't by then got married to the man I was living with and whose baby I had. He was also very angry that previously I had for a time lived in a huge house with my soon-to-be second husband and his former girlfriend who came with him when he followed me after I left my first husband upon hearing about his homosexual activity during our marriage.

A pack of lies or at least very erroneous assumptions was written by my ex and submitted to the agency of the court that investigates in custody cases. This was some 60 odd pages we eventually got to read. Flagrant lies were said about the man I now loved many of which we were able to prove to the court were total libel by producing documents. So much was refuted that after talking with the children the judge didn't go with the agency's recommendation to give custody to my ex-husband and instead granted me continued custody. The agency's recommendation had been made on that libelous junk that had not been investigated by anyone but us. They never bothered to check it out.

Not wanting to make it even harder on them than they already have it, for more than 30 years I have not talked about all this with the children from my first marriage. They mostly hate my second husband who was very strict and difficult at best. Somehow they find no fault with their biological dad and I know that there is a time they will have to know the truth. It's as though someone has said my first husband has immunity from any punishment or ill feelings even though our whole marriage was a lie created by him and once I knew the depth of it I had to leave him. Anything that came after that would never have happened except for those lies. All of my children from my first marriage have great compassion for their dad and some are often mad at me about their childhood anytime something goes wrong in their lives. It's been very hard to take. They can be mad at my second husband all they want but I finally left him too and after 30 years of being a scapegoat receiving the anger that should be aimed at these two men I'm sick of it. The saving grace is I know they know I will always love them no matter what and they are probably not that sure of their fathers' love. So I get the heat.

My homosexual husband used to play, quite beautifully, "My Funny Valentine" and called it our song. Eventually I understood why he chose that song, never made sense to me before I knew the truth. I miss hearing him play the piano but have absolutely no guilt at all about leaving him. He thinks I hate him but I don't. I have pity for him but that never takes precedence over what I know is the truth. Back then he didn't act swishy and now he makes it very apparent what he is because it's OK to do it now I guess. It's hard to look at him and think I was married to him. He was never who I thought he was. His lies made my life hard, very hard. But for the lies I would be in my own, paid for, home with my husband enjoying our grandchildren and a comfortable life. Instead I have no home, am poor, and face repeated anger leveled at me instead of at him.

It's good homosexuals are out of the closet now because that will prevent my story being repeated although it's my understanding that some of them are still living a lie and hurting others immeasurably. That is probably the only saving grace from the sexual revolution of the 60's that I can see.

That pretty much sums it all up.

Well, you said a lot with this recounting of your first marriage but not much about how this affected you emotionally and mentally. You have said you thought you went a little crazy after John's infidelity but might it have started earlier?

Actually you're right; I think I started losing it right after Chris told me I should have an affair with John who was the man who got Chris involved again in theater. Until then somehow I was maintaining my balance. Then I left Chris again but not before falling in love with John. The problem was that John was already living with someone at the time! He followed me when I moved and brought her with him! The situation was impossible and horrible. That was the most crazy my life ever was. I literally felt like I was in prison; did some really stupid things too.

Want to talk about that?

No, I'm too embarrassed. After we'd been apart about a year, Chris announced he had decided to be heterosexual saying he had not had the other kind of relationship for the past six months and wanted to reunite. By now the relationship with John was so devastatingly difficult that I agreed. John wanted our relationship but continued with other women. So Chris and I tried getting back together for a few months. We had sex once, after three weeks. Not having sex for me by then was not an option because while we were separated I had had a very satisfying sexual relationship with John.

I challenged Chris on the sexual state of our marriage. He admitted he had lied saying he was still a homosexual and was just trying to keep his kids. Fortunately for me the last time we had sex was May 2, 1972. I had a special reason for marking that date. It was long enough before the AIDS thing to protect me from him. After our final separation I think he was mostly with men and had several long term relationships, one of which recently ended in the AIDS death of his partner. He is now HIV positive too. Something else our four children have to deal with because of his lifestyle. He and they seem to be doing pretty well though.

What was the critical point at which you finally decided that marriage was over forever?

During that last short reunification we had a fight that got a little physical and he hurt me a little. So, I made a date to meet John at a mountain ski resort and on the way there the radio played "To Every Time There is a Season" and I knew everything was changing forever. After that I got a job, moved and decided I would have one last child, John's. What was one more when you had four already I reasoned. I wanted to have his child because I was in love with him but I never expected to marry him. I knew it was not a good idea. But, ultimately he decided he wanted to marry me, probably for our child's sake, and because I loved him more than I can say, I married him. A tragedy in the making. I was madly in love with him and he was not suited for marriage. He sort of tried for about five years and then he just fell all apart: drinking, being unfaithful, gambling, mental cruelty, some violence.

It was horrendous. My folks helped me substantially twice when I left him but we re-united and they got tired and decided to stop helping me although they let two of my kids stay with them. My eldest son stayed with them for several weeks after he was mad at me for not letting him stay out as late as he wanted and then they found they couldn't control him and just sent him to his homosexual father without even consulting me. That was facilitated by a high school counselor who was a friend of my mother's and who never even called me to let me know she was working with my son's situation. The other kid who stayed with them was my youngest daughter who actually went through high school while she lived with them. Then they took her to college and just dropped her off. All of this again without any discussion with me at all. She has told me she was terrified to be alone in that college town with no backup. That's the thing I regret most, not moving there to be near her at that time. That was a mistake I made. My youngest son and I were basically treated like lepers during this period of time. This was during the phase of my life where I was still leaving and reuniting with John.

When you started leaving John, first it was for a night at a time when he was drinking, then for a couple of weeks, then for longer, right?

Yes. Remember when we were talking about how powerful sex is? Could I live without him I wondered? I thought I could figure out how to survive but not to be with him, could I actually do that? Sex means many things to me. Orgasm is just one. The drive is to reproduce but the act is all consuming. I hear discussions about various kinds of orgasms among women. Believe me if a woman has never had a vaginal orgasm or orgasms as opposed to clitoral ones, she has not really experienced true sexual intercourse. This is such an overpowering, overwhelming, tremendous feeling that it is totally addictive. I'm sorry. This is probably embarrassing for you to hear.

It's OK, you're right about sex.

When I finally left John for more than a night, I wasn't sure I could live without him or that feeling. To my surprise and relief I was able to live without him, barely. But we reunited several times. That's putting it mildly. We got married three times and got divorced twice. And, as you know, we've been legally separated now for 10 years with a divorce pending if he signs the papers by the way. I decided to do it and gave him the no-contest papers the other day.

Hey that's news! Why didn't you tell me right off?

It still feels tentative, not sure what he's going to do or if I can go through with it. I can live without sex but not sure if I can live without him in my life in some way. Sex is not necessary for me now. It was great and all consuming but I can now do without it. Actually, I can't imagine being with any other man. I still feel married in that sense. Being celibate is something I can do, especially now I am old and few men hit on me. There are some hits though and that's nice. I remember what great sex was like and know there is almost nothing on earth that can be done to keep someone from that experience once you have such a partner. It really should be in the framework of marriage to prevent all kinds of problems, not just AIDS. If sex weren't so great, after having one child a woman would never again engage in it.

So I'm wondering when did sexual experimentation start for you?

In my childhood about the age of 10 I had a couple of exploratory sexual encounters with a boy and a girl. The former tried to insert his penis while I laughed in the dark on my back behind an apartment that was in the backyard of my family's house. We were fully clothed and it was not long after the sex talk my dad gave me so I knew what was going on but thought it was funny. I also had not started to bleed yet so I couldn't get pregnant. This was a boy I grew up with and he seemed very intent but could not figure out how to make it work. My laughing probably didn't help. It wasn't serious, just exploration. The encounter with the girl was when she showed me how to masturbate by doing it to me. That was a revelation.

My first really serious crush on a boy though was at age 11. I met him on the way to the dentist. He came over for lemonade afterwards in my backyard and when I plopped down onto the lawn chair it flipped back over on me. We always wore dresses then and that was one of the most embarrassing experiences of my life. My longest term boyfriend in high school for two years was with the super jock. He was Captain of all the teams: football, basketball and baseball. They didn't do soccer then. We went steady for two years and did a lot of "necking". My father used to say, "Is, duhhhh, Eddy coming over?" He liked to think Eddy was dumb, but he wasn't. He was in the Honor Society and the biggest jock in school. That was the relationship that ended tragically while I was on vacation because I wouldn't go all the way. So, I opted for guys who didn't push too hard because I intended to be a virgin until I was married. The girl who stole my boyfriend "had" to get married eventually, to someone else, but she turned out to be a really good wife and mother. A lot of mixed messages there don't you think?

Have to agree, seems that being a virgin has a lot of pitfalls because of ignorance and pressure to, as you call it, go all the way.

Quite frankly, it's nice not to be concerned with sex any more. It is, without a doubt in my mind, the single most powerful experience human beings encounter and causes us to do a lot of stupid things. Sex is a profound, animal need. It's completely overwhelming, feared, worshipped, at the core of much of what we do, and in my generational values very private. I sometimes am amazed when I look at different people to think they actually engage in it. Watching Clinton on TV and knowing he has engaged in a certain kind of sexual activity with someone other than his wife is so odd. He looks so, well, Presidential. Hard to imagine him in such a circumstance even with his wife!

It was John who made me face what, exactly, homosexuals did. He would call their acts by crude names and I would scream, "Don't say that!" That's how hard that was to face. He made me face it and it was needed. It's so easy to ignore stuff like that and ignoring is the pathway to destruction. He made sure I couldn't deny what homosexuality was about. You can't run from the truth, it's there and it will affect you, somehow or another even if you don't know it. Ignoring is a form of denial. Seems I have a pattern of that don't I?

But these sexual matters are not why you were in denial about your son's illness which we have already figured out.

That gets to the other part of sex for women. Childbirth. For some it's harder than for others, but for most women giving birth is the single most excruciating and fabulous moment of their lives. If I had not had a tubaligation after my fifth child I would have continued to have more babies I'm sure. It's our biological destiny. Lots of women today choose not to have children. OK by me, but they miss out on the best thing our sex can do, help create a human being.

Childless women have done a lot of important stuff though, I'm sure you know that.

Guess so but not having a child on purpose is so limiting I think. Never talked all that much about the deliveries although there was some sharing with friends. All five of them are endlessly fascinating to recapitulate, but there is something that makes us forget our delivery experiences most of the time, some hormone. Thank goodness! Super trauma for both sides. Every time I was in labor again I'd think, "Oh yeah, I remember this!"

I wonder if that very hormone helps you to deny or forget other stuff more than you should. What do you think of that idea?

Interesting line of thought. Maybe the more kids you have the more you get into denial because of that hormone. Don't know but do know I felt like I lost 20% of my thinking ability every time I had a child because a part of my brain seemed to be taken over by unending watchfulness over that child! After I had just one child I could never again play chess the way I had been able to before that time.

What about now that they're grown, can you play chess again?

I could always play but not as well and that's never changed. They're being grown makes no difference, they're still in a large part of my brain.

Whenever I think of having a baby I go back to the one delivery in particular that was very traumatic. It was not that hard a delivery *per se*, but after the birth I noticed the saddle block paralysis began to creep up. I think the table was tilted slightly with my head down. Maybe that caused it. I realized it as my arms were getting numb and I mentioned it to the doctor. He said, "You're just getting cold because we keep it cold in here." After awhile I could tell it was not just being cold and said again, "I'm getting paralyzed!" He denied it again. I insisted. He denied it again. I insisted again and was getting very agitated.

Then he just told the nurses to take me to my room and leave me alone. Which they did! They did not even put sanitary pads on me. I asked one question, "When will the block wear off?" They said, "Two hours, and you have to lie down or you'll get a really bad headache." I refused to do so, and insisted on being propped up in a sitting position, hoping the stuff would fall back down my spinal column. My husband, the homosexual, sat right there announcing the time regularly. I just kept thinking, "I WILL NOT DIE!!!!!" I saw the doctor outside my window walking back to his office and I thought, "How could you desert me like this?" The paralysis slowly faded away and normal life went on. Boy was I in a mess. For weeks I wanted to talk about that experience but no one would let me, so I gave up trying to talk about it until I had my fifth child. Then I asked the head of the OB/GYN clinic for Loma Linda Medical University if I had really been in danger. He simply said, "Yes." He told me they should have watched me all the time and been prepared to put me on a breathing machine. Finally! Someone admitted something very wrong had happened. That delivery when I almost died was the only time Chris watched a delivery. John would never think of being present at a birth. Somehow I blamed Chris for what happened. That's strange but I do. Now I regard that experience as having robbed me and my youngest daughter of the first moments of bonding after her birth. Focused on survival, my mind was not on my baby as it was the other times I delivered babies. I regret that terribly.

Maybe you'd like to talk about your other children?

I don't think so, because they're OK. Our relationships are all different but we are OK and they are doing well in their lives although they are learning how difficult life can be. There is guilt there but not anything I can explore right now. I have to help the last one, the one who is not fine and get through that, and then I can deal more with my children who don't need me that much. I know they're really mad I have to give the youngest one so much attention, but that's how it is.

OK, maybe that's for another time. It's good to stay focused and get through to your original goals before going off onto other matters UNLESS talking about your other children helps with the goals. We're talking about some of the trauma right now that you thought you might want to process better. How were the other deliveries?

The other ones of real note were the one with the bad nurse and the one with the old Navy doctor. Everything was so compartmentalized then that a single person can screw stuff up and no one of their peers would even know it unless told. And, usually, they tend to "stand up" for their medical peer when they find out something irregular. Like those nurses probably knew I shouldn't be alone but followed the doctor's instructions anyway after my fourth delivery.

The bad nurse was during my second delivery. She literally sat on my back in order to keep me from having the baby before the doctor got to the delivery room! Fortunately, he had seen me not long before while I was in the labor room and he was still in the hospital and came quickly. That was in a Catholic hospital and the nun who came to observe the delivery clearly knew about this nurse because she flat out told her to get away from me. Later, in recovery, I asked that nurse why she sat on my back. She said, "I don't deliver babies!" I said, "What would you do if it came out without the doctor, let it fall on the floor?" She was a very nasty person in other ways too.

During my third delivery the old Navy doctor did the most unimaginable stuff to try to reposition the baby, like putting this awful, big hook inside me. I still cannot believe that happened. In extremis, there is nothing a delivering mother can do or say but cooperate and hope they don't kill her and/or the baby. They do what they want, even today when it is supposed to be more geared to choice. Ultimately they do what they want or think is best at a certain point. We just have to hope they choose the right thing. Anyway, after all that probing around with a big hook, the old Navy doctor ordered the nurse to give me PIT to hurry things up. After that, he ordered her to give me an enema! I had tried to tell him PIT worked really quickly on me. Any fool could see what that would mean. I practically had the baby in the toilet! He messed up the saddle block too because one side was paralyzed and one wasn't.

I was present at the birth of my children and I have to tell you it was, by far, the most terrified I have ever been and the most useless I have ever felt. I did the stuff, helped my wife breathe, rubbed her back and so on, but it was all I could do to be there even though it was absolutely the most astounding thing I have ever witnessed. I kept thinking, "I'm so glad I don't have to do this!"

Good for you, you know what it's like, sort of. There is nothing like being the one doing it though. I've watched two of my daughters and one of my daughters-in-law deliver babies and watching is nothing like doing it. There is no way to even explain or describe it really. Women talk about these things among each other a little but the mess and extremity are things no one really wants to hear about. We all want controlled situations, clean houses, nice clothes, mannerly behavior and nothing untoward to reach our eyes or ears. But those other things, like our deliveries are what make us what we are. In my case: tough. I am very tough. You either fall apart or get tough. Before I had a child I thought I was so delicate! Women have to be really tough physically to survive giving birth.

But I'm old now and I have many wounds, physical and mental. I need peace, simplicity, kindness and a measure of security. Otherwise, I don't know, I suppose I would eventually get nuts or die. Pretty simple really. Life is hard and this point comes to us all somewhere along the way. I lasted in it all for 58 years. And we have only just scratched the surface of this wound stuff so far.

A few years later the old Navy doctor wanted to take my uterus and my ovaries out. This was before I had my fifth child. Because I had a period that lasted a month I needed a D and C. He also told me I had a cyst on my right ovary and it should probably come out and that the rest should come out at the same time to prevent me getting cancer in the future. He wanted me to sign something that said he could go ahead and take it all out when he did the D and C if, when he examined me better at that time, he thought it was necessary. I said, "No." I figured he could examine me and we'd talk about it.

He came in after I woke up from the D and C and told me the cyst was the size of an orange and I should have signed the papers and it would have all been over now. He said I had to come back in a week to have surgery. So I went to the pre-op appointment at his office the day before I was supposed to be operated on and after he examined me he just left the room. His nurse came back and told me that the cyst was gone. Women had kinda stopped having babies about that time because of the "population explosion" or something and I think that he just needed work really because ovarian cysts that come and go are actually quite common.

I appreciate your sharing all this with me and I know it's hard on you to remember it. I hope it helped to have someone listen, finally.

It makes me tired to think about those deliveries and the corrective surgery I had two years ago to repair the damage done to my body from them. Over 100 stitches he told me. I can't imagine how women had 10 and more babies. It is completely beyond me. On the other hand, I know many, many women have died in childbirth throughout human history and I survived quite well really and all my children survived and are pretty healthy and good looking. It's such a violent, inexorable, excruciating and yet wonderful experience to give birth to a child, let alone five of them. The love a normal mother has for her child goes way off the scale. Men know this is something they better not mess with or reap the fury of an enraged tigress. Yet, they still try to do it, because they're often jealous of their own kids, but that's another story for another time. Time's up I see. Same time next week?

OK. See you next week Susan.

SESSION FIVE

One Week Later

Last time you talked about your deliveries. Are there other physically traumatic events in your life? It's good to talk about them because like you mentioned, people don't often want to hear about it. I'll listen to it for you. That's part of what I do.

Yes, there's something else, a big lifelong trauma. It's amusing to me when someone says, "You're smothering me!" or "I feel smothered!" I take those words very literally. All my life I have been smothered to one degree or another physically. My mom says I was officially diagnosed at the age of two with asthma. Then the prognosis was that I would probably outgrow it. I didn't. So, I have never known what it would feel like to just run full tilt or do anything vigorously physical and not wind up gasping for breath.

To make it worse, mostly my gasping for breath was often viewed by others as psychological, something I was "doing" because I was in a snit or something. When I was young the problem was actually Fluffy my cat. Turns out I am very allergic to cats among other things. I adored her as my pet for seven years, roughly from when I was five until I was 12. She was soft and wonderful. I could throw a chain across the kitchen floor and she would retrieve it in her mouth just like a dog. She had five litters of kittens. My dad ran over one of the first litter even though I told him there was a kitten under a wheel. He didn't believe me. It was cut in half, both halves wiggling for awhile.

Children should be listened to, they often speak the truth. That must have been a pretty hard thing to see especially when you tried to stop it.

95

I can still see the two halves of that adorable kitten wiggling and the middle all squashed. That's when I knew what death was.

All this time with Fluffy and her kittens I was wheezing, wheezing, wheezing and wheezing. Sometimes I was taken to emergency rooms or doctor's offices and given adrenaline. That's a miracle relief! I was given an inhaler, an old style one with a bulb, but that was thrown away and the medicine poured down the sink in the midst of an attack because my dad said, "It's all in your head." That scene is forever etched in my memory. It was unbelievably cruel to me but I knew that the attitude was that I wheezed on purpose because I was unhappy or something, so it's easy to forgive the ignorance of the action.

Later in my second marriage that same attitude prevailed. John felt that when I got over an attack it was because he, personally, made it go away. Later I learned that manic depressives have a magical sense of themselves. In my family there was not only me but one of my sons and one of my daughters also afflicted with asthma. He more or less grew out of it maybe because of John's pushing him in athletics despite his asthma but she didn't grow out of it. Additionally, she suffered from severe eczema and kids at school called her "leprosy lady". Unbelievable!

People in stores would stop me and say, "Why don't you take that poor child to the doctor?!" I would then explain she had been to many doctors who only knew how to give her steroids to clear it up and it was dangerous to give a growing child a lot of steroids. Taking food out of her diet resulted in a conviction that she was allergic to eggs and she hated tuna or any other fish for that matter because it made her throat itch. She had sores and scabs and itched unbearably. Benadryl, baby aspirin, oatmeal baths, Calamine lotion helped very little. This was 30 years ago remember. Vaseline helped her but we were told never to let her use it because infection could result with the germs trapped inside with her raw tissue. She is a beauty though and has now figured out how to manage her disability. She also suffers from having the, "It must be in your head," attitude aimed at her and is embarrassed that she can't visit friends in their houses if they have pets. Few friends really understand this. I know. She cannot be around fragrances or smokers either and this upsets people too.

They always told me, "You can't die from asthma, so don't worry!" Maybe that's what doctors' told them. I was 45 before I knew you actually could die from it. Many, many, many times I remember wheezing horribly, not getting any air and being in a physical panic which of course makes it worse, and in terrible psychological distress from the lack of remedy for my condition. My grandmother was the only one who understood. She had it too. Around her the panic would recede as she put me in a quiet, cool, dark room with a bunch of pillows to prop me up, lots of water and calmly said to me, "It will be all right." Then she wouldn't let anyone come near me. Being still during an attack and not having any interaction is imperative. They treated her the same way as they did me. They thought it must be in her head, she was just being manipulative or something. Never in my life have I deliberately held my breath. Being able to breathe is too precious to me to deliberately limit it for any reason whatsoever. Going underwater takes a supreme effort of will.

Imagine never being able to run, to do aerobics, to dance more than one dance at a time, to have to stop sex right in the middle of it sometimes for lack of breath! You live with it. People know it's a big thing, not being able to breathe, but they can't relate to it because it's not visible until you drop over. The Bible says life is in the breath and it is. Without oxygen for several minutes you die. Sometimes it has been so bad I couldn't even call the ambulance or talk in order to tell anyone what was wrong. Fortunately for me, one of my kids stayed in the home until age 20 and went through it with me. Now I live alone but there is a new medicine that keeps me more or less stabilized and I always have prednisone and my electric nebulizer close at hand just in case.

The worst asthma attack I ever had was when my youngest son and I were living in a little trailer and I had made the mistake of trying to live with a cat again which proves I must have thought it was in my head too until it was proven wrong a year later by tests I initiated. Soon after that I was sternly counseled by a pulmonary specialist about not ignoring my condition and winding up in emergency rooms all over the place. That was a form of denial but it came from how I had been trained to think about it, not from myself. He could tell by my actions that I had been programmed to think it was in my head somehow, that I didn't regard it as a disease to be managed. He educated me, finally.

Is that very worst attack vividly etched in your memory?

Oh yes, I remember that very well. That night I had already been to the emergency room once. Had to bum a ride because the car was broken down. They did what they do now, nebulizer treatment with oxygen and albuterol and then tell you to go see your doctor. I bummed a ride home with another ER visitor in a car that had a dog in it. Then I went home and ate a baked sweet potato. About 20 minutes later very suddenly the world's air disappeared. I only had time to tell my son to take the quarter off the counter and go to the pay phone to call 911 for an ambulance. He left immediately. I stumbled outside looking for the air that had disappeared, just couldn't be in an enclosed place. Then my mind told me to take my clothes off to get

LAIRD SMITH

more air. Actually the body does breathe through the pores I found out later but I refused to do that, no matter what.

It was so bad I screamed out in my mind to the Savior, "Help! Let me die or take over my body! I can't stand it!" I stopped being conscious at that point. Possibly about five minutes had elapsed since the onset to when I passed out but I'm not sure. I didn't know anything else until I woke up on a treatment table in ER with three people working over me. My mind woke up first and I couldn't move or open my eyes or make a noise for awhile. I came back into my head thinking, "Oh, that's what I have to do." Then I got one eye open and the nurse noticed and said, "She's back!" The paramedic was pacing in my line of sight. He stopped at that announcement, relaxed and disappeared.

What was it you had to do?

I don't know. Never remembered once I was awake but I know I came back with that thought. I heard later that it took about 15 minutes for them to arrive and my son had led the ambulance in from the front of the trailer park. He told me that when they got to me I was sitting on a little stool with my back against the trailer with my eyes wide open, white as a sheet, and not breathing at all. They told me to breathe. I didn't. So, they carried me into the ambulance and tried to force oxygen into me.

My son told me later he thought I was dead. He rode with me in the ambulance and waited in the corridor while they worked on me. Afterwards they admitted me and let him spend the night for free in the room next door, even fed him too. If he had not been there and done the right thing I would have died. He was 12. While they worked on me he read a publication about how babies were made and born sitting outside the ER door. That's how he got some education about that.

Now that is another major trauma he suffered and might also be why the mental illness continued instead of going dormant. The idea of losing a mother, especially after in essence losing his father and his siblings too, is pretty big for a 12-year-old. Was there any other family around to help?

No. We were in the same town where my parents lived with my youngest daughter, but they had gone to see my sister about four hours away for the weekend. We had just returned to town and really weren't in touch with anyone else we knew. No one in my family ever wants to hear about these things, these near death experiences. It's the credo that we don't talk about them for some reason. I need to talk about them. It's really big, you know!

I know.

Two weeks after that happened the car was fixed. I walked across town and left my trailer pink slip with a parts store as collateral for the car part I needed and a nice man in the trailer park fixed the car for nothing, no strings at all. I paid for the parts in a week and got my pink slip back. My folks wouldn't loan me the money. Don't ask me why because three days after it was fixed it was Christmas and they handed me a $125 check then.

So I lived, the car was fixed and there was a land sitting job waiting and I hooked up the trailer, or rather my son did it because he was the one who did that, and I started the car and began pulling it to a remote area in the hills. Couldn't afford to stay in that trailer park. But I made a wrong turn going up a steep hill pulling that trailer on a narrow mountain road. The car wouldn't pull the trailer up more than half way, so I had to try to back down. Well, that is not my forte and I wound up jamming the trailer into the side of the hill and over the shoulder and the floor was ripped out. So then we were homeless.

We took everything out of it we could get and loaded up the car. The bummer is my folks would not let us stay for awhile in their three bedroom home. They insisted we go to a shelter, so we did. It was a domestic violence shelter because there was no homeless shelter nearby at that time. They let us in because they considered us emotionally abused because of my parents' refusal to help. If someone who was a domestic violence victim wanted housing we would have had to leave.

My parents hated John, my remaining son's father, and were frustrated and angry that I had reconciled repeatedly with him so they stopped helping us. Before that my dad came down South once to get me and the kids from Lake Arrowhead where I had run to once to a rich friend's house on the lake. That was the time I was afraid the Doberman was going to hurt our son. She tried to bite him several years later too but John jumped between them, growled at her until she pulled back. John finally had her put down because she growled at him a few years later.

Before going to the shelter when we were homeless, we stayed in a renovated bus on the land we were going to for several days without heat. When we saw the trailer again it was totally stripped. The stove was gone, the cabinets were gone, the roof was gone and the sides were gone. All that was left was the frame and the axle. My father gave those remains to a neighbor who made a hauling trailer out of them. Don't know why he didn't sell it to him and give us the money. We surely needed it. He was just concerned about it staying there on the side of the road and being a nuisance I think.

This "worst asthma attack" and subsequent events has a good ending though. After six weeks in the shelter where I had to go to the hospital once, we spent a week in someone's home where we were treated badly. We left there and spent two weeks in a vacant apartment in disrepair and without heat being told it was soon to be renovated. Then we were suddenly awarded a housing voucher! I had applied two years before and our homelessness bumped us up on the list. That couldn't happen today because homelessness no longer gives anyone a priority on the lists. That's one of Clinton's recent innovations with the housing department I believe.

We rented a new two bedroom town house a few blocks from the ocean and stayed there 18 months. It took a few months of rest for me to be able to work again and then I started by doing some home health care work part time and also worked part time as a waitress in a Chinese restaurant next door. Always loved working in Chinese restaurants, you get to take home food! And I love Chinese food. My son had a good time there, fishing and popping abalone off rocks, and he made a friend. Those 18 months were good. We also belonged to the gem and mineral society and he learned to make jewelry. Eventually, I found a good job that utilized my background and BA degree. That lasted nine months because I remarried John and we relocated to be with him. Most of my jobs lasted between six months and a year. There are various reasons for this. Some are my fault, some are other people's fault and some are circumstantial. Anyway, that story was the worst it got for us and we rebuilt our lives, physically and emotionally.

What happened next?

Within two years John and I got together for about two months. Before that we had got remarried two times which ended badly. Once John was living with his mother who wanted he and I to live in that broken down bread truck that was now in her back yard but she let our son be inside her house. That's when the really serious attack by the Doberman on our son happened. We heard him scream and we both bolted to the back door where he was backed into the wall and the dog was trying to get at him with teeth bared while John's mother tried to hold her back on a leash. Just as we got there she got loose and went for him. John jumped in between and growled at her. After awhile the dog backed up and it was over. I wouldn't stay there after that so we wound up in a friend's remote cabin in a desert canyon.

There was where he hurt me the worst. He gave me what's called a "Mouse" and the entire left side of my face was black and purple. I basically passed out and was in a daze for a day. It scared our son so much he ran over to the nearest neighbor and called the Sheriff who sent a helicopter over our house. By the time they got there, John had me up and outside at a table "playing" cards. They saw it appeared I was OK and left. I was actually in a very big daze. John left after that to go see his mom for a few days who was more than an hour away and I moved us out, before he got back, to my friend's house where we stayed for two weeks with our stuff in her garage. Then he came there to get us to be with him again. I had actually found a place he didn't like. Then he left again, coming back a few days later and proceeded to assure my friend he was fine but I wouldn't see him or talk with him. I packed a few things for me and our son and we left on a Greyhound bus. I set up a life again, and then about a year later John came to see us after convincing me that the Mormon Church had made a new man of him, which after about two months proved not to be true.

Is that one of the times you remarried?

Yes, we were actually married the second time in a Mormon church, not a Temple but the stake church. Then he had to return to his mom's house over a legal matter and we went with him and visited with her. We, including her, although she was very ill, all returned to our house. She left after about a week, visiting family for the last time as she returned to her house. The end result is he left again to make a court date in the pickup he traded for an old used car I was buying. When he came back we had moved to another town with the help of the Mormons and ultimately we lived in the round house I told you about another time where he was so emotionally abusive. After that, some other moves related to me trying to get work. Then finally, after the death of John's mother from cancer, my son and I finally ended up in the trailer where I had that worst asthma attack of my life.

My mother-in-law was diagnosed with cervical cancer in '78. I took her to the radiation treatments after which she was very ill. Then they performed something new where they implanted nuclear material into her uterus because the cancer had involved the uterine wall. Finally she had to have a colonoscopy because of necrotic tissue in her bowel from the radiation. She then went on to live for about five more years but ultimately the cancer had spread to her lung which they took out. When she died I think it was because the cancer had gone to her brain but I'm not sure because I wasn't there for the removal of her lung and then her death two months later. John stayed with her during that time. While I was the one caring for her I learned that to really do that well you simply had to love the person. It just happens. Before that we'd been distant because she started living with us from the time she heard we were married and I resented that. With her illness I literally had to learn to love her and our relationship at the end was loving but I couldn't live with her son although I tried over and over again.

Some time after her death there was a contact with John again which resulted in our traveling down to see him to try to help his legal situation by showing he had a family. Finally, after he refused a temporary judge which caused a continuance of his court case, John decided to go into the VA Hospital to evade the problem. He got a pass to leave for a few days and we all went back to my house. I had taken with me a cute ribboned wand my youngest daughter had made when she was little that I found in John's mother's two-car garage where he had stored all our stuff. I wanted to give it to my daughter. John had told me I could look in there for stuff but when he saw it he had a fit. He was furious I had taken something. Then I took him back to the hospital when his pass was over.

Then what did you do?

His reaction to my taking that wand more than anything made me aware we had to get away from him again. I took him back to the hospital knowing I would return home to pack and leave for New Mexico which was a recommendation a psychiatrist I'd seen once about our situation had made saying that it would be good for my youngest because three of his siblings were there. John was discharged eventually from the hospital because he wouldn't take medication and was finally found guilty and spent some months in county jail for an event that happened in his mother's house that a visitor had perpetrated. He eventually returned to that house, lost it, reconnected with me and came to see us in New Mexico where his behavior caused a judge to tell him to leave the state which he did. He went to another state and I didn't hear from him for a long time.

There's even more to this saga isn't there? And somewhere in there you were legally separated right?

Yes and I don't want to relive it now. All in all because I'm not materialistic or ambitious in the worldly sense I haven't done that good of a job of taking care of myself or my kids when their fathers didn't. I surely tried. But I never once yielded my sense of ethics. It's just not in me to do that. I have integrity. Why I don't know, but I know that I do. Subordinating oneself by giving up one's ethics just isn't right. Looking back it sure doesn't appear, objectively, that I ran my life ethically, but I did. It quite literally became a choice of lesser evils to progress out of the mess that befell me and my children as a result of Chris coming out of the closet and John not being able to be a consistent husband or parent because of what I now understand was his mental illness. Those years I was totally overwhelmed in that marriage and then I began to leave, to leave, to leave, to leave, with five children in the home, then four, then three, then two, then one.

So, did he sign the papers for the divorce, by the way?

Yes, he did actually. And I filed them. So, it's done. He feels really bad about it though. It meant something to him that we were still married even though we didn't live together or even have all that much contact. I don't feel any different really but it's symbolic, it was needed for lots of reasons. Will have to spend time feeling this through.

Well, you two don't seem to have much trouble getting remarried if you ever decided to do it again later on for some reason. I was wondering if thinking about that gun thing led you to a final decision.

Maybe it did, I'm not sure because I really didn't think about it much again. Like I told you I could tell my mind was trying to forget it and I pretty much did but you pulled it to the surface at one of our meetings and maybe that was the final straw which I had been ignoring, denying, before.

OK, just wondered. Let's get back to the asthma.

All the stress of the circumstances of both marriages and trying to raise five children no doubt made my asthma worse. But the smothering also got worse because, I think, as I got older I went into menopause and that had an impact on it. Then I started having to take prednisone from time to time.

Eventually, a pulmonary specialist prescribed a home nebulizer. It wound up going to work with me during difficult times. Then, after a three day hospital stay a new doctor told me about a new medication I should be taking and as long as I can take two puffs of that twice a day, along with my other two inhalers, I can breathe pretty good. If I miss one time I feel it and start huffing and puffing. I'm also too heavy now which doesn't help. Can't walk far though or up hill. Two years ago I got so debilitated from asthma that I had to stop working. I haven't regained my stamina but I have fewer bouts of huffing and puffing and am not so terribly exhausted now that I'm not trying to be part of the workforce. During my 30s, 40s, and 50s until two years ago, I was always exhausted. When I stopped working, my youngest son took over my business and I still had some income for awhile. He sold that, paying off $3000 of my debts by the way.

This is the son with the mental illness? How did he do with the business?

Yes, him. He didn't do well running it but he did a great job of selling it to someone else! Running it was just too much activity and stress for me or him. Added to the asthma for the past 30 years is high blood pressure which went untreated for about 10 years. Then a tachycardia disease set in when I was about 45 too. Then came arthritis and degenerative disk and joint disease. Until I was 56 I worked anyway, but now I need to be less active.

They say asthma is getting to be an epidemic. Pollution is no doubt the cause.

Imagine someone putting a pillow over your face when you are lying down and you can't get any air and this happens repeatedly throughout your lifetime and often suddenly requiring hospitalization. That's how it is. Usually to look at us asthmatics someone doesn't realize what we're going through. Once it's to the point of stiff, high-held shoulders, sitting straight up, shallow breaths, people begin to get a clue something's wrong, that we need to go to the ER.

When it is the very worst there is no wheezing because not much air is getting in and out and some doctors still don't know this. I've gone to an ER getting almost no air and have been told I wasn't wheezing so I wasn't having an asthma attack! Somehow I get out or write "no wheezing when really bad". Once a doctor made me spend six hours in that state in a short hallway with closed doors, refusing to give me any medication. That was extreme torture and I couldn't do anything about it. Finally the shift changed and the new doctor got on it. That mistreatment put me in the hospital for three days.

I never really knew what happens to the lungs during an asthma attack until I was 45 when that doctor explained how it worked and made me address my condition. What happens is that the muscles of the lungs, around the bronchi, clinch up, sort of like a Charlie horse. Also, the air sacks begin secreting mucous, and the tissues become inflamed and swollen. All of this is in response to something in the air that the body is allergic to. Pretty awful huh?

I'll say. That must have had an enormous effect on you all your life.

Sometimes I day dream about being able to run, ski, walk in marathons, do regular exercises and most of all to have clear, free airways. When I was little I always wanted to be a ballerina. I took a few ballet lessons but it was stopped I'm told because I wanted it to stop but I don't remember that. Doesn't matter, because I would never have had the stamina to really be a ballerina. I also have flat feet so that vocation wouldn't have ever worked out for me. All we did was the basic exercises and no dancing at all in those few lessons. I just loved toe shoes and wanted a pair every year for Christmas. I would go downtown to the shoe store and try them on, telling the clerk that was what I wanted for Christmas. I never got them.

Later I painted toe shoes. Mostly, though, I painted landscapes as though from a height. I don't know why from a height. Wide open spaces and long vistas are my favorite scenes. While I love the ocean because you can see forever, the desert provides more to me in that sense. As for the mountains, having trees all around me bothers me, probably because I feel a little smothered. Also, I don't like small spaces. The idea of being stuck in a small space is appalling. I am claustrophobic I guess but it comes from the asthma. When I'm in an airplane, before it even leaves the ground, I turn on the airflow and point it directly at me. Once I was in a seat with a broken air nozzle and I was very uncomfortable for that entire plane trip.

Someone who has never had impaired breathing, and endured this repeatedly throughout his or her life, would never understand the courage and stamina it takes to go ahead in the face of it. It's a real disability which has no outside look to it to gain its victims some measure of understanding and compassion. There are many, even doctors, who still think it's "in your head". It's not in my head, it's in my lungs and it has been an enormous burden to bear for an entire lifetime. It is tiring, life threatening, misunderstood, expensive to medicate, engenders little compassion and often receives unmitigated disdain, curtails all really active vocations and avocations, dictates where you can go and how long you can stay, makes you very vulnerable to the need to be around someone who knows what's happening in order to get the medical help needed and it's terribly embarrassing to pull out your spray in public.

Often movies portray asthmatics as psychologically weird and show them using their sprays at tense moments. If they are male they make them effeminate or psychotic. Underlying it all is the feeling that it's "in your head". There have been friends my entire life whom I cannot visit in their home for long because they have a cat or dog, and they never really understand. Somehow, it's thought that asthmatics are misfits or at best not smiled upon by the gods and they could really just stop it if they would just get their head right. That's quite an image to constantly fight by refusing to receive it, by calmly doing what you have to do, by making sure there is some loved one around who will help and not put a trip on you, and to forgive all the people who refuse to acknowledge you have a disability that is very difficult and deserves kindness.

So being a ballerina was a dream too but you knew you couldn't do it because of the asthma so you didn't really work on that becoming a reality.

105

Besides not being able to be a ballerina the biggest regret I have about being an asthmatic is that I could not really travel to remote places, hike up to Machu Picchu for instance. Can't hike period, can't even walk uphill more than about 30 feet without stopping, and can't be in remote places because there is no hospital nearby just in case. Oh well, never had the money to travel anyway! And I can't have a pet, except fish, or a poodle. Had a miniature poodle once because I'm not allergic to poodle hair, it doesn't shed. She was killed by a car when she was five and I miss her very much. A friend bred them and gave her to me. Not a dog I could ever really afford to buy.

This condition has been very limiting but that's the pathway I was dealt and that's okay with me. Still, I know a lot of what it has cost me. Mainly, I wish people would understand asthma better and be kinder to its victims. Being smothered, being suffocated repeatedly is no fun.

Do you think there are some psychological aspects to asthma?

I think it is a weakness in the lungs and like all weaknesses of the body it gets worse under stress. Some people have a touchy tummy. Often their tummy hurts from fried or spicy food but if they are very tired, or stressed out, it will be worse. It's that way with asthma and every other chronic condition people have. Well, I'm sure this was a bit boring but I hope that you learned something about asthma and maybe you will be more compassionate about it.

I did learn a lot, but my six-year-old daughter has it too so I already know a lot of what you told me and I certainly have compassion. The fact there is an epidemic of asthma lately is also letting us know that it's triggered by something, pollution probably.

Be kind to her and give her a lot of space and peace when she has an attack and let her have the medicine that will make it better. Not being able to breathe is terrible. I see the clock says it's time to go. I'll be back at the same time, next week, OK? Is there anything you want me to think about for next time?

Your son suffered a lot of trauma along with you and some rejection too it seems. Could we talk about how you felt about that? I think that's part of the guilt you have now about his illness and his having to endure how hard your lives were.

Right, I'll think on that. Bye Bob.

SESSION SIX

One Week Later

Remember what I asked you to think about?

Yeah. Our life was hard on my youngest son. Maybe it was harder than being with his father would have been. I'll never know. I haven't really tried to tell you how terrifying his father could be and sometimes how really bizarre. One time I saw from a window how he literally forced our son to lie to him at the age of about six because his father just wouldn't accept the truth. That was very bad. Sort of like getting a confession from someone by torturing them. The torture was mental and psychological but had the threat of being physical which he did often enough as well I have since learned.

You've only heard about some of what I now call "The Odyssey". We moved at least 52 times by the time my son was 18-years-old. Full household moves. There were other relocations, escapes, as well. I could go through all of them and tell you why we moved. Often we could no longer afford where we were and had to scale down and then when it got better we moved to a nicer location. Sometimes it had to do with the reconciliations with John. Our son needed a Dad so I tried again and again. When the reconciliations failed, we were usually the ones that had to go away because John would never leave where his stuff was and he always kept just about everything. Then it was start over time.

Sometimes it had to do with heartsickness and just getting somewhere else, a new location and opportunity. Sometimes it was to get close to a loved one who was in need or from whom we were alienated and we needed to correct that. All in all it was interesting, very tiring, and gave us both a desire to be in one place for awhile. I remember eight moves while growing up which was considered a lot back then but that's nothing like what has gone on for me and my youngest child since 1980.

You were gypsies in a sense. That can work if you consider it a natural part of your life and not always an emergency requiring a move. I'm sure you had reasons for why you moved but I've no doubt at all that it was very hard on him not to have a secure home location.

After we had been homeless that time and my folks wouldn't help us, he told me that he thought we were going to die but then he saw we were all right. That's when he developed faith that Yahweh was watching over us and that we would always be OK. I always knew we'd be OK somehow, not sure why, maybe it was faith or maybe it was denial, refusing to think that we might not be OK.

To keep some integrity and not give in to bad stuff in a work place often required a change of job. And that frequently required moving. I've also had a supervisor call me into his office, then lock both his doors and proceed to kiss me! He was the boss' son by the way. I just laughed. It was unbelievably funny to me. That was apparently a good response because he stopped and let me go. Then I once worked for someone for seven weeks and never got paid. It goes on and on.

These job impasses can get really difficult, and I try for as long as I can to keep the job but eventually it's just the right thing to do to leave. For instance, when I realized it would be best, I saw to it that a domestic violence shelter on an Indian Reservation was put in the hands of Native Americans instead of the WASP women, like me, who were always imported to be the Executive Director. There were Native American women there who had the education and experience to run it with just a little training. I provided the training and maneuvered the situation to the point of leaving them in charge and the Board of Directors had to accept the new regime.

So, that time you stacked the deck on them?

Boy, I hate Boards of Directors. I actually told them what I was doing and at the last board meeting I attended I told them I was leaving before the next one. They just said I couldn't do that and refused to relate to it. Kinda like how I dealt with my son's mental illness: denial. I hear they were really shocked that I actually left just as I said I was going to do, but not before I had trained those women to do the work without me or anyone like me. I started out thinking I would stay there but saw what was needed.

I was right to leave too because after that change the shelter got $20,000 from a Tribal entity instead of the $10,000 they gave the place when I ran it and submitted the very same grant proposal. Some of the Tribe had resented Anglos running the place and responded positively once a Native American woman was doing it. Those women who ran the shelter loved me for doing that and I loved them too. Also, the new Program Manager was appointed to the Tribe's domestic violence legislation committee. They never would have appointed an Anglo to that committee. I'm proud of doing that. But it cost me thousands of dollars again, caused another move, and aborted a career I had chosen.

During the time I was there I had to counsel women sometimes because the regular counselor wasn't getting through. One of these women had a five-year-old daughter who had been sodomized by her uncle, the woman's brother. The mother was in a total state of denial, just couldn't relate to it at all. The way she felt, she told me, was that she was in a room she couldn't get out of because there was no door and no window.

All I had to do was assure her repeatedly that there was a way out and she would find it. After awhile she did because she announced suddenly at a meeting that there was now a doorway in the room. Her little girl came into my office one day, though, and looked me in the eyes and said, "I'm bad." I told her she was not bad at all, she was a little girl and she was not bad.

In these kinds of circumstances I always wonder what will become of the child. Can't know for years usually. Can only hope you got through.

I'm good with little children, so maybe I did, I hope I did.

You've had some really interesting job experiences.

Was once hired by a nun to run a wonderful homeless program for mentally ill women over the age of 45. She'd started the program while she was also running a homeless shelter she set up that was well known and very busy. In the program I would run, there were nine women and the funding said they should get case management towards the goal of getting them settled in their own homes within 18 months. When I came aboard, a week before the incumbent left at the nun's request, the program was about to fail because there was no case management and a grant accounting was due soon. Then this wonderful woman, the nun, died suddenly while she was at a retreat!

There was a scramble for power and an older woman on the board decided she wanted her protégé, who was a CPA, to run the shelter, to take my job!

She point blank asked me to train the CPA to run it. I declined explaining that four years of education and eight years of experience was not something I could "teach" a CPA. The old biddy engineered a special board meeting with barely a quorum and I was to appear on an hour's notice. Knowing she was moving against me, I took with me the accounting that I was working on and handed it to an attorney on the board who then told me, "I want you to know I think you are a very professional person." That hateful woman passed a prepared statement to me and demanded I sign it. I didn't sign her statement, shoved it back to her and, having brought some paper and carbon, I wrote simply, "I resign," and signed and dated it. Don't know what happened with the program after that but case management was in place by then, provided by myself with a directive to the board that they needed to hire a part time case manager which was the failing point when I came aboard. I made them pay me a month's salary when I resigned because I had a contract. That was a truly horrible experience for me and for the program residents. I could have fought it but she had convinced some of the board that I came a week early and got paid for it when I shouldn't have. The truth was the dead nun asked me to come aboard a week early because she was so worried about the funding being lost because the program was not being run correctly. However, I couldn't prove that. I went to clean my desk out and those poor ladies were so shook up. One very nice board member came over and consoled them. Not sure where she stood but she was nice. I had just bought that new car I told you my daughter co-signed for and I broke my leg and ankle about two weeks later and wound up on disability for six months.

You've mixed it up with some major connivers it appears. But this made a lot of moves and changes go on in your lives.

During those times we lived in very nice places with swimming pools, in a homeless shelter, in a new town home near the ocean, in various and sundry apartments and houses, and we always had what we needed. That is what it taught me and my youngest son. We can be okay. We will be provided for. There will be a job, a place to live, food on the table. So, then I and he can trust in that and take some chances in life. I could do some real work in society, not just go after the bucks and the goodies. It also made me flexible but I know being homeless scared him a lot. Too much to put a child through, let alone one that turns out to have had mental illness symptoms since the age of five! The mentally ill women I worked with didn't tip me to his condition though. I still went on in denial about it.

Change is hard even if it is good change.

110

When I was in high school in the 50s, one teacher often said the one skill we needed to survive in the coming years was to be able to cope with change. I didn't really understand that then but I do now. Change is happening so fast now, so pervasive and everywhere that people must be able to learn new things, go anywhere, live in any circumstances, be assertive with bureaucracies, recognize the need for change and be able to respond to survive, to grow and to still remain sane. Once you fail to do this you are frozen in time. You might be safe or not but no longer able to grow or respond. That's fine if that works for you. For me, I took it a day at a time, met the priorities that appeared evident and was ready to move mentally and physically if that was required, but now that I am older I recognize I have more limitations and have to factor those into my responses. A child probably felt the same way I do now that I'm old and I failed to realize that.

It had its toll on me too. There is a lot of stress in taking a stand which causes your life to change suddenly and dramatically. Now my alternatives are becoming more and more limited. Most of my activity is from a home base. It's nice these new limitations have coincided with the advent of the internet because that allows me to communicate, to do research and to stay informed without going out of my house! It reserves my physical energy while still giving me mental stimulation.

There's something nice I have noticed, about growing old though. I call it the Gentle Conspiracy. It has to do with being an old woman, something that happens.

So what is this conspiracy?

All of you who aren't old women don't know that we are always operating together, always in communication in each other's presence and usually without words or even obvious body language. It's a secret. It's what saves us from anguish as we get older and get treated worse. All old women are the low people on the totem pole anywhere, anytime. So, we turn from being the natural competitors of our youth to being natural allies when we grow old. That's a big change. The gentle conspiracy is hard to explain and I don't know if I even should. You shrinks might ruin the secrecy and that's important because as we old women become aware of the reality of the conspiracy we get some relief. To know about the conspiracy in advance might ruin the nice surprise we get when almost everyone deserts us except for a few who still have natural affection. The very few who really love us. Some of us are lucky. We still get the token stuff. You know, birthday presents, holiday presents, a little money if we need it very desperately here and there. Don't forget, when we were young we received accolades and gifts galore often for

111

our favors. Get old and that's all gone no matter how much cosmetic surgery you get or hair dye you use.

Truly, the conspiracy should be uncovered naturally like all important things, not learned from a book or a course. Let's leave it at the fact that all we old women help each other psychologically and sometimes materially at the drop of the veiled abuse hat and we don't need to know each other to do it either. We are also clever about it.

Can you at least give me an example just so I'll understand what you are talking about?

OK, one. Just before I couldn't work any more I did a clerical job for an art gallery. The manager was a snobbish creep who decided to take exception to something really stupid about how I did the job. I had delivered the goods and a bill and wanted to be paid. While he was beginning to berate me, before paying me, in walked a middle aged couple with an old woman in tow. I took them to be customers. The gallery manager continued in their presence with this line of attack as I just stood there. Very casually the old woman walked up near to him and asked him if he had done something. He got very flustered and said, "Uh, no." She gave him a hard look and made it clear he needed to do it right away. He completely forgot his chastisement of me. He just took out the checkbook and wrote me one handing it to me as he rushed off. She looked my way and gave me a small smile. I gave her one back. She was the gallery owner.

I see, and these types of things happen often between older women?

Yep, I do it too now. It just seems to come naturally.

Thanks for sharing that, it's amazing actually. To be honest I'm going to watch for it. Back to your odyssey with your son. These moves had more than the physical and mental stress ramifications though, I'm sure.

That's part of why I'm helping my son any way I can because I know I messed up, hurt him with all those moves. These other ramifications you allude to I call "places" for lack of a better word. There are geographical places, places in the mind, places in the dynamics between people, and often the circumstances themselves can be places like being "between a rock and a hard place" suggests. The mental places have divisions within themselves. There are memories which are places. There are ethical positions or places in the mind which create dynamic new places when interacting with other people. There are rational places where our mind keeps secure our defense mechanisms while constructing reality to be what we need it to be. And there is a spiritual place where we commune with our Maker and retreat from the physical if we are aware of it. That place is called the Kingdom of Heaven.

Some of these places can be seen with the physical eyes and some require the "third eye" to see. All these places, and more, interact to make us who we are, to place us at a point in time and space at any given moment as the world and everyone else's places affect us and we them. To be physically alive is to react to stimulus and then to take an appropriate position given our understanding and sets. Yielding to indicated inner and outer motion makes up our pathway from one place to another throughout our lives. These mental, spiritual and physical dynamics are what psychologists and sociologists try to understand. It's impossible to find a norm, though, because every person's pathway is idiosyncratic, impelled by his or her "places".

You have almost developed a whole new way to look at psychosocial dynamics. Maybe you should pursue this professionally.

John has an idea about life that he calls the "Tumbleweed Theory" that shows all the pathways one can take. The difference between his theory and what I know is the Truth is that no matter how many decisions we make as we go along various changes in our pathway, there is a predetermined end arranged by the Will of Yahweh. Before anyone would listen to this place thing, let alone the knowledge of Yahweh and how He works in our lives, I'd have to get an MA at least in psychology and religion and I don't see that happening. Too much in the way right now. So far all I've been able to do is start a website with lectures about aspects of the Gospel. It's at *www. soundingthetrumpet.com* if you have an interest.

If I had an interest it would be because I'm wondering how you managed to come through all you have and still be as sane and competent as you really are. Something made that possible and it wasn't psychotherapy and it wasn't because someone rescued you and finally treated you and your child right.

We were rescued by learning the TRUTH about what's going on, Yahweh's purpose. By actually having it proved to us and pretty much at the same time. So he and I survived probably because of this intervention at just the right time. I was physically and spiritually ill to the point of desperation when I was invited to my first class.

Another place, just at the right time for the two of you to begin a journey back to stability it seems.

That's right. Another example of these "place" dynamics would be to look at why I took my son out of school in the 5th grade. It started with the fact he couldn't read! Something was wrong. Additionally, the moves always made him "new" and that was always a bad "place" for him to be because of the conflict with the homegrown kids who were often group bullies. Teachers weren't much better. They chose off the new kid too and often humiliated him. The situation required my intervention as a parent. First I tried the teacher, and then I went to the principal. When there was no movement in this dynamic or resolution offered, I went to the Superintendent of Schools. He listened and said, "We have a new program, home schooling, with a very good teacher, why don't you put him in that?" So I did. Thus he entered a new and unique place for his education and circumstances.

So when was this?

In 1983.

The teacher was great. She gave credit for life experiences. That meant I could take my son with me everywhere and he would see how life got conducted. Also, she let me incorporate the Bible into his reading lessons. We agreed that the biggest problem was to get him reading. I inserted fantasy books too because he liked those stories. Additionally, I explored what his experience was when trying to read. Turns out the letters bounced around on the page. Other indicators began to reveal he was dyslexic. I had had one child with this problem who overcame it in the 7th grade so I knew a little about it. The schools pretty much stood pat on the topic back then, "We don't recognize it."

The home school teacher also gave my son tests to see what his style of learning was. Turns out he was math oriented, learned best by hearing rather than seeing or writing, and performed best in the late afternoon. Do you see the "places" scenario evolving here? He was at a place he couldn't read and had a bad social place. The school system was at a place it was trying a new program, home schooling. I was at a place where I had knowledge about a problem the schools weren't dealing with at that time. My son was at the mercy of many things including his place in the sibling order, his place in the family in regard to who his father was, his place in his peer group as a new kid and in the age level where there is extensive bullying, and on and on. This construct involved too many places for a kid that age to cope with. I was seen as an interfering mother by many people but it was required to give him a chance to survive all he was confronted with, which, by the way, was all my fault because I unilaterally decided to have him in the first "place". That set all types of things in motion that weren't good for him.

It gets worse for him when you see the places his mother, me, was in: single mom, poor, shunned by family, trying to recover from abuse, afflicted by recurrent suffocations, balancing priorities as allowed by others. By that last I mean my other minor child was a priority to me but I was in a position of little contact because she preferred to live with my parents and I had been informed by authorities that she was of an age to do what she wanted. My son, on the other hand, was openly told he should never expect to live with them because they wouldn't allow it and that was because they hated his father!

This whole complex of "places" converged and created what our lives were then. My son and I did the best we could at any given time to deal with our circumstances, to make the place we were in better. To an outsider it looked awful. Indeed it often was awful. But in our hearts and minds we were doing what we could given the priorities and ethical constructs that I, the parent, operated by and was teaching him. There is a degree of beauty and pride in being able to do that in spite of everything.

I'm always amazed at some of the positions people take which make no sense at all, especially as regards innocent children. He suffered from the anger which was really directed at his father! That's that hydraulic displacement model you mentioned when you did the Freud analysis several sessions ago.

Yes and it was clear as a bell to me and sometimes even to those who were doing it. But we survived. He learned to read, was enrolled in several schools over time in order to play football and so on. And he played on the soccer and little league teams for his age. His experience in those activities was different, though, because he was not one of the "in crowd," one of the kids with secure families who had lived in the town forever. He was in a different "place". Those kids got called to bat more often, got more praise and fewer expressions of displeasure. Coaches are often horribly unfair to kids like my son, especially if they only have a Mom to try to intercede for them.

It was hard for him. It was hard for me. But we have a pride in surviving it, in proceeding forward and in refusing to accept a negative view of us that was often expressed. If we had accepted that view I doubt we could have survived. This builds integrity and strength of character or it destroys you. On the other hand, once humbled like this a person is always aware of the level playing field so to speak. That is a valuable lesson. Additionally, someone caught in these kind of "places" is frequently more selfless than others, able to give more, able to forgive more, able to understand more.

So, these "places" are always developing, converging, coagulating, creating a complex environment that is more than physical and in which we must operate as individuals. Such dynamics are constantly flowing and changing. New input, old output, opportunities, and revelations push the comprehension into new dimensions, new "places". The Odyssey, as I call it, was occasioned by the steady influence of an enormous amount of coordinated "places" in our minds, hearts and even our souls. They led us to new places and other experiences. But we could never get out of some "places": family position is a key one I find doesn't change. This is why the current lack of traditional families in our society is having horrible ramifications. With a father and mother, in the same town, with the same friends, in the same school system, with a positive extended family experience and so forth, a child obviously has a far better chance not only to survive but to see a pathway to excelling in his or her life and "places" by being readily accepted by others.

Even though there are so many broken families now, I know what you are saying is true. If the family lasts long enough, say until the kid is about 11, and it was an acceptable family situation from the outside view, then the child and single parent might make it unscathed but only if they stay put, not if they go elsewhere to start over. And that is really hard to do, to stay put when everything around you reminds you of what has been lost or you really can't afford to keep things the same which is the case 95% of the time it seems to me.

Our culture has done a terrible thing to children by the breakdown of the family. The results are evident. The reasons are now easy to see but the cure is almost impossible to imagine. There is very little real commitment to marriage and the raising of children any more. There is a deep core belief that everyone should do his or her "thing" and put their individual happiness above everything. The extended family has broken up severely or become almost perverted in its ingrown attitudes. People frozen by these circumstances never grow or change. They act out the "places" they have been taught rather than find their new idiosyncratic "places". This odyssey my son and I went on was a microcosm of what is happening in our culture of broken families.

The America I knew as a child is foreign to the one I see today. Children now come home to no supervision, some children roam the streets getting in trouble and forming alliances that precede family loyalty. Over minor matters children are pulling guns out and killing each other rather than having a fistfight or taking the problem to their parents.

Part of this is because grandparents are not devoting themselves to their families as they once did when they lived within a warm nest of approval and respect. They are now usually abandoned by families when in dire need or themselves abandon their families when they are needed and instead go off searching for their own fun and happiness.

The people who still have natural affection and value the meaning of family and child rearing are often ridiculed as not with it, or worse, they are impeded and castigated by their family members who have grown unconcerned and self-righteous about their views, their needs, their time, their money, their everything which they don't want to share with anyone except maybe a sexual partner.

A sign of the times, broken families make broken children?

It creates odysseys like the one my son and I shared. While interesting, they are also dangerous. While in some way free, they also keep one locked out of mainstream society. It would be better to do it the right way. One father, one mother, one set of siblings, one home, one school system, one set of friends, one town with its attractions, and one extended family set if possible. This simplicity is better for children. Add to that the positive effects of parents who are good role models and you have the basis for consistency which will create unselfish and well balanced young people to grow into the leaders of a culture. Without that you have, quite simply, a lot of chaos.

Are you OK, you almost look ill. Want to stop?

That would be good, it was very tiring to do and it's even tiring to talk about it because I have emotions and reactions to it that wear me out. I'll be all right. See you next week.

SESSION SEVEN

One Week Later

On a social level, how have you been a part of this democratic nation? I can't help but wonder if in the face of all you've told me if you were ever able to participate as a citizen. That is, what political stuff have you been involved with or were you just too busy to be involved? I mean by this to suggest that with your attitudes and beliefs political action might have been the answer and am wondering if that was something you tried?

Before I answer that let me back track to make a point that will make more sense of my history of or lack of political involvement.

In the 8th grade I had a memorable history teacher. We had problems, he and I. His test questions supposedly only had true and false answers, but to my mind the answers were ambiguous. He couldn't think beyond the obvious and see what I saw in the questions and answers. Besides, the basic problem, for me, was, "Who really knows what went on for sure anyway?" That teacher, as most history teachers do, bought into whatever the then current textbook version was of "history". I never have.

Then in my second year in college I took a course called "Western Civilization". My teacher was remarkable for more than his albinism. He was the first and last albino human being I ever saw. He taught the "climate of opinion" in various eras rather than trying to buy into anyone's exact recounting of events. I gained from that class a good understanding of how our current society developed, that wars were fought throughout history, that technology had been changing the face of civilization but that ideas drove people to take the actions which change their times.

That same year I had a philosophy professor who was apparently an existentialist and it showed. His job was to teach us a survey of different philosophies over time. It was an intro course. What he actually tried to do was tell everyone to be either pragmatic or existential and tried to prove the rest was hogwash. I was offended by this and fought with him openly in class. It has always been my supposition that you have to know where you stand on ethical and moral issues in order to be acting from a place of integrity, that you just can't act expediently and have any integrity. What he suggested was a good way to annihilate the idea of integrity it seemed to me.

An English professor that same year in college was the best teacher I ever had bar none. His name was Mr. Piggott and I took American Literature from him. He also taught my parents by the way. Reading "The Scarlet Letter" again under his guidance, for instance, was a revelation. "Why was the illegitimate child named Pearl?" he would ask. Then he would remind us of the Pearl of Great Price parable. He tied together the various levels of the book and pointed out that reading a great work of literature could simply be fun or it could be mind blowing by simply seeing the author's philosophy, metaphors and subtext instead of just the story. Reading has never been the same for me and I am glad of it. From his mind-opening tutelage I now think of things such as the idea that every event is a place in one's life and that life is composed of all these places. We literally travel from one place to another like a string of pearls.

Anyway, I mention all this to let you know from where I come intellectually so my political posture can be understood, maybe. I mean, I gave the whole political thing a chance, dove right into it even. Then, as events developed I evaluated them and took a position based on my values, my integrity. Having a distinct position I then lived from that point of view. You see what I mean? Or would you comment as my father often does, "You over analyze everything!"

In my profession we would never accuse someone who evaluates their life of over analyzing unless they just sat around doing only that and ultimately became catatonic.

It doesn't matter what my father thinks in reality because that's just the way I am. So, why do we get educated anyway if not to understand what's going on and develop a point of view based on our basic values? Learning how to think rationally was always my goal in my education through my sophomore year in college anyway. After that I just wanted to finish a BA for employment purposes and figured out how to do it as quickly as I could with what I had already. Cold blooded and effectively I did it on purpose and I knew it wasn't an education. I challenged courses. I took 35 units a quarter after fighting hard with the department chairman to allow me to ruin my own education. I took comprehensive courses where I read 15 books and took a six hour test with questions that correlated them all, and so forth.

And that's how you managed to get your BA during all this stuff that went on in your life?

That's how but deep down I know that learning to think, once you know how to read, is where it's at. Oh, I have to interject that I hate math which is a hard science but you know what? My youngest son does it differently from how they teach it and gets the same answers. He's brilliant at math. So, even math can be intuited if it is your forte. Had to teach myself algebra to take the one math course required for my BA, statistics for social science. Then I promptly forgot it, both the algebra and all those stupid formulas. Remember, I think in words. Like I said at our first meeting my mentally ill son used to think almost exclusively in numbers. I can't even imagine thinking that way. He like his dad is a person of few words.

I've known people who said little because they took everything they said very seriously. They did not want to present a false image or lead anyone astray or make commitments they couldn't keep. Are they like that?

Yes, but their verbal communications don't really convey the depth of what they are trying to say. Oftentimes what they say will seem so wrong but when the right questions are asked it turns out that the concepts they are trying to share are actually extremely complicated and insightful, not wrong.

So, about politics and you?

My political activity started when I was 20. That was in 1960. At that time I couldn't even vote. It wasn't until June of 1970 Congress lowered the voting age to 18 from 21 and the Supreme Court upheld it that same year. But Chris was a political science major in college so we became involved in political organizations before we could vote. The first thing we did was to become involved with the election of John F. Kennedy. Oh, how we young people loved that man. And, I would like to mention, it was not until a good 20 years later that there was talk of his "extra-marital affairs", Marilyn Monroe, etc., and I am not sure I believe all that. Sure was nothing like that mentioned then! I remember seeing him, live on TV, say, "Ask not what your country can do for you but what you can do for your country!" It brought tears. He correlated patriotism and politics. Nowadays, patriots are mostly considered to be in the military, but not back then. Camelot in the White House! Wow, Pierre Salinger must have been a truly great press secretary.

When I opened my door one day, there stood my across-the-street neighbor whom I barely knew. She looked strange and just said, "The President's been shot." Then she left and I turned on the TV. You know, the Gen Xer's would be stupefied to turn back time and see how that affected us! The TV was on day and night for two days and I cried the whole time. It was one of the most overwhelming experiences of my life. Then, to top it off, right there on live TV they let Lee Harvey Oswald be killed by Jack Ruby. I remember commenting as they brought him out that he should have more protection. The next thing you knew he was dead. Poor Marina Oswald, to have a husband who would do such a thing! I felt such pity for her, almost as much as for Jackie. Never did understand how Jackie could stand up let alone go through that whole ordeal without a public tear. I would have been a total basket case. That was my first clue that high political office changed things, changed marriages apparently, changed priorities I guess. Just never could understand her but I do admire her.

Well, I got past that but secretly I wondered if Lyndon Johnson was somehow to blame. On a vacation to New Mexico my in-laws had a book called "None Dare Call it Treason" and I read it. It postulated that Johnson was behind it all. Everyone was trying to make sense of it. Then they had that lonnnnnnnnnng investigation and when it was over they locked up all the investigative material until I forget when! We were all appalled. How could they do that? We were not given the information for National Security purposes they said. Did that mean the Russians killed him and we couldn't be trusted to know that because we might say "nuke 'em"? Well everyone knows the continuing saga and the movie made by Oliver Stone about a decade ago about all this. But still no one of us plain old citizens knows what the Warren Commission found out. And what about all those people associated with the whole thing that died? Way beyond the realm of probability. I am still interested but it was a long time ago wasn't it? And besides, there's the other stuff. You know, the other assassinations that followed.

After Jack Kennedy was killed (we didn't call him John by the way, we all used his nickname Jack), we entered into the political scene more assertively. Chris had completed his BA and was now teaching school with a secret desire to run for office and to go into the Foreign Service ultimately. I joined the Eleanor Roosevelt Democratic Club. Never heard the bad moral stuff about her or her husband or Eisenhower until 20 years later either, so is it really true? I have to doubt it but maybe it is. During the course of our political club activity I met Governor George Brown and Jess Unruh, Treasurer of the State of California, at a cocktail party. The thing I remember most about that party is the huge powdered-sugar-coated strawberries. The Governor was awfully jovial in a stern sort of way and Unruh was scary.

Another time I was part of a group of about five people who met Mrs. Medger Evers in her hotel room. I was invited because of my membership in the Eleanor Roosevelt Democratic Club, but why me I don't know. Remember, her husband was the first well known man who was assassinated in the beginning of the Civil Rights movement. They killed Martin Luther King, Jr. later. The object of this meeting with her was to talk her into running for office. There was much discussion. She mostly listened. She is a quiet woman. Her one comment was that she had a concern that running for office might not be good for her children. Then I said the only thing I had to offer, being a mother myself. "Your children come first and if it wouldn't be good for them you shouldn't do it." She smiled. The rest of them looked at me funny.

This is the Mrs. Medger Evers as depicted by Whoopi Goldberg in the "Ghosts of Mississippi" movie?

The same. It wasn't until years later I even understood why they looked at me funny. It was self-evident to me and should have been to them that what I said was true. Prioritizing is the single most important, continuing mental activity that people should engage in as far as I'm concerned. She didn't run. She knew how to prioritize. Those people who came to her motel room were just after Democratic power. According to the movie the last thing Medger Evers said to his wife was to take care of their children.

So you really did do some political stuff.

Very busy at it for awhile. Then one day our club sponsored a big meeting for the Democratic Presidential Nomination campaign contender, Robert Kennedy. He was a shoe in. There were about 300 people in the audience that day and I sat next to one of my club sisters. He hadn't stopped speaking yet when she suddenly whispered, "Come on, want to meet him?" I nodded "Yes!" She was from Hyannis port and she knew the Kennedy's.

We got up and left before he was finished speaking and she took me through back corridors of the hotel and we wound up at the bottom of a service staircase. Suddenly he came down that staircase and stopped while she introduced me to him. We shook hands. He had the most beautiful color of blue eyes. They were turquoise and exactly the color of the commemorative stamp they made years later. I was so impressed with Bobby that I got Chris to take me to Whittier where he was going to be in a parade later that day. We watched him as Rosie Grier held him onto the flatbed truck to keep him from being pulled off it when people grabbed to touch him and shake his hands. There were thousands of people of color there and they loved him. The next night Chris woke me up and said, "Robert Kennedy's been shot." He'd been watching TV when it happened. So that's how Nixon got on the scene. Bobby Kennedy would have won, he would have been President.

It was hard but I still decided to be involved. I grew up in a family that hated Nixon. So, I naturally wanted to see him defeated. I did volunteer work a bit, not as much as before, but I certainly voted. Then, when two weeks before the second Nixon election, he finally ended the Vietnam War I wanted to puke. He was still elected to my complete astonishment! I was sure he would be defeated for blatantly ending a war for political purposes, when he no doubt could have done it much sooner. I decided the election had to be fixed or else people were so stupid it didn't matter any more. I have never voted again. As far as I'm concerned there's something rotten in Denmark. That's my own personal opinion. I don't get on a soapbox about it and I don't know who to blame but I've dropped out of it.

You arrived at conclusions about the whole political process and reacted on those conclusions. But what if you're wrong?

I'm not. Nonetheless, the political stuff going on today is known to me and I have reactions. Was watching C-span one day and someone called up to say something to the effect that they'd heard talk that the whole Lewinsky thing was a diversion, a smoke screen, to get people's attention away from something else that's going on. The only thing I could think of that would warrant such an elaborate fiasco would be that a comet or asteroid was about to hit the earth and that John Glenn's coming shuttle flight really had something to do with that and his presence was to capture media attention away from what the flight was really about. But that's a giant leap into fantasy. I did notice that just before the launch finally happened someone in flight control said, "May the wings of Discovery carry us into the future." It struck me so odd I wrote it down and I never heard mention of this again.

You think about all this stuff but you don't act politically any more because you basically think it's rigged, right?

You got it. Anyway, it's all completely beyond me, who has no power at all to do anything about the whole now global thing going on.

What about politics on a smaller scale, at the water cooler for instance, or in a club?

As far as office politics goes, I cannot abide that or participate. There is no reason at all for those kinds of charades so far as I can see except to gain certain people an advantage that is possibly not even earned. I am not a political animal. I am not politically correct. What I do, what I say, whatever the reaction, I will deal with it.

The whole spin mentality comes from merging politics with propaganda. When they taught us about propaganda I saw that it meant governments actually warped the truth and even lied for advantage. Spin goes a step further and is at core an attempt to avoid a glaring truth and shape people's opinions to match whatever the current power mongers want them to think. Spin and propaganda share a common ancestral point of view, how to make a lie palatable. And this is the fabric of which politics is now made whether it is in the office or at the national or even international level.

And you hate lies, don't you? No one likes to be lied to but you seem more angry than usual at the idea of being lied to. Why is that do you think?

Actually that came to me the other day. Apparently counseling opens up the thought processes and stuff gets revealed when you're alone too. So, anyway, when I was five there was a play house on our porch. The porch was an old fashioned one, about five feet high off the ground. The porch wrapped around the house, which had been partitioned into two apartments, and the play house was in the corner of the porch. We played on the playhouse. We actually got on the roof and would crawl over it and dangle our feet until they touched the banister and then get down from there. I was in the dangling part of this maneuver when I asked one of the girls I played with if my feet were right over the banister and she said, "Yes." So I dropped down a little. My feet never even touched it. She laughed as I fell about six feet to the ground from that position onto cement. I broke my arm. This girl was known to be a liar, she lied all the time. That time she lied to me and I got hurt.

So that's it. You learned early and graphically that lies hurt other people.

Guess so. I didn't believe in lying before that happened but hating lying by others was probably due to that.

The truth is not really too admired any more. It's often quite unpleasant. Like, the fact that biological terrorism is now the major threat hanging over our head is seldom really discussed in depth. It is too ugly to contemplate.

We'd much rather deny it exists most of the time. Seems denial is the fad. Wonder where all this denial is taking us?

The truth is usually not expedient for pragmatic points of view. That's where expedience and pragmatism get you. Black is no longer black and white is no longer white. There is now only gray according to most people. I don't buy it, there is a real black or evil and a real white or good and gray is simply a mixture of the two and when you mix them they are no longer pure. And I'm not talking races! Human beings are humans whatever color their skin is and in my experience black human beings are often a lot nicer than white ones.

You can't see any reason why the truth might be covered up for our own benefit? For instance, to prevent panic?

Lies are bad, truth is good period. Purity is an interesting word. Can I use your dictionary there? Thanks. (Thumbs through pages.) Let's see, according to this *Webster's New World College Dictionary* purity means the quality or condition of being pure, freedom from adulterating matter, cleanness or clearness, freedom from evil or sin, innocence, chastity, freedom from corrupting elements. I still think we should strive for purity in our ethics and morals when interacting with others. Quaint way to think in this day and age I'm sure.

I can't say I would be able to handle the truth about a really cataclysmic event very well. Maybe it would be easier to not know and go on in ignorance.

Why? Wouldn't you want to get yourself right, enjoy your children more and so on? Oh well, just call me eccentric. What does *Webster* say about eccentric? (Thumbs through more pages.) Let's see, oh yes, the number four definition is "deviating from the norm, as in conduct." That makes me a deviant I guess. I'd rather be that than the norm I see taking hold today. We deviants of this type have a hard time of it out there in the world. We people who say there is a right and wrong, a good and a bad, are very unpopular.

So why haven't you attempted to leave the county, see if somewhere else is better?

Even though I refuse to be involved politically because of what appears to me to be going on, I still recognize this is a very great country with a wonderful Constitution. It just got off track somehow. Getting money and

125

having stuff is the official American quest now, the so-called American dream. The dream used to be a good job, a home, a decent car and enough to feed your family. Now it means a lot more. Get rich, buy everything you want, spoil your kids rotten, have a mansion, and eat out most of the time, go on fabulous vacations and much, much more. For instance, people are able to actually spend thousands of dollars now on Christmas presents. They go into debt for all of this and if their situation changes they're ruined. The American concept as espoused by the Declaration of Independence is still good, it's the people who have proceeded to override its basic tenants and replace them with greed.

We got greedy, we got arrogant, we got selfish, we got inconsiderate, we got insensitive and we became the proverbial "Ugly American" at home and abroad. And the rest of the world has to let us be because we also got very, very powerful. No one to stand up to us. And yet I am proud to be an American and happy I was born in this country. I really am. But I am not blind either and only time will tell how this all turns out.

It seems we're at a dead end and I'd like to quit early today if it's OK with you.

Yeah, sure. Same-o, same-o next week?

Okay, see you then.

SESSION EIGHT

One Week Later

So, from what we discussed last week it seems that a lot of people are maybe in denial, not just you. There's certainly a lot that isn't nice to look at today, but we have to in order to fix stuff. I still wonder if you could just get involved and help with that? It might give you some satisfaction.

Things have gotten to the point that there is a kind of gridlock. Nothing seems to get fixed really, just talked about. I really don't think a tired old woman could have any impact on this situation. Besides it usually takes men to make major changes. That's just the way it is. I do know, though, that this type of frustration is usually one that brings the worst out in men. Women can go with gridlock for a long time before they lose it but men really resent it. Moreover, men are different from women when they are deeply upset. Most men are silent about wrongs done to them for quite a long time. They seldom scream out loud, unless they have a devastating physical injury, or even talk about what is bothering them. But men have emotional reactions just like women do and they always come out eventually. Their best reaction is to make an attempt within normal channels to make changes that would ameliorate a gridlock situation. There's one of those big words. Oddly, first I was taught big words, and then I was told not to use them when I was a journalist! Words are my stock in trade though and I can't resist using the right word even if it is a big one. I mean the right word can really say just what you mean. Do you mind? I hope not.

Not at all although few people talk like you do.

127

In my experience most people have trouble addressing what is causing the big problem in their lives in a realistic and calm fashion. Some men can do it and they become the great men of history. Few women are, frankly, able to control their emotions enough to react coherently and definitively to really devastating situations. They can get physically and mentally incapacitated by their emotions more quickly than men do it seems to me.

I think one of the ways men scream is with violence, domestic or otherwise. And it happens often. More among men than women, although in these days women are becoming more violent. When I grew up, girls having physical fights were a rarity and very frowned upon, but now it is not uncommon for a woman to even fight with a man. But that's another topic and what I consider an aberration of our contemporary times.

As a woman I wouldn't really know how men feel inside or what they think but I have suffered their anger in many forms. Their ego seems to demand that they always have the upper hand around a woman. This probably has a physiological basis. I figure they have to get it up, to be rather blunt, and without good ego strength it doesn't happen. So, ego is very, very important to them, more than to women I think, especially old women.

(Chuckle)

One easy way for anyone to acquire a kind of bolster to their ego is to lord it over someone else and some men do that to other men, to women, to children, to animals. Minorities have always been handy for them to lord it over too. All types of men are subject to doing this, not just white men. And, to be fair, there are women that do it too. I am convinced, though, that real ego strength doesn't require putting someone else down and very strong men and women don't do that.

The "getting it up" part is blunt but probably true to one degree or another.

No doubt women's lib has made it harder on men ego-wise. I've been wondering about this new Viagra thing. Used to be that impotence was a rarity but now it's fairly common apparently. Imagine designing a drug so men can get an erection regardless of real sexual attraction which is the usual cause of that physiological state! Really seems that something is wrong somewhere that such a drug is even needed. I hear even non-erectile dysfunction men want to take it too. What happened to romance? Kinda seems like the equivalent to breast implants in women.

I didn't have a brother. That would have been nice. I would have understood men better. Also, a brother would have been my very own male to talk to in confidence, one who would always feel protective about me and would engage other men if my welfare called for it. My father has never engaged Chris or John about their problems and how they affected me. He has just taken his anger out on me, and in John's case, our child. If I had had a brother he might have taken Chris or John on, physically if necessary, to make my life better. A brother might have also understood what was wrong with Chris and privately told him to leave me alone or else. I would have been furious if I knew of such intercession, and very sad because I was in love, but it would have worked I think.

Although, if I had been saved from these two relationships of pain, the five children produced by them wouldn't be alive. So, it's okay with me. For these five reasons, I realize it wasn't in the cards for me to have a brother who would have impeded the circumstances that allowed my children to be born. They were destined to be born and I am glad they were and love them very much.

It's interesting to note that today women don't necessarily need men to have children what with *in vitro* impregnation and so on. There are also surrogate mothers and even women who ask men they like to father their children but don't want them involved with raising them. Because of the way a lot of men love variety in sexual conquests, they aren't always too bothered by all this.

Aren't those a lot of really odd circumstances, though, into which a child might be born? Can't help but to affect their lives and not always in a good way. Men have responsibility in this matter of how children are brought into this world just as women do.

Now in the case of John, he wasn't given the chance to comment about my having his child although he did always say he wanted me to be the mother of his child. But that could have just been a line. I decided to get pregnant by myself so it's not on his head how hard it was for our son. Besides, John was quite literally screwed up by his military service during the Vietnam era and not really able to be a good husband or father because of that. It doesn't help that he was involved in that military arena, stationed at Guam, during a time when Americans didn't even know we were involved in a conflict in Vietnam, Cambodia, and Laos. He has fewer VA benefits because of that too. He's very intelligent and saw and maybe did things that basically boggled his mind. So he was left with the mind of a brilliant thinker without the ability to actualize anything because he is literally bound and gagged by the emotional trauma of his military service. He needs but gets none of the disability benefits of doing that service. There are a lot of men in this category. They got the grief but not the benefits. And along with other Vietnam vets they also got to realize later that it was not a righteous war anyway which is really a bummer.

I see a lot of these men. There are lots of them who are totally dropped out, barely surviving and have no one but others like themselves to relate to.

That's because some men came out of the conflict okay but some didn't, a lot didn't. The reaction of the country to their service was different from World War II service. The actual fighting was different. I used to wonder about this and once asked a Vietnam vet who was a stranger to me what made it different. His answers told me there was disillusionment on a grand scale. They went to serve their country and found out later the whole thing was a sham. The powers that be wouldn't let them win the war. They were not trained well and the enemy's guerrilla warfare was a shock. The fact children were involved in sabotage was startling. And napalm. That was new and terrible. Special Forces were being used in truly horrendous ways. And back home there were demonstrations against our men even being there. What a confusing, horrific, dehumanizing and violent mess.

So in addition to being bi-polar your husband has a lot in his mind from that time, stuff that makes it hard to live a normal life or feel OK about himself even.

Yeah and there are other terrible scenarios about surviving Vietnam too. I have a son-in-law, 14 years older than my daughter, who is a Vietnam vet. He was damaged, his life changed, but he never fell into violence or self-pity but his life is sketchy and he's been married three times, so it affected him too. He was a health nut, very active, and paid attention to his body. He also looked a good 10 years younger than he was. Then one day, 30 years after Vietnam he develops a lump on his neck.

Seems he was exposed to Agent Orange when he was in-country. With a lot of help from advocates the cancer was deemed service related. One more year and it would have been denied as service related. 30 years was the cut off for that. So his healthiness, his ability to ward it off so long almost ruined his chance to get VA help. He finally did get a 100% disability award. He also had to go through seven weeks of radiation and a radical neck dissection and lost the ability to swallow forever. It's a wound from his service. It just showed up 30 years late that's all. Pretty devastating to him and his family. I was there during the hard part, it was terrible.

He told me of an interesting experience over there so long ago. One night they were being fired on and he was in a trench. There was a lull and he stood up to take a look. There was something behind him on which his shadow appeared. He heard a bullet zip by him and strike his shadow. It passed right by his neck on the side where he ultimately got the cancer. Pretty weird. A shadow wound which manifested 30 years later.

Your son-in-law came back damaged but not violent apparently. You're letting me know why you have a hard time just letting go of your husband. You know he got a raw deal.

Like I said, men scream differently from women. Some men get very grumpy when distressed, just plain nasty but under control. They can also become very fixated on something and talk it into the ground over and over and over and over. Additionally, they may become very inappropriate with the distribution of this information, like calling radio shows and laying it out for everyone, sometimes in an agitated state. I have witnessed all these types of reactions myself.

Women are more circumspect. They might tell someone where to get off but they will seldom put something considered beyond the pale out for mass consumption, even if they believe in it deeply. Occasionally, they do, but rarely. When they have children still in the home, they are very careful to keep a reasonable profile and not to alienate the community. Men aren't so careful in my experience, not if they are really worked up about something. They'll sometimes take a stand come hell or high water.

An example was John's insistence that we live in a house for another year after it had been foreclosed on and auctioned off on the courthouse steps. He believed the VA should have done something to help him. It was a VA loan and you know what? Now they will do something, consider refinancing. Before it was over for us, though, we were living with two children in the breezeway. Good thing it was the desert. Even after the children and I finally left he stayed there another six months. That's pretty much when I had to give up on him. As far as I was concerned, it was his fault we lost the house and his stand wasn't righteous, it was his anger at himself and the VA loan system. It was a scream.

Sounds like his whole life since the war has been a scream of one kind or another.

I wonder what he would say about that because as far as he is concerned real men don't scream at all. Probably I should explain that I really do think the sexes are very different. The roles people play, based on the biology in which they are encapsulated, are very different. Once I asked a Kindergarten teacher whom I admired and taught two of my children to tell me from her observation of young children what she thought was the basic difference between male and female. She was married to a Tibetan lama by the way, not that it makes any difference but it's interesting. She thought about my question for awhile and then said, "Little girls are always trying to find their best friend and little boys are always trying to find out where they fit in the pecking order of the boys they interact with." The pecking order, it's always about the pecking order with men. This is the norm we're talking about, the average. I think men are hard wired that way. There are, of course, obvious differences which occur among both male and female including homosexuality.

Speaking of which I have an idea about homosexuality, in regards to the male rather than the female, which I think has relevance to how it happens. You know how baby ducks will imprint whatever animal they see first and follow it as their "mother"? I think sexuality is imprinted as well. This imprinting would occur when the first real sexual event occurs, that is, when a bipartisan orgasm is achieved which is always mind blowing for everyone whenever it is.

There is no way to explain in advance what a full-fledged bipartisan orgasm feels like, it has to be experienced and whoever and whatever sex the cooperative sexual agent is at that first experience might be imprinted on the brain as how to re-achieve the same feeling. Thus, experimentation in adolescents is probably not good but conventional sexual activity at an appropriate emotional age, hopefully married and/or monogamous, is important. This is just a theory I have based on what I know about Chris.

The high school affair he had, you think it imprinted him to be homosexual?

Could be, couldn't it? He was able to have sex with me, a woman, but he preferred that first experience, that first mind-blowing experience. It's obviously more complicated than that. But the simplistic idea is that maybe he just got imprinted regardless of whatever other stuff was involved in him being homosexual. Or I wonder if his homosexuality is a scream of some sort? If so, it's fear. Fear of what though?

Hard to say if homosexual preference is a scream from the psyche but it's an intriguing idea. You want to know what caused it don't you? What made him that way, what kept him from preferring you?

Obviously I've given it a lot of thought and I knew him and his background really well when we married, except for that high school affair that he told me about, finally, after four years of marriage and two children. It's not only because I was hurt by it that I'm interested though. I'm a social worker at heart. What can help someone is of interest to me. To know what could help, one needs to find out what caused the problem. I just think that way because I'm a social services burn-out. For five years I did my very best to help people that needed welfare, interpreting laws and regulations to their very best benefit, and still there was so very little I was really able to do. Did you know that people sometimes go to a welfare department requesting a specific, one-time type of help and they can't get it?

Not really, I do refer people to social services but I'm not real clear how they go about providing help.

For instance, a lady whose husband was to get his disability soon knew she only needed a certain amount of money to help pay the rent and they could make it then. But she literally had to apply for the whole gamut. There is no mechanism in the welfare system to let responsible people apply for just what they need.

I was a fraud investigator for one year. It became very clear to me that 98% of the people on welfare, at least 30 years ago, were not frauding even if it looked like it at first. Then there were the other 2% that we looked at who were actually, deliberately, committing fraud. So sure am I that the system is a terrible mess that I wrote a paper while getting my BA arguing that the only real way to change the welfare system was to scrap it and start over. Furthermore, I think that the system itself inspires fraud. Frankly, you could just open an office and hand out money up to a certain amount to people who come for specific reasons and you would be better off. The whole thing is an enormous dehumanizing industry. Many welfare workers seemed to be unaware that but for the clients they serve they would be out of a job. I saw tremendous prejudice against the clients that was very ugly on occasion. Still, when my whole world fell apart after leaving first Chris and later John, I had to apply for help. As soon as I put things together I got off AFDC. If I lost a job I would apply for unemployment insurance and AFDC again if I had to until I got another job. This system, as bad as it was, allowed me to continue to feed and house my children at least three times for several months. There wasn't anyone else offering to do it.

So, it's bad but it's all people have in those circumstances?

Yes, that's right, but we could have made it more humane. Instead it's been made to be less helpful all the time. Clinton really took a shot at mothers when he basically said they all have to go to work. Originally the whole idea of AFDC was an effort to allow single mothers to stay at home with their children until they went to school. Now it's called TANF and they have to agree to work, often in state supported and very low income jobs.

You must have an opinion about how we got into this mess regarding families.

As far as I can see, the breakup of families was, in large part, created by the so-called sexual revolution. When it became OK to have sex out of marriage, to live together before marriage, it inferred that people had a right to act out sexually. That took various forms but mostly it meant that if a marriage got stale sexually the partners, or one of them, could feel it was OK to have affairs. Those affairs eventually eroded the fabric of the marriage creating emotional barriers that usually end the marriage. Even women began to think they could experiment sexually and some marriages even got into wife swapping as a whole ideology which would supposedly keep the marriage from floundering. These attitudes are the single most devastating thing that has happened to our country. From there it is easy to do other immoral things like the corruption we now see in our government. That's just doing stuff to unknown people and easier to do than hurting a spouse. Broken marriages make broken families which make a broken nation.

You really think sexual immorality is at the heart of many other corrupt practices?

I do and my spiritual beliefs are that adultery is a physical manifestation of "whoring after false gods" in fact. Of course money is a big bugaboo, "The source of all evil is the LOVE of money." That's whoring after money and often having a lot of money means power and power means that someone can really call his or her sexual shots quite well values being what they are now. We used to call women who married for money "Gold Diggers" and then they were considered to be very bad. Now that's often the norm with younger women from what I hear.

Whatever caused it we can both agree it is devastating to children.

Children with single parents lose out in so many ways. Not only do they not have the other parent around daily, but the parent they have has to work so hard they basically lose that one too. Latchkey children often wind up in gangs who become their families. In 1990-91 I worked for an agency that focused on gangs and I began to really understand the importance of good role models for youngsters and that they absolutely must have trust for and support from their parents or they look for it elsewhere. Simple and yet so complicated is this family thing that has so drastically affected our nation.

Young boys become young men who become older men. If they didn't have a good role model what can they do? All kinds of dysfunction happens and then "screaming" sets in. Mentor programs like "Big Brothers and Sisters" are good and helpful but they really are only a drop in the bucket of role modeling and commitment that a young person needs. Mostly, the women keep the kids in a breakup. Mostly, women can't make as much money as men. Mostly, fathers no longer in the home pay little attention to parenting and all too frequently they don't give money or effort toward that parenting. When they are with their kids they tend to buy them a lot of stuff to assuage their guilt instead of parenting them. Those fathers that do stay involved suffer greatly because they seldom see their children. If fathers do pay child support, it doesn't make up for what a woman can't get in pay unless she has other help such as her parents. The kids frequently suffer in a poverty environment and are raised by a mostly absent and exhausted mother. No role model for boys and not enough attention because of the priority to keep food on the table and a roof over their heads which is essential but not enough to raise stable men or women for that matter.

You're even saying that the single parent thing is causing boys and girls to grow up without the understanding of how to be stable men and women!

I am and my experience with my own sons who needed a good father role model that they didn't get tells me it's true. My sons are literally having to figure out how to be stable men all on their own as adults by noticing the way stable men act. My oldest son at the age of 33 is starting to redefine himself consciously because of what life has dealt him.

One of the ways men scream, by the way, is to deny financial and emotional support for the children after a divorce. There's that word denial again in a different context. This goes back to the dictatorial, "Do and be what I want or I won't support you." Women can't understand how men can be so mean and cruel, but it's based on anger.

It does seem today that in the Yuppie relationship there is a better understanding about the responsibilities of a marital relationship and parenting by both parents. Men help out more in the home because the wife is working. That's good but it's not always good enough when both parents work, not for the kids it isn't. If those marriages fail they probably do a joint custody thing and what a nightmare for kids unless the parents are really organized and good at it as well as not acrimonious toward the other parent. I'm not saying all ex-spouses are unable to do what's necessary to keep the children growing into healthy people but I am saying most aren't able to do it.

So do you think people should stay married for the kids? And if so why didn't you do that?

Used to be people did stay married for the kids. I stayed in my first marriage as long as I did for the kids but once I found that note I just didn't want Chris to raise our son. It was going to be hard enough on our son when he learned about his father's homosexuality later. He didn't need to also be around what I consider a deviant type of man in the meantime to have that as a role model. It wasn't until Chris became overt that I could justify that I had to get out, especially for our son. That's back when people got married forever. To break it up was an enormous shattering of ideals, self image and practical circumstances.

Course this is definitely passé now, doing anything for the kids. Now, people decide not to have kids. Selfish. Good thing everyone doesn't feel that way. I used to have a plaque that said, "Most of the people who favor birth control have already been born." You could add abortion to that today.

If my mother had aborted me, I wouldn't be here! Pretty simple, yes? Guess it's apparent I'm Pro-Life and consider abortion to be murder. A woman sure does have control over her body and the control should be in not having sex or to have it responsibly if you don't want a kid! It's really easy today to keep from getting pregnant so what is the excuse for doing that and then murdering the baby? I better not get started on that. Murderous selfishness, pure and simple. I do know some women who took precautions and got pregnant anyway, but they all had the baby rather than abort it.

So, you left Chris because you didn't want him to raise your son. If you had had all daughters would you have stayed?

Probably and would have been a very miserable woman.

Going back to abortion just a minute, I wonder how men deal with that. I mean, if he wants the kid and she aborts it? Think that might produce a little, teeny, weenie bit of anger? Still no excuse for violence, but understandable if a man bearing that pain would march out some of his other ways to scream, like verbal, mental and psychological cruelty. That's no fun. Men are masters at driving women nuts and women go nuts pretty easily because they are, let's face it, more emotional than men. So who do you think will win that game? They can beat us women up in so many ways.

Or a man hurt in that way who doesn't become abusive might turn it on himself. My son, the one who had trouble with drugs lost two children to abortions women had despite what he wanted. And these women had stated they wanted to have children and to marry him! He lost another child to spontaneous miscarriage. That final loss hurt him too but it didn't hurt his self esteem at least.

I've known some men in that position and they are first of all deeply sad and hurt that a woman would abort their child. It's a terrible emotional assault on the man himself, not just the losing of a child. That is, unless he is in favor of aborting an unwanted pregnancy and plenty of men are in that category too.

Those kinds of men are just as irresponsible as the women who get pregnant and abort the baby in this day and age of easy contraception. When I got pregnant with John's child I did it deliberately and never hid that fact and before I decided to do it I had used contraception. I also did not expect for us to get married but I did want to be with him for as long as I could.

Course I know men complain that they don't understand women, but they do understand very well how to hurt us deliberately. Doesn't take a rocket scientist to know a woman hates to be cheated on just as a man hates it. Women are sometimes more willing to put up with infidelity though because a woman has much less finance producing ability, usually, especially if she has been a homemaker instead of pursuing a career.

A woman with children is very handicapped in her work situation. She not only needs babysitters but also has to be absent from work because of childhood illnesses and school situations, and so on. There are also certain situations in which a woman needs a man's protection. Men can play with that whole field of things and literally decimate a woman who doesn't behave exactly as he dictates. On the other hand he can get along quite nicely without a particular woman, especially if he does not have the kids produced from a failed marriage.

Some of your views are the ones you grew up with, some are from your experience but isn't there maybe another view, a modern view of how best to be married and raise children, even if divorce appears on the horizon?

You think I have a conventional, old-fashioned view of women? You put a man and a woman together and 90% of the time the man is physically stronger, makes more money even if he has the exact same job, doesn't give birth or have the related problems of child care, has a much easier and safer time being sexually promiscuous, and usually isn't taken advantage of by other men, like mechanics for instance. Reality is reality, fair or not. Sure, a woman can choose a career and selfishly make sure she gets there by getting the education required, moving up the career ladder, working 60 or more hours a week, and agreeing to travel all over the place if required. In this scenario what has to give? Obviously, she can't really have children during all this or, if she does, they might be neglected to say nothing about the impossibility of having a partner who needs so little attention. The men I have observed start getting really angry and dysfunctional if they don't get steady attention. Then the silent screaming begins.

I think I see where this is going. The silent screaming can take the form of violence, domestic violence.

Why do we have the increase of wife and child abuse and even killing by men? Because that's one way to relieve anger and a lot of men are pretty angry down deep. Other stuff doesn't help a man stay away from violence either, like feminism, affirmative action that discriminates against white men, and the fast pace of life created by technology, among other things. Maybe the wife was great and the children beautiful and well-behaved, maybe the anger was even at something else. Men are complicated and powerful beings. They have the capacity to plan in a very calculated way. It is recognized from studies that they are more calculating, some say logical, than women. They are also usually much stronger physically. Put all this together with anger and you get violence sometimes. Not good, and definitely increasing.

Now you're giving an apologia for domestic violence instigated by men which includes the change in roles that women have achieved in the last 40 or so years. I'm sure you're not saying domestic violence is to be expected but you're on a fine line here.

Violence anywhere, anytime, is never OK as far as I'm concerned but men need to scream and they don't have the cultural largess to scream out loud. So, they scream in other ways. I'm just saying that's how it is, not that it's good how it is. Of course it isn't good but we need to understand it to have a hope of stopping it.

Sometimes the men who are most powerful in their particular pecking order get together and scream in unison. That's when you have a war. Usually over power, territory and money. Sometimes, they say it's over a woman. Remember the Helen of Troy story? I suspect there was more to that than

Helen. Back then women were property and not really taken that seriously. Imagine being considered property, like a chair or a horse or a house or a slave! Every woman knows innately that slavery of any kind is wrong period.

Men are power mongers. It's in their nature. Deny them the ability to have real power in at least one arena and they get weird. You can only hope, as a woman, that you find one who knows how to use power beneficially and doesn't need to put down someone for his specific and often hidden ego reasons. If you have a man like that staying home would be great. Women must be wondering why they ever wanted to go out and work so hard. Being a homemaker was a busy and tiring job but it had a degree of freedom from all the stresses related to earning income in order to pay the bills, of not having to report somewhere everyday because you have to, and so on.

You know you are talking to a man, and I don't necessarily agree with all this. I think lots of women love working and they actually find it preferable to staying home and changing diapers, cleaning and so on. And I really don't know that I seek power of any kind!

Do I hear a little bit of screaming in there? Remember the hierarchy idea of the kindergarten teacher I told you about? She saw the seeking by five-year-old boys to find every male's placement in the Kindergarten power structure, pure and simple. Sometimes they fit in and accept what power is given them in the structure. Sometimes they want more and do inappropriate things to get it. Take that far enough and you have a rapist of women, the environment, or something. So, we get to the state the world is in today. It's the fault of men, there's no doubt about it. Women would have never got us to this point we're at today. They just would never put themselves in so much danger and they know when to keep quiet. Even I can keep quiet at times. I don't yield but I know when I better keep quiet at least. We know how to do that and you men don't often enough that we have wars.

Maybe in the past but men's and women's roles are changing.

That's true but the biological thing is still there, the will to conquer, the will to get as high in the pecking order as possible, the need to have ego massaging in order to be able to get it up. I do, though, see Generation X men fighting this power-seeking in themselves. They are trying to not rape the world, trying hard to give women power cheerfully. This is good but they are not the mainstream. In fact, they are anti-establishment because the establishment got us where we are today. These male Xer's worry about the ozone, global warming, eating more vegetables instead of killing animals for money although they admit they would have no problem killing an animal if they had nothing else to eat, and so forth. I notice, though, that they do some other stuff that is not good for them, like take drugs, maybe because they are fighting this power struggle inside themselves. In my disabled son's generation he has already lost three friends, one a best friend, to suicide. It's the final scream perhaps.

Who knows? I don't, but I see things that give me ideas about all this. Been through some stuff you know. Lots of it. Weathered the storm, still around, still trying to figure it out. But I don't hide from all of it or get in one groove and stay there, frozen in time. We human beings have the capacity to learn, learn, learn, and hopefully, to grow, grow, grow for as long as we live.

So where do you think it will all go, this change in women's and men's roles?

We women want a little more of the power, a little more equality, but we have to remember that men are men and they can scream in ways that hurt us. So, we have to respect them and their power. We have to. Stupid not to. "Wait until you get old," I would tell a young woman who doubts this. Just wait! Then you'll really see the power they have. A young woman has the power of the sexuality of her youth to exert some control or influence over men. Not so when she is old. That's why love and commitment are important, or you may as well decide to be alone when you're old. If the love and commitment aren't there men roam. My mother-in-law used to say, "A stiff dick has no conscience." Crude but to the point. To get into a man's head enough to make his conscience interfere with his natural inclinations requires love and commitment.

I respect men. I know what they can do firsthand. That doesn't mean I don't resist them trying to get me to do wrong things or that I'm always quiet. But I respect how and when to rebel. Some stuff is not important enough, some is. Timing is the key to any kind of useful rebellion against a man by a woman. Pick the wrong time and you're finished before you begin. They often have this weird ability, too, to take something you say to them, usually as a rhetorical question, and later come out with it as their own! Truly amazing. Maybe that's the essence of being a help mate, knowing when and how to pose a question that brings a point of view later to a man which allows him to think he got to that idea all by himself. We don't have to take the credit. They care more about that than women. My problem is I am not very good at communicating anything but my real thoughts and feelings whatever they are at any particular time. But, as I said, I can be quiet, there are times

I have been quiet for hours in the face of terrible stuff that I desired greatly to respond to completely.

Is that the proverbial "walking on eggs" syndrome you're talking about when you say there are times you are quiet?

Yes, and having to live that way most of the time is a terrible drain. At least on me it is. My mother-in-law used to tell me, "I just don't pay attention to anything they say." She didn't take most of what men say seriously and just ignored them basically even when they were loud. That seems so disrespectful but in a way wise.

Anyway, I sure don't want any of them screaming at me in any way at all any more. They are on their own now insofar as my intervention is concerned. I tried to deal with my father, with my husbands and with my sons frankly and completely honestly. Not too effective. Now, I mostly listen to them when they want to spout off except for an occasional question unless it's so important I have to say more and then I will usually get some emotional flak aimed at me.

That being the case, I don't know how you could ever possibly live with your husband again!

Well the thing is he is getting old, rather quickly. He is also a bundle of guilt for his bad treatment of me and he wants to be nice to me. That doesn't mean he could actually do it but I am less afraid he would lose it and hurt me. He really knows how to push someone's buttons though. He knows the buttons and he will push them. But he seems to be mellowing greatly and eager to be nice now. You get a lot less courageous the older you get, man or woman I think. Getting feeble is interesting. It's okay I guess.

Without a man in my life, I am much more peaceful and content. I'm in charge of my own time and thoughts at all times. Priorities become very clear and easy to actualize without opposition. This can only happen for me because there isn't a man to interface with me and who would probably try to control what I do, how I do it, and when I do it. The worst of all is when men try to control what we think and insist we will think the way they want us to, or else! Or else the silent screaming begins. Mental cruelty. Men don't seem to appreciate that a woman will do or be how a man wants so long as she can keep her integrity intact because she loves him and that she doesn't really have to agree with him. They often insist on that and that's the stage for a terrible psychological bind that usually ends in divorce.

Even the few marriages I see that endure have this problem. The man trying to control everything, to be in charge. Most marriages that continue require the woman to give in to a degree unless the power differential is in the woman's favor. Those are the best marriages, where the man is more in love with the woman than vice versa. Then she continues to have some power, to be able to exert her will sometimes. Never had one of those marriages. That would have been nice, but it usually doesn't happen unless you are a raving beauty and I'm not, nor are most women.

You have been very open in this meeting in particular. You are not hiding anything but you are still not clear what to do about your husband are you, even though you've given him papers to sign and even filed them? I think you actually know how to help your son and are doing that but his father is another thing altogether. Why do you even want to try to be with him?

He needs someone who he can trust while he gets older and older and he trusts me more than anyone in his life. He knows I will, even if he backs me into a corner, tell him the truth as I see it. He knows I do love him and forgive him even though he doesn't forgive himself. He has many acquaintances but usually even when he thinks he has found someone to trust they are just lying in order to use him in some way and he is disappointed in the end. He doesn't really know how to be friends with other men because he is so competitive with them.

Those are good answers but could you really do it and stay sane and happy enough yourself?

I could if the rest of my family wouldn't disown me but some would and that'd be very hurtful because we all get along pretty well right now and that took a long time to achieve. One thing of the things John told me has really stuck with me, an old gypsy saying, "Give me a life I can live with." I have that now. For the first time. Before I had a life I had to live with in spite of everything men did to me and that I stupidly did to myself. It was hard.

The really negative part of being with John is that unhappy men, and women too, self medicate a lot with alcohol and drugs. Happy people don't kill themselves by degrees. Enough anger without ventilation or remedy breeds depression. Depression requires alleviation. One alleviation is suicide and/or homicide. Another alleviation is alcohol and/or drugs. That whole thing is bigger than men, that's everyone. Would he finally be able to relax and just be, accept himself and me and be calm and peaceful? Alcohol is his drug of choice last I heard but he does other drugs and that would have to stop for us to be together because it's too dangerous in many ways.

Now you've given me a lot to think about. My first reaction is that you would be crazy to try to be with him. The other is that you love him, he needs someone and is hurting for probably all his life and somehow trusts you which is rare in his type of person. Additionally, he is older just as you are and older people sometimes manage to keep the heat at a bearable level even when they couldn't when younger. But your family repercussions are a big problem and that may be why it actually cannot be ultimately. Although, Biblically a man and wife are instructed to abandon everyone for each other.

Only if they live in peace though. The head of the man is Yahshua and then the man can be the head of the woman but if Yahshua isn't in the mix and there is constant trouble and fighting then it's not really a marriage is it because marriage at its most basic is a unity and there is no fighting in unity. And could we, would we live in peace?

I see it's time to stop now. It sure goes fast, for me anyway. See you next week.

SESSION NINE

One Week Later

I wanted to bring to your attention that you haven't really talked about anything much you might have done wrong in your second marriage, the one that's actually finalized again in divorce now. What part did you play in all this besides getting involved with someone who probably wasn't good husband material anyway, having his child even, and you knew it?

I have always been too willful. That has changed now but only because of my spiritual belief which has literally changed me in that way. My entire life before that was willful.

There is also the fact that for four years I escaped responsibility, the only time in my life I remember doing that. I smoked pot. All the time. Things just got worse. And I knew it. But I didn't know what to do about it and just escaped. Was totally unable to decide what to do although I knew something had to be done and soon. Finally, events were bad enough for my children that I had the resolve to start leaving a bad situation. I suspect that if I had not had children I would never have left, never have found a reason to do so because I was so completely overwhelmed. Although, I have to tell you I was literally told once, by the Creator, to "get up and leave." So, maybe that's the real reason I finally began leaving.

We still had the house then so when I started leaving it meant leaving my home, meant dragging children around, meant trying to secure some kind of financial means, and it meant enduring continuing emotional abuse from loved ones who didn't understand what I was going through and who didn't want to hear about it. Had to leave twice, first one didn't stick. Second really did but even then I tried several reconciliations when he claimed he got "religion". They didn't work. Needless to say he offered no help at all after I left. Oh, I take that back, he sent me a wadded up coat once in a box because he was worried I was cold.

Every time I left there was a complete upheaval of circumstances. Sometimes I was able to take some stuff but usually nothing but a few clothes and personal possessions. My children are still angry about the loss of memorabilia. Finally, he just sat in his deceased mother's house with a two car garage full of the stuff and wasn't able to make any payments on the house so was forced to leave and most of the stuff was lost. What he managed to get out was literally stolen by the people who helped him get it out.

You lost almost all your personal stuff? How did that affect you?

Early on I just let all the stuff go. Fortunately, I'm not materialistic and live in the now so losing stuff was never that great a burden on me. A mutual friend once told me that my husband kept it all thinking I would come back to him to get it. I don't agree. I think he just thought everything was really his and in his anger at our leaving he decided we should be punished by not being allowed to have it. Didn't bother me that much and I taught the kids that stuff is just stuff. None of them is a miser of stuff and there's a freedom in that. That's another thing he was, a miser of stuff. This is some sort of psychological problem. He couldn't even throw away scraps of paper. Can you imagine the stuff that stacked up over the years? What a dirty mess.

Pack ratting usually bespeaks of someone who has lost so much that is important though intangible that they can't stand to lose anything at all any more.

Well he lost pretty much all of it. To fight off his demons his great escape was alcohol until 1978. Alcohol actually brings on demons I think but maybe they were more bearable than his regular ones. Then he turned to marijuana with some alcohol thrown in. He was leaving the alcohol mostly alone the past few years but now he's drinking more since I gave him the papers. When we talk on the phone I can tell if he has been drinking.

Two of my children flirted with the escape of alcohol but they seem to have it under control now. Three of my children have been involved to one degree or another with drugs or marijuana. The FDA doesn't agree that marijuana is a drug so not sure what category to put it in other than medicinal. Two of those three managed to get that under control too. Only one had a really big problem with self-medication.

What about you now?

I drink red wine at night sometimes when I can afford it. It helps me sleep and the doctors say it's good for my heart and blood pressure. But for those four years that I escaped with pot, I was at a total loss. Everything was a mess. After I came back from the first time that I really left for awhile, eventually the house was finally auctioned off, we were still living in it, there was no steady income, food was scarce, the heater was broken, we were down to two children there in the breezeway, and I quite literally didn't know what to do. Did get some financial assistance which it took forever for him to agree to. There was no possibility of me getting a job because of all the flak he had put out over the talk radio. Finally, I just got in a car and left, then returned, then left again. Later on I returned a couple of times for several weeks with one child, his, to see if he really had changed like he claimed. No such luck.

When did the leaving start really?

The first escapes were overnight stays at motels when I knew he was drinking or, if we had no money, staying all night in the car in a church parking lot near the house. At first he was very contrite about these situations, he even told me I should leave when he was drinking. Then after he started smoking pot he began to put together a whole set of rationalizations which made all his wrong doing my, the children's and my parents' fault. He began not to feel sorry for what he did that was wrong because, as he saw it, we were to blame.

Has that changed at all?

Nowadays he says he was to blame and is surprised I will even speak to him. Then once in awhile he'll trot out the rationalizations again, these are times he's under stress. Can't talk to him then, at all.

Not that I didn't do wrong too. Just not sure what it was I did besides having our baby before we were married and staying with him too long. He was unfaithful, I wasn't; he couldn't work, I did; only he got drunk and violent until the end when I slapped back at him a few times; he gambled our slim resources, I didn't. So what was his beef? He says the other four children, my parents, society, other people, etc. Then just one year ago when we had one long decent talk he told me, "I told you I know it's always the man's fault." Who knows what he really thinks, but then I think he's three different people, literally three different personalities. That must be hard for him. It was sure hard on me.

Marijuana may not be a drug and so far as I'm concerned it should be legalized even though I don't do it any more, but regular use seems to cause some people, like me, to drift, to not pay attention, to forget, to not address issues that need addressing. As far as hard drugs are concerned they are just plain terrible. They can kill the user and sometimes others. They turn nice people into liars and thieves. Luckily I didn't go that route, too much self respect I think.

Hard drugs are decimating our society. In 1991 I wrote a drug demand reduction curriculum for 6th graders. National Guardsmen would go into the schools and teach it to the kids along with other activities like map making, survival skills, and so on. This helps but it's not enough. A complete education about the dangers of hard drug use needs to be given to 3rd and 4th graders because by the 6th grade they will already have been introduced to peer pressure to use drugs and they will know how to get them. They need to know at a very young age about these things. We adults putting our heads in the sand about this definitely won't help. Isn't this so very sad?

Yes it is.

My kids were never taught about drugs. It wasn't a problem in the schools or on the streets then. My last child is part of the generation that was exposed to drugs at a young age without any real education about the horrible effects of hard drug use. My work for drug demand reduction was an attempt to understand the problem myself so I could teach my child. It is almost too horrible to think about but we must, we really must.

Young people today are literally bombarded with peer pressure to do "bad" stuff: drug use, early sex, stealing, drinking, and cigarettes. All bad, and some illegal, escapes. How can we expect these young people to resist these pressures if they have little attention because of working, often single, parents, and when they have very little practical education about these matters,? In the 50s the pressure was to be "good". Now the pressure is to be "bad". The situation is of epidemic proportions. These are the people who will run our country in a few years. Some can't read or write. Most don't have any real ethical foundation other than not getting caught. Most terrible of all, the usual idealism of youth is fading in the face of reality. Youth is where idealism is naturally apparent and when there is strength of character there is a willingness to attack large problems. Without youthful idealism and character what can change?

The young ones who refuse to be hypocrites literally drop out, refuse to engage this society, find niches within populations of like thinkers, and remain kind, non-violent, ecologically sane, and build their own life without hunger for possessions or power. Ever hear of the Rainbows? This is a loose confederation of these young, and some older, people. Most would call them hippies and there is a remarkable prejudice against them by establishment persons. They meet regularly, in the open not in convention centers, to trade goods, ideas and supportive embraces.

They came here to the Taos area a couple of years ago didn't they? Were up in the mountains by Tres Piedras or something weren't they?

Yeah, that was a Rainbow Gathering. They happen all over the U.S. They not only have a philosophy but there is a complete culture about how they gather together, how they travel together, how to get wrong doers to toe the mark, what is expected of each other, and they are devoted to not hurting the earth. Wherever they gather, they leave it in a condition that defies they were ever there at all. They are gypsies with few possessions, complete dropouts from society as we know it. They'll take low wage jobs for awhile to get what they need and then hit the road again. Sometimes when they have children they tend to stay put for awhile but not always. They espouse differing spiritual ideas but all seem to be in pursuit of the spiritual meaning of life. They have no pride of possessions. Just what they need is their creed. They also have a rather strange way of policing each other. Confrontation is discouraged and instead "lessons" are contrived. Sometimes lessons are staged by a conspiracy of friends to teach someone something. This is scary to me but accepted by them it appears.

Anyway, this group is quite intellectual and non-threatening in reality if not in the mental fears of the establishment. It is organized, non-judgmental, non-political, in touch with Mother Earth, and blatant in its refusal to become part of mainstream America. A Rainbow Gathering is a giant celebration of their lifestyle and a time for visiting with each other. They get by on little and they love art, music and nature.

This is much bigger apparently than I ever thought. It just goes on like this, pretty much inoffensively except for an occasional bad apple and the rest of us are completely in the dark about it?

Yep. Is the Rainbow way another great escape? Probably. I would go that way if I could. I can't because of my medical conditions. If I could I would. I prefer them to what I see in society today. Guess I'm a borderline, old Rainbow. They like me and I like them. They are welcome in my home. I am welcome in their locations which go from tents and sheds to mobile units and rented rooms. But I don't think I would ever consider using marijuana again which is a staple for Rainbows, even though a doctor told me she would prescribe it for me because she thought it would help my asthma. The last few times I smoked it I got so paranoid. Who needs that!

The only thing is I really do get too uptight, too easily. Reacting to small things like they are some of the past things I've been through. I really don't like this because I believe in living in the now and that is pulling the past in. Maybe I just don't have the patience I used to have. Used to understand everyone, why they did what they did, forgive them and go on. Now, I find myself wanting to shout, "Cut it out! Count your blessings!" I also feel compelled to reveal lies in my presence. How can you trust anyone if you know they lie?

This is the affective disorder that the Social Security doctors uncovered in you?

They saw it, that my abilities to transact business and remain successfully at a job site are impeded by my ethical structure and my over reaction based on past wrongs inflicted on me.

I have a new escape though that's socially acceptable. The internet. Taught myself enough to make rudimentary web pages. I make web pages for family and a few for clients although I'm falling behind the tech changes. Also my computer is losing its ability to really be viable for this and I can't afford the needed changes. But I enjoy it and learn a lot because it's a great research tool. I also keep in touch with various people through email, some of whom I have never even met. It's fascinating, on the cutting edge and keeps me informed. People are starting to get their news over the internet as well. Recently newspapers began a celebrity filled TV ad campaign to "teach your child to read a newspaper a day—that's where it all begins!" Boy are they scared or what?

Anyway, that's my escape now. It meets my needs: for information, to be creative, to write, to have contact with others. And it is sedentary which is basically what my health conditions require. Works for me and isn't hurting anyone so why not? I have to have a reason to be on the net though. I really don't "surf". When I go online it's for a specific reason.

My talent has always been writing. I have always written stuff. If I get mad at someone I will often write them a scathing, long letter. Used to send those letters but finally learned they were actually for my benefit, to get it out of me, and now I throw them away, usually. No matter what job I had my writing skills were always utilized. Manuals, grant proposals, procedures, policies, reports, correspondence, narrations, case studies, newsletters, press releases, it goes on and on.

For myself I write whatever seems to just come at the time. This has included poems and a fantasy novel I wrote in 1973 when no one was publishing that genre'. I no longer have it because my husband took it. He kept all my copies of news, feature, interview, stories I wrote for printed media too. I have the poems. So does he. Also wrote a teleplay and produced it with a grant. Don't have that either but I could rewrite it if I wanted to. Got it produced but couldn't get it edited. Then something happened to the tapes and they aren't good enough to edit now. Really sorry about that. Would love to have seen the finished product. Was an exciting, very creative and limits pushing undertaking. Someone did a documentary of us producing the teleplay. Never got to see that. The tech crew was from LA City College.

Sounds like writing has always been your solace, how to be useful, how to make your thoughts known, how to ventilate, how to do lots of things that give you pleasure and self esteem. That's good, that's really good, and maybe what has saved you from just giving up.

Writing is a great outlet. It can be a powerful statement. It can be for many eyes or just one set of eyes. It can be regurgitation of emotions. It can be beautiful. It can logically construct a system of thought. It is a way to communicate to oneself or others, to organize one's thoughts. Often I learn a lot when I try to write about a particular event or idea. Just writing it helps to show the errors or fuzziness of thoughts I am having and I am forced to account for these and find new answers to old questions. Writing also, for me, is a learning tool. If I write notes I will remember better. It seems to secure it in my brain. Some people learn by hearing, some by seeing. I learn by hearing or seeing and then writing.

This is really useful. This is the stuff that you need to know about yourself as you continue to get older. This is the joy of retiring, to do what you like to do, what gives you pleasure.

I also paint, sometimes. Not enough. It is the best pure emotional regurgitation I have found for myself. Can't explain how it works. I pick a subject to paint and just do it. The doing of it, the hand movements, the colors used, whatever, seems to pull out from me whatever is in there lurking about currently. Twice I have painted persons in tree trunks without knowing it. Later they were pointed out to me by others who were observant. From an art therapist I worked with once, I learned they think tree trunks in art represent the artist's ego. In my first painting with a tree trunk that had a person in it, the person was stretched out on it like a torture rack. In the other painting the trunk had two people embracing in it. They reflect my life experiences when I painted them but I never knew I painted those figures there until they were seen by others. Don't have those paintings either. I also have a third painting of a tree and in that I can see a woman on one knee with a shadowy figure behind her helping to keep her from falling. Telling you this makes me realize I need to paint. I really do. Will let you know next time we meet if I keep this resolution to paint again.

Good idea, see you next week.

SESSION TEN

Two Weeks Later

Missed you last week Susan. So, how is your son doing, how is your relationship with your ex-husband going, and have you painted anything yet?

Just didn't feel a need to come last week and I think that's a positive. What do you think?

Sometimes that's it and sometimes it's just the reverse. Hard to know until I see how it's going for you.

Well my son's doing really well and he has a wife now! They seem to feel complete with each other and both have hard backgrounds and some mental illness that is under control. I think they feel they have found their mate, someone who will accept them and love them regardless of their illness. He is also inventing lots of stuff, even got a website to sell one of his product ideas.

My husband started smoking again, is drinking even more and is really very sad about the divorce. Can't seem to think of him as being my ex-husband. I'm trying to stay in touch but have to be careful not to be caught up in trying to rescue him from whatever develops. He's a grown man and pretty stable on his meds now.

I haven't painted yet, maybe during the coming week I will. Some new information surfaced in my family this past week. It raises other questions too that I will now have to explore and deal with appropriately, not just for me but for those involved.

That's pretty vague.

I'm not ready to talk about this new personal situation. Hasn't totally sunk in. My mind hasn't cogitated it enough yet to really discuss the matter. It hasn't washed through my being yet. I think I'll try to handle this on my own. In fact I want to talk about my belief structure today and I think I don't really need to come any more, at least for now. Maybe later when this new information has sunk in I might have to talk with you about it. I don't know.

I think you're right. We've traveled through a bunch of stuff. Some was just pure ventilation, some was very revealing even to yourself, and you've achieved some resolution. You got the divorce and you don't seem as guilt ridden about denying your son's mental illness for so long. I sense you are in a different place now, ready to just help him get on with his life instead of beating yourself up over your failure to see his illness because of your own needs. So, OK, I'm ready to hear about your beliefs. In fact I'm interested to see what has helped you spiritually to get through all this.

The search for TRUTH in capital letters has involved my mind since I was 16. At 17 I had a vague, visionary experience causing me to believe there was a Supreme, though impersonal, Force at work. God didn't seem the right word for this Force. When I went to college I learned a term that seemed to fill the bill. It was coined by Henri Bergson, *Élan Vital* or Life Force. I still hold with that truth of an *Élan Vital* with the major exception that I now know it is not an impersonal force and He/She has an actual name, Yahweh. Quite literally, this force caused me to be created, and planned to what end my life would go by having the innate power to make that happen. Even the smallest grain of sand has this in common with me.

Therefore, it is inescapable to arrive at the conclusion that the physical plane and everything in it is completely interrelated. Throw in the fact that there is really no time, just physical motion which man has chosen to harness mentally as a concept called time, and you have a really confusing concept for a physical, doomed-to-die being. That makes it imperative to address the spiritual or metaphysical, where there is no time, and no death.

Before I go further there is something more to tell you about The Odyssey I mentioned before, where there were so many moves for me and my youngest son. This same period of time had as its main focus beyond survival a search for the TRUTH. My life had become so very difficult that I needed to answer basic questions in order to survive it mentally. For 15 years the very search helped me make the trek back to sanity in my life. My youngest child shared this search with me.

I felt the only salvation for my circumstance, in view of my ethical structure and life path, was for me to know the TRUTH.

So what do you mean, TRUTH in capital letters? I mean, generally what do you mean by that?

What do I mean by the TRUTH? Well, how big questions are answered and how they must all be interrelated and have a collateral cause in order, *ipso facto*, to be the TRUTH. What does everything flow from? How does it all make sense? Questions like, "Why was I born?" "What happens after death?" "Is there a God?" "Why is there evil and pain?" And, the answers must work together, like a tapestry, to be the ultimate TRUTH.

By 1978 I had arrived at the conclusion that, unless there were a God and a purpose to all this, human kind was clearly going to destroy itself. My search began as a desire for the human race to continue. Remember, I was a child of the cold war and had lived 20 years under the threat of nuclear annihilation. Today we know that threat is less and the greater threat is the ecological damage we have done to the planet but we have known for some time we might be bringing about our own demise as a species.

So, to use one of your big words, the nihilistic path the world was on started your search for TRUTH beyond the *Élan Vital* belief you had?

Yes. I came to this conclusion about seeing that Mankind was going to make itself extinct after entering into the world of work, having left the safe nest and enclosed world of my home. In my work I had tried assiduously to make the world better for suffering people. I was now 38, had five children, and my life was a complete mess just like the world. Seeing and admitting that I had almost no willful impact at all on the world outside myself or on my very own small world, my mind screamed out, "Why don't you do something about this!"

To whom did I scream? To that impersonal *Élan Vital* which tells me I innately knew there was something personal to scream out to.

An answer came back into my mind, "I have a plan."

"What plan?" I demanded.

"My son," came back the answer.

I was totally shocked. In fact I shouted back, "You mean, that's true?!!!" I was appalled. That story was one I had derided many a time.

You actually communicated with something or someone?

Yes, those answers to my questions were impressed upon my mind. That began the search. I had already learned about basic different religious beliefs and the one that I had never given any credence to at all was Christianity and it supposedly had something to do with the Son of God. So, I decided to find out just what they had to say about this Son. The search started with the Episcopalian Church on the corner by our house. This is where my two youngest children were baptized at my husband's insistence once he knew I was on the search. That church fell out right away when I found out the baptism was to be done in the back of the church because we had no money to donate to them in order to have it in the front of the church. That couldn't be right.

Be aware before I continue that this ends up as an indictment against Christianity including Catholicism and Protestant churches and all derivations of the same.

Then the great exodus began, leaving my husband. The only time I actually heard clear, quiet, words in my mind from the *Élan Vital* which I now called God was after my husband had hit me, again. That still small voice in my mind. The words were, "Get up and leave." I think I mentioned this to you once before. My body got up and left without any decision from me. When He speaks it is. Before I knew what was happening, my body got up off the floor, left the room, got my keys and kids and drove away, very fast. The exodus was on. I left for hours the first time, then I left to go 800 miles away for three weeks, then for two months at which point I chose off the Grace Baptist Church first just because someone mentioned it and I liked the word Grace. That fell out for lack of concern to get us there and lack of structure. It was, I found out, more social than anything.

Next I went to the Lutheran Church into which I had been baptized at age seven. That was done at the little church across from our home. My folks didn't go but encouraged me to attend Sunday school, probably to have some free time to themselves. My Godmother was into it though. She played a strong hand in that Baptism at which she gave me my first Bible. I'm in touch with her now after many, many years too.

So at a much older 38, and after some intense studies with the Lutheran church, some reading of the Bible, and asking disconcerting questions of the Lutheran pastor, that dogma also fell out. Turns out it's a lot like the Episcopalians except for one thing. This time it was more over the baptism issue than money. They sprinkled. I had read Jesus was immersed and so why didn't they do that? 12 years later I found out that the Bible repeatedly testifies to the fact that the New Covenant has nothing to do with being immersed in water but rather talks of being immersed in the Holy Spirit and fire, so my complaint against the sprinklers was not really correct either.

Water cleansing was only ever given to Israel and all of the Mosaic Law was over at Pentecost. Yahshua died on the cross, was buried three days and then resurrected. Then He spent 40 days among His disciples being seen by 150 people before ascending into heaven after telling them to wait together for 10 days. On that 53rd day after his death the Holy Spirit was poured out at Pentecost ushering in the new, spiritual, covenant.

As for my son and the Lutheran Church, he gave the minister's son a black eye during the Christmas pageant of which they were both a part. At least that church gave us shelter for a couple of days, even though I had left that fold, when we returned to town after my decision to attempt another reconciliation with John. Next I trooped myself and my child down to the Assembly of God Church where I discovered they did immerse in water of which at the time I thought myself and my child were in need.

When I requested the pastor to baptize us his response was, "We'll have another baptism in the spring probably." It was early winter. I noticed that in the Bible water immersion was an immediate thing when requested of John the Baptist and others before Pentecost so I was taken aback.

Then, two weeks later the pastor announced that we would be able to be baptized in water sooner as it turned out. This was because a congregation member was getting married and the espoused needed to be baptized. The soon to be spouse was more important than we to the Assembly of God, obviously, and erroneously I was sure, but God had found a way to overcome their error is how I thought. Further, I was told that there was a plan for us to be baptized by an assistant pastor. This had to do with our lack of importance I suppose because no one had mentioned money. I had met this assistant pastor and something about him bothered me so I refused to have him do it. Many times in my life I have been told not to go on first impressions but after a long life I have found that first impressions are actually very good so long as a definite prejudice is not involved.

Anyway, after some argument, my refusal of the assistant pastor was honored and we were baptized by the full pastor. About two weeks later the assistant pastor was arrested for child molestation. Still I studied with them, at every study group they put forth, for more than six months trying to find the TRUTH. The final problem came when they refused to talk about two books of the Bible which I was curious about, Genesis and Revelation. There was this big problem about evolution and carbon dating, and what on earth did Revelation mean? Absolute refusal to discuss those books drove me away. "We can't understand all that now," was their excuse.

About this time, I got a flyer in the mail advertising a free, extensive study of the Book of Revelation offered by the Seventh Day Adventist Church. They would even give you a free Bible. I was always collecting Bibles and giving them to others as well so another one would be good. One time I had 17 of them. We began to study with that dogma.

It was a nice period of time. This is a very pleasant church. They have their own schools, two of which my son attended over time. However, they think you must be baptized by them to be saved, not recognizing any other water baptism, and they have dietary laws. The laws were probably good for people in the health sense but they didn't seem to me to be a spiritual matter because we are now under the new Covenant and the New Testament clearly said it wasn't what you put in your mouth but what came out of it that defiled a person.

The Revelation study basically made sense on one point, that there is a correlation between the Book of Daniel and the Book of Revelation. The rest of the stuff they presented was based on the ideas of Elizabeth White and others and they didn't hang together in my mind. They talked a lot about Babylon and equated that with the World today and they said the Whore of Babylon was the Catholic Church. Remember Babylon means confusion? Well what they had to say was confused. This denomination, as a protestant church, is a daughter of the Catholic Church, "gone out from her" and they didn't seem to see that by their own teaching that made them part of the Whore in Revelation because "her daughters" are also lumped into that epithet.

Then one evening at a vespers session, something happened that tore it for me. A man appeared at the back of the chapel, in the hallway. He said, "Excuse me, but me and my friend are traveling through your town and we ran out of gas. Could you give us $5 to continue our trip?" It got very quiet. The elders were there, well dressed, well fed. No one offered anything. I had 27 cents and knew that wouldn't help much.

Then the pastor said, "That sort of thing is taken care of by the Assembly of God Church. You should give them a call." The man remonstrated that it was night time and any call to that church would produce nothing until the next day. He explained he had come into this church because the lights were on. The physical ones were but the spiritual ones were not apparently. He was told again to go to the Assembly of God Church. He finally left. That was it for the Adventists. None of them that had plenty would simply put their hand into their pocket and take out $5 for the man.

Within a short time the pastor was in the hospital with a quintuple bypass surgery by the way. I met with him not long after he came home to discuss the Sabbath which I did intend to keep after I left that church. So, I took that information with me and went on my way. Right after this, contact with my husband suddenly happened again and he stated that he had found the RIGHT church! He said the Mormon Church had made a difference in him and that he was now part of the Aaronic Priesthood working toward becoming a Melchizedek Priest. That sounded promising. He re-entered our life, we got married again in the Mormon Church, not in one of their Temples. You can't do that until you earn it. And so we became happy Mormons, for about six weeks.

John had a court appearance in the South that he had to make so he left. He took with him the old pickup truck he had traded my car for and left us without transportation. I also was left with the final $125 payment on my car which he had traded. I was able to pay that finally, but I stopped being responsible for his debts after that and made it legal by filing for legal separation. Anyway, before he left that time we appeared in a play together, "Death Takes a Holiday". He got embarrassingly drunk at the closing party, and stayed drunk mostly until he left. He even went to the Mormon Church drunk.

My son and I had to move several times after that, one of which was paid for by the Mormon Church which also fed us, very well. You know, right up to this day I have always known I could call them up and say I need housing or food and they would provide it! Once I left them though I never asked. They consider all baptized Mormons to be a part of them forever.

You got baptized again?

Yes, they baptized us too and were worried about mine because my left toe didn't quite get immersed the way they thought it should. They regard anyone who leaves them as just fallen away and are always waiting for any of us to come back. We are definitely in their data base.

Another thing they do is to have their congregation keep a year of storage food at all times. They have wonderful family events and are helpful to each other. Of course, they don't have much use for anyone but other Mormons, really. Their young missionaries go door to door trying to gain converts with a rather canned pitch but lots of youthful enthusiasm and commitment. They also use TV a lot to proselytize but until you are one of them they are distant. There again, though, being part of the in group got your children advanced in the church and being part of the out group got them passed over even if you were in the church itself. My child saw this right away and refused to go to "that church." Took me longer to give them up because they were so supportive.

Finally, with the fact nagging at me that Joseph Smith had not only championed polygamy but he had also predicted a date for the return of the Messiah which didn't happen, two other factors came into play which led me to leave them. One day I got a call from the school. My son had been injured in a wrestling match and was on the way to the hospital which happened to be right across the street from our apartment, fortunately as I had no car. A broken neck they said! As the ambulance arrived I was there to say, "Pray, pray, pray, pray, pray." Then I called our elder, the Mormon man assigned to us to help us if we needed it. His wife answered and after I explained I wanted a healing team to come now to the hospital, she said, "Well, he's at a pizza party now, but when he returns I'll tell him."

They got there several hours later, after the diagnosis changed from a broken neck to dislocated cervical vertebrae and I had taken my child home. Then they anointed him. A bit late I thought. Even then, I continued to give them a chance. I had decided that the church could be right and some of the people wrong. To understand what ultimately happened to make me turn my back on the Mormon Church you have to know about another experience I had.

There were hard times, very sad and emotionally debilitating times through this entire odyssey. Often I would feel a dark despair and be in tears. I had learned that when this happened if I would read the Bible I would get calm and even peaceful. So, one day during a particularly emotionally traumatic time, I took my Bible, went into my bedroom, and as I was lying down on my bed I opened it at the same time I looked out the window. The breeze was moving the trees in a gentle, calming way and I sighed loudly. Loudly enough that I noticed it. The next instant I looked down at the Bible which I had opened at random when I laid down. My eyes immediately alighted on, "I know your every sigh."

That's when I knew the *Élan Vital* definitely, definitely wasn't impersonal. It was so personal that that event was planned to give me a witness of several things: He/She knew me, the Bible is a witness and has several levels of understanding in it of which some are idiosyncratic to the reader, and that the physical creation was a gift, also a witness. Actually I admit this last revelation about the physical creation as a witness and a gift just came to me now in relating this to you. Ever since then the Bible has had a value to me that goes beyond words, mine or it's. No lie, this happened exactly as I've told you.

I'll take your word for it but it's pretty far out.

So, now the Bible itself did the Mormons in. How? Well, I set down and asked this God, now personal, to reveal to me through the Bible whether or not the Mormon Church was THE CHURCH which had THE TRUTH. I then opened the Bible at random. It opened to and my eyes alighted on, "False prophets . . . ," Jeremiah 14. That did it for me.

So, now you can see things are getting pretty heavy because I have begun to believe what the Bible tells me ahead of any person. This meant a lot of things. For instance, there's lots of stuff in the Old Testament, mostly revealed to me by the Seventh Day Adventists that make me wonder what I should be doing. But, the New Testament clearly debunked any food laws so I didn't buy that. But keeping the Sabbath seemed to be needed to be done as near as I could make out. I kept it even when doing the Mormon thing.

For eight years I kept the Sabbath. Looking back, I think that erroneous effort was nonetheless a proverbial Godsend. Keeping it meant that for the first time in my entire life I could, according to God, really rest one day a week. No cooking to speak of, no trips, no housecleaning, no nothing unless the proverbial donkey was in the ditch and then effort was allowed. Once I had to move on a Sabbath, it was required. Keeping Sabbath gave me time to take stock of my life, to get some center as the psychologists call it and balance in my life. It cleared my mind. It may have kept me from going insane.

The odyssey continued and after the end of the Mormon adventure it became really ugly. The search was getting harder. There were bad things that happened then that I just recently found out about. The bad stuff that I did know about was enough, any more and I might have just imploded or something. The homeless situation happened within months of the end of the Mormon time. I knew they could and would get us out of that, but I never called because I knew they were wrong. I was tempted though, I admit it. I ate better with their free food than I ever had in my life or my children's lives. Just ordered up whatever I wanted and it was delivered right to my door. That is pretty amazing and no other church came anywhere near that type of support.

My big smothering event happened within months of leaving the Mormons. You know, where I died and they brought me back. My mother-in-law died right after we left the Mormons and naturally my husband became even more deranged. My other minor child had a chance to reunite with us and elected, greatly supported by other family members, not to do so. I couldn't find one good job for quite awhile and once I had five part time jobs, all of which required different attire, and some of which were split shifts.

Did you ever think all of this was a message to go back to the Mormons?

No, actually I never did. I was convinced they were wrong. Eventually our lives stabilized and miraculously we were in the town house near the ocean. I found a Sabbath keeping group which did not try to keep the food laws.

Additionally, they took a clear stand on what Christian's call the "Rapture". There are three versions of this and I began a study of this topic to find out for myself which was correct, a study that ended with no clear result because there really is no support in the Bible for a rapture. That's why they can't agree on this point: because there is no proof for any of their ideas although they will site II Thessalonians and Revelations to try to support it. The word "rapture" is nowhere in the Bible.

We actually stayed in that place 18 months, healed, and had good associations with this group. They called themselves the Bereans because they supposedly prove everything before believing it, their namesakes being a praised group in the Bible which studied before just accepting anything. These modern Bereans didn't really prove anything much but they were mostly nice people. They were more our social life than anything else.

Actually, I had by now almost given up on finding THE TRUTH and decided that no one really had it and we just had to do the best we could. I believed that the Messiah would come back sometime, that we should keep Sabbath, and that we should do all the good works we could while there was time. I also believed the Bible was a mystical witness to the reality of a personal God.

Meanwhile I read everything I could get from the Worldwide Church of God and found the prophecy dogma very interesting. The founder died two months after I turned on to that group and they began to splinter. They would visit the area occasionally and we went to their meeting. This is when my son requested to be baptized again. He never believed in the Assembly of God baptism and was mad at them for saying, "And Satan will never bother you again." He already knew that was a lie. Also he never really accepted the Mormons at all because of the way they treated him. Anyway, I requested baptism for my 12-year-old son from the Worldwide Church of God and they refused. They don't baptize young people. That pretty much ended my association with them. That had left the Bereans. Soon after this and another failed reunion with my husband, we moved to another state to be near three of my other, grown children.

Another reunion?

Yes, he was being tried and wound up in jail as I told you before. He had decided to go into the VA mental hospital because of legal trouble. He refused to do what was necessary to get his mom's house into his name although I had a lawyer who was prepared to make it happen. John did say if our son and I would stay there he could keep it. I didn't understand that and his only explanation was that we had some income, welfare and unemployment right then. I think now that it was because my name might have been on the deed. I had to sign something in order for his mom to get the house that

161

included my income information. Anyway, because he wouldn't cooperate I finally decided that whole thing was going nowhere and my son and I came to New Mexico.

Once there my spiritual attitude stayed pretty much the same until I learned something new. I had sought a Sabbath keeping group and found one. It was an offshoot of the Worldwide Church of God. In fact, the son of the recently deceased founder of Worldwide was the leader of this group. His name was Garner Ted or Ted Garner I forget which. He wasn't at this group but they followed his teachings. While attending this group, I heard talk of another Sabbath keeping group which was frowned upon because they used the name Yahweh instead of just saying God. They also called Jesus by the name of Yahshua. This was very interesting to me because I had heard a "Jews for Jesus" lecturer and he had mentioned that Jesus' name was really Yehshua. The Jews say Yeh because they are afraid to say Yah. The more I thought about it the more amazed I was that we were not calling Him by His real name! Seems pretty disrespectful. Additionally, I suddenly realized that God really wasn't a name. It had occurred to me before but I hadn't pursued the thought. It was like saying doctor, or man, or lawyer, in short it's a title not a name.

If God had a name, why not use it? If Yahshua was the Messiah's name why call him Jesus? So a study began about the names. It was very revealing. There is and has never been a J in the Hebrew, Greek or Latin alphabets nor is there any letter or symbol that makes the sound of the letter J, and there was no J in the English language until 1400 years after the death of the Messiah! What a mass delusion! It was clear to me there was an evil entity at work here. It had taken me a long time to really believe in Satan. This cinched it. Only a supernatural power could pull off such a hoax for hundreds of years.

Oh, about Satan. I spent a long time denying that there is such an entity. Denial again. I could believe in God and a Messiah but not in an evil entity oddly enough. Boy did he have fun with me! Finally, it was so clear that something evil was at work in the world and in my life that I couldn't deny it any more. I figured that entity was probably the one they called Satan. Something is definitely very wrong in the world, big time wrong, and everyone knows it. Ignoring that truth gives Satan a lot of power and a clear road to deceiving people.

During this time I got a good job on an Indian Reservation and learned a lot about Native American religion. Then I got another job with an order of brothers and priests of the Catholic Church. In fact, it was the Servants of the *Paraclete* who worked with psychologically disturbed priests and brothers. They have achieved national, probably international fame, for their work with pedophile priests. While I was there, I decided to find out more about the Catholic Church. All I knew was that when I asked my Catholic girlhood friend to explain purgatory she couldn't but I still thought their ceremonies were beautiful and mysterious and I wanted to join them at about the age of nine. My mother said, "No." I never really knew why but I'm glad she kept me out of that church. During my college days I learned about the inquisitions. That pretty much put the Catholic Church on my you-know-what list. Remember that Tyrone Power movie, "Captain of Castile?" They actually had the inquisition chop off his sister's head in that movie. And we all know about the burnings, Joan of Arc for one.

So, now as an adult I gave the Catholic Church another chance. The parish priest at the Servants gave me a Catholic Bible which has several more books in it than a Protestant Bible. I attended Catholic services and found that they are very programmed and unclear. Finally, when they really couldn't answer any of my questions at all, never wanted to discuss the Bible, and continued in this vague manner, someone finally told me there had been a big change in the church in 1962. This resulted from something called Vatican II. Seems there was a Vatican I in 300 AD or something and since then there had never been another until 1962! At the time I thought, "What on earth happened then to make this come about?" Seems Catholics everywhere were pretty much adrift because so much had changed: Latin was no longer used in services, meat could be eaten on Friday, and everyone was answerable suddenly to "his own conscience". Then there was this recent phenomena of many, many priests being found to be pedophiles. I have personally met many Catholics who are distraught and no longer go to church because their priest was found to be of this ilk, often being put in jail, more often being sent to the Servants for therapy after some poor parish pays a huge settlement on a victim. The state of the Catholic Church is decay, chaos, confusion, despair and worse. So, that ended my foray into trying to understand them. It's impossible anyway because every order, every priest or brother has a great deal of largess. I won't even go into the idea of black priests, bank debacles or the Vatican's allowing Nazi's to flee under the cloak of its diplomatic immunity when the war ended.

Something really odd happened before I left the Servants. One morning I got up and found I had forgotten to turn off my crock pot. While I messed with it the lid tilted and a blast of very hot steam hit the center of my forehead. It caused a burn. So, I went to work with this burn on my forehead. Much to my surprise everyone there had a black mark on their foreheads! It was Ash Wednesday they told me and they celebrate by doing that. Funny, I had the burn, they had the ashes. I was actually the only non-Catholic person there.

Again did this make you wonder if maybe they were the right church?

No, quite the contrary. My burn was real. Everyone else's was make believe. Anyway, all through this learning about the Catholic Church I began to call God by His Name of Yahweh and stopped calling Yahshua by the erroneous name of Jesus. Still the group that used the proper names was wrong too in almost everything else!! What a mess. Trying to find the TRUTH is like trying to find the proverbial needle in the haystack for sure!!! The pastor of this group agreed with me that the names were being lost and when the "Rapture", which I still thought might be true, occurred the names would then be lost to the remaining people. This is because the names were taken out of the Bible more than 6,000 times when the *King James Version* was written in 1611. I own a Xerox copy of that Bible now.

So, I decided we should put the names back in. He was all for this and I turned my life over to do this magnanimous thing for those poor souls who were left after the "Rapture". Wasn't I noble? In the meantime my child's life is disintegrating and I didn't know what to do about it. That's another story, his story, and he says he might tell it eventually. Someone else will put it on paper because his dyslexia makes him unable to write easily.

Well, to make a long story short, this pastor, I found out later, knew there was already a Bible, several in fact, that had put the true names back into the Old and New Testaments. One of these, the *Holy Name Bible*, is actually a *Scofield King James* teachers' Bible that the names were put back into by a Jew named A. B. Traina. He took a couple of liberties though and certain Scriptures are better read in the *King James*, but in that one you also have to insert the true names everywhere. Anyway, this man wanted to create a new Bible with his own dogma inserted as a teaching Bible. His ideas were few, confused, and patently idiosyncratic to himself. Before I knew about the *Holy Name Bible*, I actually left the project over his "dogma" and the fact that the Bible he wanted to use as the base for his new Bible was the *Living Bible* which I don't think of as a real Bible at all. It was two months later before I found out about the *Holy Name Bible*. I called him up right away to let him know there was a good Bible with the names back in it. He said he knew it! By that time I had been exposed to the TRUTH which is where I also found the *Holy Name Bible* which isn't in print any more. I got one of the last ones. I didn't call myself a Christian any more. Now I was and still am a Yahshuan. But that guy did reveal the names to me and that's important.

Okay, I told you all that and won't go into the rest of it because my intention was not to convert or teach you but to let you know the extent to which I went on a search for the TRUTH. This is important to understand me and what I did, why I did it, what I did wrong and why. It's necessary to give you an understanding of the type of person I am. The lengths that I'll go to. This has caused error in my life from a practical point of view but the search led to something. It led to my peace of mind, to a feeling of comfort in spite of my life, to a resignation to a greater purpose which has used my life, given it meaning. Do you see what I mean? What creates peace in a difficult life anyway? That's the question and I have the answer. It's not like the bumper sticker, "I found it", though, because it finds you.

When I had no where else to go, had no where else to search, had spiritual and physical illness lying heavily on me, TRUTH came in search of me. It appeared as a casual invitation that, thankfully, I accepted. This is part of the miracle and mystery of life. The inner man or woman is the one that can live on, not the outward, physical being which is temporary and obviously corrupts. The inner person is who can be saved. The person inside our skin, our soul, searches for spiritual food and is unable to mature until that food finds him or her. That is why the Messiah said, "I am the bread of life." He is the spiritual food we need. We are all lost sheep in need of spiritual feeding. Where I learned the TRUTH it is still being taught but the organization itself and most of its other class locations have gone sour, apostatized.

So, I made a website to tell the TRUTH for those who might be led to find it that way, *www.soundingthetrumpet.com*. One thing I will tell you now is that this TRUTH can be proven quite easily when it's revealed to a disciple who is shown where the witnesses are in the Scripture and in creation. Basically the key to understanding the Bible and finding the truth ". . . line upon line, precept upon precept . . ." is in the Tabernacle Pattern. Faith is not blind. In Hebrews 11:1 the Bible says faith is evidence and substance but the dictionary says it's blind. Another of Satan's tricks.

Because I have this body of knowledge in my mind and heart I now know that bad acts toward me are not really personal, they arise from the influence of evil entities upon individuals. The spirit guiding each of us recognizes the spirit guiding another and spiritual warfare which affects the physical realm is the result when one person has an evil spirit (part of Satan's minions) and the other has the Holy Spirit guiding the person. It's a matter of who you want to be controlled by: Satan or the Holy Spirit, it's really that simple. There is the matter, as well, of the evil spirits fighting among themselves for control of a person or situation, more than one can be trying to get control.

Also, this TRUTH is written down, in a textbook, which was sent to all the world leaders, secular and religious, including the Vatican in 1961. No one has ever been able to refute what it teaches. So clear is it that I really believe it produced Vatican II when it was read by the Pope who then made an effort to clean up some of the Church's errors, without much success I might add.

So, basically you are saying that Christianity is wrong as a dogma, in fact so wrong that it is called the Whore of Babylon in the Bible, but that you do believe in a Savior whose name is not Jesus but is Yahshua?

Yes, and that's just the beginning. It's very beautiful.

Between our sessions I have often thought, "Oh, I should have said this or that." There is so much more to be said about what has happened, but somehow what has come out is adequate. I want to thank you for listening to it. I know it's your job but it's still nice to have someone listen. No one would ever listen to it. No one can listen to it all because it would take as long to tell it as it took to live it in detail. And there are deep things of dark and light that have not been mentioned but enough got out that I am no longer bursting with it anyway. My goals have been met. I learned some of the reasons I was in denial about even more than my son's illness, and I expressed some of the trauma that I have endured. And I now have an ex-husband.

I think I can say thanks and goodbye, for now anyway.

Bye, it's been interesting to know you Susan. Good luck.

THE JOURNAL

Providing Support and Hoping to Publish

THE JOURNAL

Five Years After Therapy

August 23, 2003

Last night I realized that I like to hear baseball, not to pay attention to it but as a background sound. It's a yesteryear sound of cheering and happy shouts, and of horns going "Ta ta ta, da ta da!" It's the sound of how it used to be.

I have decided to keep a journal. Not every day because I just can't be that methodical and not every day is that interesting. Because I'm deeply involved with my son and his wife, providing case management basically and emotional support while medication trials continue for him, I've begun to think I might write something for publication about this whole experience of learning about mental illness and trying to help loved ones who suffer from it. There is enormous discrimination, lack of understanding, and downright prejudice spewed onto people who exhibit mental illness symptoms. Long ago it was worse, people were even kept in closets or hospitals rightly dubbed "snake pits". There was even a famous movie called that, "The Snake Pit," telling about how horrible the mentally ill were treated. They had almost no chance of getting better. Now there is hope because of the helpful medication produced by the decade of the brain—the 1990's—which saw great research progress in understanding brain chemistry and function. One thing has become really clear to me: people with brain disease need advocacy from loved ones because the systems in place currently simply aren't good enough yet to get them to where they need to be.

My thought is that eventually I will offer relevant stuff from this journal to the National Alliance on Mental Illness (NAMI) to use as a case study about a family dealing with mental illness in a loved one. Our family has different reactions running from absolutely refusing to believe my youngest son has a mental illness diagnosis or fearing it to the degree of refusing help or contact, to real concern and some attempt at understanding what is going on with him. This gamut of reaction is very common in families. The negative attitudes are very hurtful and create a climate of poor self esteem for the mentally ill person and separation from loved ones just when he or she needs real support.

Guess if I'm serious about this I have to keep this focus in mind as I write in this journal. And I need to train myself never to mention names because if any of this is published it would be really hard to go through it and get them out and anonymity would be best I think. So, I'm going to write with a primary focus on the whole gestalt of my family which includes a mentally ill person who is now on medication trials and one who is only made worse by psychotropic medication.

One bad thing about all the new psychotropic medications that I must mention is that they all have side effects. Also, my daughter-in-law is one of those people who has a mirror effect or reversal effect when she takes most medications psychotropic or otherwise. This literally means that the best known medications for her diagnosis, which is bi-polar, actually make her worse so when she has become deeply depressed, in the throes of hyper-mania, or cycling between the two many times a day it's really hard to treat her, to help her back into stability. I know this is true because I've seen her on many psychotropics but last year a psychiatrist insisted that she take Depakote, which she'd never had yet. Depakote is a fairly new drug used to reduce mood swings but it sent her straight into mania. After taking it even a week we felt it was making her mental state much worse but the psychiatrist insisted it takes longer for its benefits to take hold so she continued on this medication. Before she got off that med she was cycling in and out and had become a totally different and confused personality, whereas before the Depakote was introduced she was stable. Then to make matters even worse she had a miscarriage. Her other medical professionals told her the miscarriage was probably due to the Depakote! I was at the meeting with the psychiatrist when my son and daughter-in-law told him they were trying to get pregnant. This meeting was before he prescribed Depakote. He must have been ignorant of the fact that it could cause a miscarriage because he didn't take her off it even when they told him she was, in fact, pregnant.

Most mentally ill people are disabled and on Medicaid and/or Medicare. As such they are very limited as to their choice of psychiatrist unless they have a rich family member who will help them get really good care. All they had was me and I have no money either. I'm committed to them and have case management background but that didn't keep them from suffering the loss of a child and her subsequent mental decompensation. Depakote not only made her mental state much worse but from what we were told by other medical professionals it also killed their first child! They both felt it was a boy and they named him David.

She got well again, after months of agony, and she stays away from the psychiatrist. This same psychiatrist, who is the only one available for them, does seem to have figured out my son's medication regimen and is now fine-tuning dosages by evaluating him every month. My son's lucky, the medicines have the appropriate affect on him but some didn't work as well as others which he now knows. While there are remedies now for mental illnesses, they don't work on everyone and there are obviously varying degrees of competence in the field of psychiatry.

So, this is a new writing project I am undertaking by means of this journal: chronicling our family and all the other things that happen in it while still maintaining support for my mentally ill son and his wife. I am more than a little upset at some of the attitudes my flesh and blood have demonstrated about mental illness but, hopefully, over time they will learn that it truly is an illness and if you love the sufferer you owe it to him or her and to yourself to grow and become part of the answer instead of part of the problem. It boils down to treating the matter exactly as you would if a loved one had cancer or diabetes or any other chronic disease.

It was a difficult year but my son and his wife have been so stable recently that they are trying to get pregnant again. Their child will be my seventh grandchild. I've committed to help them if they need it. They will be very loving parents and will adore their child. My other children are doing pretty much the same as always. They call and I listen and comment with their best interests at heart which they know so it helps them feel better usually. My eldest brings her kids by for a couple of days when she and her husband go to the Red River Rally. It's fun with the kids and I try not to worry about their parents riding their Harleys all over the place with no helmets.

Life is pretty good for me actually and I'm up to taking on this new project of following the family process as it involves the two in it who are mentally ill but something is bugging me that I can't put my finger on yet so I'm going to keep writing about other things too. I've done a painting for each of my children and I'm still doing web work for those of them who have sites. One of them bought me a new computer which has helped a lot and I'm having fun with that.

My ex-husband and I communicate from time to time but he is going downhill slowly, drinking more. Can't get too involved because he has lots of strange people in and out of his trailer and I fear they are taking advantage of him but there's nothing I can do about it. He let that happen when I was with him too but certain types of people he kept out such as heroin addicts for instance. I set up Meals on Wheels for him so he has one square meal a day at least and I encourage him to keep track of his health. They say he'll live to be a 110 probably. He's not crazy now which is good. Whoops, not supposed to say "crazy". That's one of NAMI's goals, to call mental illness exactly that or brain disease and don't call it "nuts" or "crazy" and so on. They are jumping all over the media about this and I agree they are right. Not using demeaning words is the first step away from discrimination and prejudice. I'll try again. Psychotropic medicine works for my ex-husband too. In fact what works so well with him is what they started our son on first and they are both still taking it. It's still hard to call him my EX-husband.

Our country won the "Iraqi Freedom" war. Not sure how I felt about all that but when I saw Sadam's statue knocked over on TV I was elated that we had brought him down, but they don't seem to be finding any weapons of mass destruction and that's why we went there. That's not what's nagging at me though. I think what is bothering me is I'm still trying to get a grip on 9/11. There is so much fear now. A different type of feeling is in the air. People are going on about their lives again, even traveling but it's not fun. It's strained. The last time I flew to see my folks it was unpleasant. Security in the airport even had me take my shoes off and ran some device up and down my body. I'm not too worried about the Homeland Security thing because I have nothing to hide so I don't care but am wondering where all this is going. They got a lot of Al Quaida in Afghanistan but not bin Laden himself.

Still bugged too about the election. That whole mess was so terrible. Chads. Crap. Can't believe the Supreme Court actually went so far as to make a final decision on who would be President and then it seems to have turned out that Gore got the most votes. Feel vindicated in what I thought all along, it's rigged with the Electoral College being the basis of the problem. It really makes me mad.

There were two snipers killing people in the Beltway last fall but they were finally caught. Poor Laci Peterson and her son were found and her husband Scott is being tried for their murders. We're all still trying to figure out how Columbine could have in '99 and there have been more school and job site shootings since then. There have also been some devastating earthquakes and everyone's worried about the North Koreans and Iran getting the nuclear bomb.

The long and short of it is that since 9/11 a dread has settled over the country and we've experienced a loss of freedoms because Homeland Security feels it needs more access to personal information to make sure we are not attacked again. Everyone is still shell shocked about more than 3,000 people being killed in the World Trade Center while we watched on live TV and we're all wondering what's next.

Many people have lost fortunes in the stock market, including one of our friends who is now learning to be poor. The economy is in shreds with the lowest interest rates in something like 50 years, a huge tax relief bill was just passed, former Governor Gary Johnson is attempting to scale Mount Everest on about the 50th anniversary of Sir Hillary's success, and the Matrix Reloaded just came out.

My life is more settled, peaceful, and less frantic. The knowledge of the TRUTH has gained me the stability and comfort needed to get my life into balance. I have that gypsy slogan "Give me a life I can live with" and more right now but there is still this unease.

Currently, my needs and desires are simple and I have nestled into this little cottage in the foothills of the Northern NM Sangre de Cristo mountains at about 8500 feet. In October I will have been here for the longest time in any place since the loss of our home. It is quiet, peaceful, very beautiful, and friendly here. I get Meals on Wheels too unless I feel well enough to go to the Senior Center to eat so I don't have to cook that much.

I still worry about getting frozen in time. Don't ever want that to happen. I can see it in people's eyes when they freeze up. My father is frozen, has been for awhile. Lots of people I meet are. Hopefully, I will never stop seeing reality, being aware of possibilities, knowing priorities, and having integrity but for now I am finally allowed to rest.

I was here three years when 9/11 hit. That was a day like the one when Kennedy was assassinated. No one will ever forget it who lived through it. I awoke to the phone ringing. It was one of my daughters and she said, "We're at war!" I said, "With whom?" She said, "I don't know," then went on to explain what was happening. I saw the second plane go in. I saw the first tower go down and then the second. I had been in NY City two months before and was driven past those towers. My youngest daughter took pictures of them behind me while I was standing on the Statue of Liberty pedestal. Hadn't developed the film by 9/11 and after that it was two months before I could bear to have it done. Knew someone who toured the towers on 9/10. My youngest daughter knew some people who died in the towers.

June 15, 2004

Haven't touched this journal again until now, almost a year later. So much for good intentions and my new found project! But now I'm really serious about it because my daughter-in-law had their beautiful baby boy in March. My son and the baby are fine but my daughter-in-law has post partum psychosis and we literally have to move them in with me to make sure the baby is taken care of well enough. I was gone for three weeks for my youngest daughter's wedding and tried to manage this from New York! Barely kept the thing together. I found out over the internet that two out of every five bi-polar women get post partum psychosis when they give birth. That was a shock and totally new information to me. The medical doctor is calling it post-partum depression but my daughter-in-law is out of touch with reality so it's definitely psychosis. This is the beginning of a long process of support until she returns to her right mind.

The wedding was really something, on a yacht. After 9/11 the firemen got the flag off this particular boat, called The Star of America, to raise at ground zero. All of the family attended the wedding except my youngest son, his wife and their baby which hurt them a lot and no doubt added to her irrationality and paranoia. They couldn't afford to fly and the car they were going to travel across the country in got a problem that made it impossible. Maybe it was for the best because who knows what might have happened if they had tried that trip. They could have flown in the same time period as me, though, if the family had helped them to do so. A ticket was bought for me or I wouldn't have been able to attend either.

I house sat for my daughter and new son-in-law while they went on a two week honeymoon and something odd happened. My asthma got markedly better. The dogs didn't bother me! Thought I would have to take Prednisone all the time but I didn't, my daily meds kept the asthma at bay.

When I got back it became clear my son is having a really hard time because of what's happening with his wife but he is completely committed to his son. He is now being the baby's primary caregiver. It's scary because people are watching and concerned. That's why we all have to live together so the baby is OK and everyone knows it.

Will probably move them to California if possible because this last time she was hospitalized for a few days a doctor told her she should go there because marijuana is what helps focus her and it's legal there. We have very little to operate on but we're pooling resources and have the beginning of a plan.

June 20, 2004

I flew out to California for a few days and checked out rentals as well as visiting my folks who are getting old, in their 80's now. My father announced to me and my sister that he would be dead in a year and he told us how we should support our mother when it happens. About two weeks later I was told by him over the phone that the doctor said there had been a mistake and he might have another 10 years in him. This is another reason to move to California, to be near my folks.

It will be hard for us to get to California: trucks cost more, gas costs more, rents are higher but I think we might make it. Will try to put it together.

August 2, 2004

Today was my 4th grandson's birthday, he's eight. Everyone was totally gaga and still in amazed shock. No one can take their eyes off him, or their hands for that matter with good reason. Yesterday he came home from the hospital where he'd been for about a month. He was in the intensive care unit for three weeks. The doctor told me privately, twice, it was a miracle he lived; a nurse told me they call him "Miracle Boy." My eldest daughter went through this very long ordeal with flying colors. She lost it once and I was there to follow her around to keep her safe as she raced down hospital corridors crying for about 10 minutes after fleeing his room because they were still "bagging" him as they call it. The doctor had a device inserted into his throat that he was squeezing rhythmically in order for my grandson to breathe. He'd been on a ventilator and they had to clean the tubing and the problem began.

When I had walked into the room there was a red crash cart next to the bed and the doctor and the ventilator technician were on either side of my grandson's bed. He'd been on a ventilator and in a chemically induced coma for many days. His platelets had fallen from 400,000 to 400 and he'd been given several infusions of them along with 20 other meds. There were IV's all over him including one in his chest they called a "central". This all happened because his appendix burst and it was four days before they diagnosed it. By then there was an abscess in his abdomen and then septicemia set in because a normal gut bacteria got into his blood stream and began destroying his platelets.

When my daughter was able to go back to the room, first she wrapped herself in the privacy curtain and peeked out, and then she flung herself onto the day bed and sobbed uncontrollably. Her husband had been called, was on the way. My middle daughter was there and started comforting her. I watched the "bagging" go on from the head of the bed and behind equipment for what seemed like hours. Then this woman came in and started by looking at the chart, then went over to my daughter and tried to pat her and talk with her. She was ignored by the medical team. She was the hospital chaplain. She came over to me and asked me if I was all right. I looked her straight in the eyes and said, "I'm perfectly fine," and I was, never been so calm in my entire life. So far as I'm concerned her presence was Satan incarnate. Her presence to me was like that of a ghoul.

My son-in-law showed up and my daughter ran over to him and stood behind him with her arms wrapped around him as he stood by the bed looking down at their son and talking with the doctor. Men are so incredibly strong. The "bagging" finally stopped and my grandson was still alive, breathing with the help of the ventilator now. That was the turning point. Today he got his presents and then went to his newly decorated room and everyone left so he could rest.

There were mistakes made and his dad is very angry. He will scream in some fashion about it, probably by means of a law suit. My daughter will just go on insisting all is the same and refuse to look back. She won't coddle my grandson. She will continue to raise him as always. He is deaf in one ear now because of nerve damage from the powerful meds they felt they had to give him but they honestly don't know why he survived. I do, it was Yahweh's will that he survive. Simple as that.

September 8, 2004

My daughter-in-law is still not well. Another hospitalization was ordered which involved the police this time. My being here to help with the baby is making all the difference insofar as his care is concerned. It's really hard for me because my daughter-in-law pretty much hates me when she's like this. When she is in her right mind she is unbelievably helpful, thoughtful, and giving. The change is completely amazing. I've had to learn to overlook how she acts and talks to me in order to continue helping her. My son's meds are stable but they make him sleep more hours than is normal and he can't wake up easily at night so I do night feedings and take care of the baby in the mornings. The baby's mama is in another world.

Today I found a place in California online and the landlady agreed to rent it to us. We told her we'd be there next Tuesday. Had already given notice. So we have to get a truck, get the stuff out of storage, pack up what's here in this house-from-hell temporary rental we're in and hit the road. Should have enough money according to what the truck rental company tells me are the miles per gallon the truck will get. I'm trying to get more money because we barely have enough and it's too much of a shoestring budget to go that far on really. But we have to go. My youngest daughter has already sent us $250 which will help.

We will get a raise in our Social Security disability SSI portion in California and the state will also pay the baby some as-yet-unknown amount because his parents are disabled. Rents are more but we have a housing voucher and that's computed on one third of our income regardless of the rents so long as they agree the rent is reasonable. Should be better because we will have more income and my daughter-in-law can legally have the one thing that helps her, marijuana. All the psychotropic medications they give her make her worse. She is so bizarre and awful on them. Any time she goes to the hospital they drug her up and don't listen to the fact those drugs don't work for her and in fact actually make her worse. In the beginning, after the miscarriage, I insisted she take psychotropics too because I didn't know what else to do but now I know they don't work for her and try to advocate with the doctors in regard to this problem. It's been hell but I trust that Yahweh will work it out and it will be better. The baby is fine. He's such an easy and delightful little guy.

September 13, 2004

Well, we're in trouble. Left yesterday about 5 p.m., got to Gallup, gassed up and when we got back on the freeway we lost track of each other. They were in the truck and I was in the car with the dog and some stuff. They had no cell but I did and suddenly I got a call from a friend because my son had called him from a pay phone and he put us in touch with each other so we could meet up. I also had a message on my phone from my eldest daughter who heard from our new landlady who said she went ahead and rented the place to someone else!!!! So here we are on the way and no where to go!! Stopped where we met up and rented a motel room for the night. Thanks to Yahweh we're back together anyway. We decided to go on in the morning and try to find a rental when we get there. Had a great breakfast which came with the room and then continued on but in Flagstaff when we stopped again for gas it became apparent that the truck is getting one half of the mileage they told me it would and we will not have enough money to get much further than to the edge of California! I went to the truck rental office and complained, talked to the regional manager and so on but it did no good. We took off again and now we're in a motel in Seligman, AZ. It's nice enough but costs $70 a night and I'm not sure what we're going to do. Not enough money to get where we were going. We have to make a plan to stay somewhere and go on later as we can.

September 15, 2004

Decided not to leave Seligman because when we got up this morning the car wouldn't start. The starter has gone out. My son pushed it to start it and nearly got a hernia today trying to do that on gravel. A muscle in his chest actually popped out and went back in eventually. We checked out of the $70 per night motel because we're running out of money and we moved the car and the truck to the park to consider what we can do. While we were hanging around there someone told us we could get a room at the Supai Motel or the Romney Motel for about $75/week.

I called my dad and he agreed to wire $300. With that we paid for two weeks and have $150 for food until more money will come into the PO Box I rented today for their checks and all our forwarded mail. My Social Security still goes to my bank account and I can get it out with the debit card. We called Social Security to give the new address and I think it was in time for the checks to get here on the 1st. I am so tired, was so glad to get into the room and have everyone safe for two weeks. Will have to unload the truck soon and put the stuff in storage, can't afford to keep it more than the week we paid for. Thanks be to Yahweh for my father's agreement to wire money and for a cheap motel. Thanks also for our Social Security which means money will be coming in again.

September 16, 2004

This will be harder than I thought because this small room with four people in it has already made her worse. She is wandering about this tiny town, saying a bunch of weird stuff. I've no idea, no one does, how long it will be before she gets back to normal if ever and she's still taking the medication they gave her at the last hospitalization which is making her worse. We're now trying to talk her out of taking it. My son's concentrating on keeping her safe and I'm concentrating on the baby. It's only two weeks and then we'll go on to California, get our money raised, stay a month in Needles and hopefully proceed to our destination on November 1st. Of course we don't have a rental now but I can work on that and am sure something will pan out.

Have gone to the storage place and they agreed to let us have two units that will hold our stuff and let us pay for the rental on the first but we have to get anything we need together because they will put a lock on both units until we pay the rental fee. My son and his wife will store the stuff tomorrow and return the truck. The car's parked in front of our room facing out and there's an incline so when we need to use it we just put it in neutral and let it roll out into the street and pop the clutch. Very, very small town with little traffic makes this possible. Even I can do it. My eldest daughter up and put $150 in my bank account and boy did we need it!!!! Now I see why Yahweh made my asthma better. I'm living with three other people and with a dog and a cat in a motel room and I am doing OK. Still have to take my daily medicine and I have my nebulizer close by but I am OK. Good thing because the nearest hospital is over an hour away. My middle daughter sent me a phone card because the cell can't be used and they want to know how we are. There's no phone service in this motel room. There's a phone but no service but the room's decent enough. I'm walking the baby around in the stroller a lot.

October 3, 2004

We're in Needles at a motel I've decided isn't good enough for the baby after checking in for one night. We will find a better one tomorrow and pay by the week. Got the Social Security thing done. She didn't come with us and my son is so worried about her. She became unmanageable. The cops sent her to the little clinic in town where they told her to get mental health help and gave her a long distance number to call. Seligman is too small to have anything like that locally and she never got through on the pay phone. Don't know what she thinks she's doing by choosing to stay there. In a way I think she's trying to free us from her behavior.

In Seligman some guy they had met who lived two blocks away had said he could fix the starter (there's no parts store in Seligman) and he took it apart at his house but didn't get it fixed so the car still needs a starter. I had to get really shrill to make him put the car back into a condition where it could be driven. Feel like they were trying to steal our car. So my son is still pushing the car to get it started. We paid for the storage before we left and we'll go back to get our stuff when it's possible.

October 4, 2004

We're in a much nicer motel with a swimming pool and a restaurant next door. I was right about that other motel because I accidentally left some clothing on the back of the bathroom door when we moved out and when I went back for it they claimed it had never been there. It's $186 a week at this nicer place and we can have the dog and the cat here. Have a microwave and small frig too. This will be OK for a month, much larger room. He's been in touch with her. She cleaned some rooms at the motel to get a room to stay in for a couple of days. They're talking about getting her here. No doubt he'll go get her tomorrow. This is one very hot town for October. Got a library card already and some books to read. The baby is doing fine and interested in everything. If my son and I hadn't been his main caregivers the baby would probably have been in a bad state because his mom isn't here but instead he's fine. My eldest daughter came through with her kids on a trip to Southern California and they stopped by to see us today. That was great and we all went swimming. I'm sure part of the reason for her trip was to check up on us and make sure we were all right.

October 5, 2004

My son made a quick trip back to Seligman to get his wife. She has finally stopped taking the meds now too. She had $400 when we left and had about $60 when he got her here. She says someone stole it. He bought a new starter at a parts store and they loaned him some tools to put it in. Was pretty easy after he had seen how the guy in Seligman got the broken one out and back in again.

Well, we almost got a place on the North coast. After talking several times with the landlord, though, he just didn't feel comfortable renting it to us without meeting us. A few days later we finally got notification on the cell phone that a low income apartment complex has a three bedroom available the first of November in the town where my middle daughter lives. I got the application when I was in California in June and faxed it back to them before we left. Have to fax them new income verification now which we recently got from Social Security. We are each getting $300 a month more in this state and the baby is getting almost $400 in TANF because his parents are disabled. He got nothing in New Mexico. I had called the state office in Santa Fe about that and I'm sure they are doing it wrong there. The baby is also getting a small Social Security check finally. So, we have somewhere to go and the deposit is not much so should work out fine. The plan is that I stay with them for a month and then get my own place close by. She definitely seems more under control now she has access to legal marijuana and not on any psychotropic medications. Also we learned today that we will be getting more money than we thought from Social Security because we're in a motel. They give extra money for food in these circumstances. In addition to that, my other son sold my old car that I gave him and he deposited $500 in my bank account so money is stacking up and that usually means Yahweh is about to move us.

November 4, 2004

We made it!!!! We drove straight through and stayed at a motel one night before they went in to sign the lease the next morning. My middle daughter paid for the motel. Then we stayed at a motel again because we couldn't get moved in enough in half a day and everyone was very tired. The next day they finished unloading and we got the truck back by 5:30 p.m. before they charged us more. They didn't charge us for gas either because they needed the truck. Right after we showed up two people came in and rented it right away. My son had already cleaned it and it was ready to go. Managed as well to get my stuff to a small storage unit until I need it. Now we settle in and I start looking for a place for December 1. We made it!!! Thanks be to Yahweh who moved my dad and my other children to help us substantially even though they are all mad at us.

November 18, 2004

I've been holed up in my room most of the time because she really does not want to be around me. This happened before when she went manic after she had the miscarriage two years ago. Usually she loves me and is very thoughtful but in this manic condition that she's still in she is hateful to me and says a lot of ugly stuff. She's pretty quiet if I make myself scarce and she likes it here but it's clear she can't wait until I leave. I hope everything will be OK. Not too sure she is up to caring for the baby but she is doing it, getting up every morning and taking care of him and the house. My son takes over at about noon and does the rest of the day. I found a place yesterday and am now working on getting the housing voucher set up which requires an inspection of it. It's about eight blocks away so I can get here soon if needed. Will leave on the first. There was enough money left to give half the deposit now to secure it.

December 28, 2004

From what we're hearing on TV tens of thousands of people have been killed in the earthquake off Northern Sumatra and the resultant tsunamis in the Indian Ocean which have devastated the coastlines of several countries. Some estimate the death toll will rise into the 100s of thousands and never be fully known. Commentators keep stating that this event is "Biblical" in nature. It's reported that the axis of the earth has shifted slightly and I'm wondering which came first, the earthquake or the axis shift? Also wondering what the effect of an unusual axis shift will be and what will be next.

March 16, 2005

Today there was a birthday party for the baby, his first one, and his mom pretty much just watched. I made the cake, his aunt and I oversaw the actual process of the party, and my son watched the baby as his party went forth on the grass in front of their place. We invited the local small kids and they were thrilled. The problem with my daughter-in-law has worsened because as her major gift to her son she decided to stop smoking cigarettes and the doctor gave her medication to help with that process which, unfortunately, had bupropion in it and, being a psychotropic, it had a very bad effect on her.

Since I had written a statement for her medical file letting it be known that all psychotropic medications have a reverse and decompensating effect on her, I am angry she was given this medication. Now her mental state is worse and we have started trying to get her to stop taking it after a week because she is obviously having a bad reaction to it. She was actually doing well before taking this med. I don't know why doctors won't listen to the fact that she simply cannot take any of that type of medication. Marijuana helps her on a day to day basis but it doesn't seem able to pull her out of psychosis once she's in it. Only time and lessened stress can do that. She can take lithium which is the old remedy for bi-polar disease and has some good effect but it blows her weight up drastically and changes her blood chemistry to the point they always take her off it so that's not useful either. Also I have personally heard a psychiatrist tell a mentally ill person not to try to stop smoking until they were very stable. It's a great stress to stop smoking and as we know a Surgeon General even admitted it's harder to stop smoking than to get off heroin! So there has been a backward slide for her into aberrant talk and behavior again

April 12, 2005

I'm really worried about the baby. He seems fine and my son says everything is fine but his wife is having a lot of trouble coping I can tell. In the state she's currently in she speaks very disrespectfully to my son and he's having trouble dealing with it. The baby seems fine though and is crawling finally! He lost two months in that department on the trip in those motels because we didn't want to put him on those motel room carpets and kept him on the bed where he couldn't really try to crawl. I've asked Yahweh to take care of the situation and please make sure the baby is safe. Other than that we are watching everything very closely and I am more involved on a day to day basis with their life again.

May 3, 2005

My son had a dream that a CPS worker was standing at their open front door. I had a dream the same night that we didn't know where the baby was and I got very alarmed. Additionally, there is some sort of problem brewing with three women my daughter-in-law has sort of befriended in the apartment complex they live in. She's still manic and when she's like that she is a gadfly and trouble is often the result. She also invited her aunt to visit them who is mentally ill too it appears and there were some major and very loud difficulties between them. The baby seems OK and my son is still providing most of the care except in the mornings.

182

May 24, 2005

I can't believe what's happened but we have the baby back now. The three women called CPS to state a concern about the baby saying they heard him crying a lot and his parents fighting all the time. Actually the baby in the apartment next to them is the one that cries a lot. The first I knew about the situation, my son called to say they were on their way to my house for a planned visit but he noticed there were two cop cars outside. The end result was that the cops stopped them when they were leaving to come over to my place. The cops called CPS after talking to the three women and my son and daughter-in-law. Ultimately the CPS worker took the baby because of the reported fighting between his parents and his mom's obvious mental instability right now. When my son called to tell me what had happened, I called right away and asked CPS to bring my grandson to me. They told me they couldn't because regardless of blood relationship they needed something called a "life scan" on anyone to whom they release a child who has been placed in protective custody. It was Friday about 4:45 p.m. and I couldn't get the life scan until Monday. So he was gone part of Friday, all of Saturday, all of Sunday, all of Monday, and then on Tuesday he was brought to me and my son who had left the apartment so the baby wouldn't be exposed to his mom until she gets all right again which was a CPS condition for returning my grandson. My son moved his stuff and the baby's stuff as needed to my place over the weekend. That was a very long four days and we will never know where he was or what happened to him there. He's 14-months-old now and never been cared for by anyone but his mother, his father, or me. It's got to have been very traumatic for him.

June 15, 2005

The baby was very glad to see us but he pinched me and bit me for about two weeks occasionally after he came back he was so mad. He would also scream if you tried to put him in the bathtub or put him on a diaper changing station in a public bathroom. My son got him used to the idea of a bath again after about a week. The CPS worker mentioned that where the baby had been was a very clean place, in fact she said she couldn't figure out how the woman there kept her white carpets spotless while taking care of young children. I'm wondering if his baths included a little too much scrubbing or something because he was terrified to get in the tub after he was returned but he had really enjoyed his baths before he was taken away. Am also wondering if he was taken to a medical facility and had a forced examination on a table, an environment that might seem similar to him as a chrome and tile bathroom with a hard and cold changing table. He also wouldn't eat anything solid for awhile. I have no idea why that is but obviously it has something to do with his being gone those four days. We finally got him to eat peeled grapes after about three days. He was eating all kinds of things before he was taken away. I think he thinks it's my fault his mom isn't here because he doesn't pinch or bite his dad. It really hurts my feelings when he hurts me but given what this child has been through I can understand why he's angry so I just tell him not to do that as nicely but firmly as I can. We will be moving to a larger apartment ASAP and I've given a 30 day notice, also part of the CPS conditions. We need at least two bedrooms and hopefully three.

Something I found very disturbing about all this, beyond the obvious, is that we were told that babies adjusted easily to being taken from their parents. This was according to the CPS worker who for years had been doing this job. All I can say is that being so tiny but very smart a 14-month-old would no doubt try to ingratiate himself to a new caregiver simply out of fear. Survival instinct would cause a small child to simply conform in order not to get any negative feedback from the strangers with whom he/she is now confronted. To say they adjust easily is missing the point of the trauma to them. My grandson has always been well treated and trusted his mom, dad, and me completely. When he came back there was an innocence that had been lost after just four days of a strange environment.

Additionally, the ring leader of the women who caused this whole thing was a notorious meth addict and dealer who had her kids with her while she engaged in these pursuits! Makes you lose faith in a child protective system that can be used by noxious persons to hurt people they don't like or are angry with who happen to be parents. Both my son and I told them the truth about the three women but it wasn't taken seriously because there were three of them. One is the drug dealer and addict, one is an addict along with her husband, and the other one is clearly mentally ill with delusions. The first two are parents with children in the home. I met and knew about them all. In my opinion I really don't think taking my grandson away was necessary although I admit I was worried about his welfare myself but not nearly like I was worried about him when he was away those four days.

July 8, 2005

We just moved into a brand new two bedroom town home. That was a minor miracle seeing as how we have a big dog and a history of recent moves. The landlord wanted to meet the dog and liked him so that was OK and since I have a voucher he knows he will get paid. He's one of the few landlords here that will take vouchers. Since the dog is a "service dog" and we have a psychiatrist's statement that my son needs him as part of his therapy, the landlord really couldn't refuse him by law but they can find other ways not to rent to someone if they don't want to for some reason. The damage deposit was $1000 and he agreed to take that in two payments. We've had to get two payday loans to accomplish all this and it will be hard to get out of that bind but we will I'm sure. Thanks to Yahweh who, as usual, takes care of us.

The baby sees his mom every week in a supervised setting at the CPS office. My son is distraught but committed to doing whatever they want to insure he keeps his son and what they want is for his mom not to live with the baby for now. She doesn't have enough money to pay the rent on their old place and will have to leave that apartment soon. My son plans to move stuff out of there whenever it becomes necessary and to clean the place. She won't be able to do any of that although she'll talk about it and make motions to do it. She's getting even worse now really fast and can't focus on much of anything. She's lost a lot of weight. She's acting even more erratic and is very depressed. They won't tell her when she can live with us again and we can't do anything about it either but wait until they clear it. I've requested that she be able to see her son more often but they are saying no for now. I've also asked them to try to help her but their focus is the baby and they don't seem too interested in helping her. It's obvious they don't believe she will get better. I believe she will get better because we went through this once before when she had the miscarriage. It took over a year but she got better finally. For now, I'm glad I am living with the baby again.

My father is dying. It's been that year that he predicted last June so now I'm wondering if he just reversed that decree after he made it so we wouldn't all treat him like he was dying for a year! I'll never know I guess. He has hospice. He refused to go to the hospital again to receive care for his severe emphysema and bronchitis. He's tired; he's 84 and he's ready to go. He knows what's happening with us but not in detail and he's glad I'm helping them keep their baby.

July 21, 2005

My dad died last night about midnight. We went down to see him three times. He told me during the last visit that he loved me. He said he wasn't always too sure he liked me, but he loved me. When he loaned us the $300 last year he had told me he loved me, that I was good girl, but that I did stupid things. He literally saved us that day. My mom read me the riot act when she found out about it. We paid them back by December.

The last time we left he went to bed and only got up once or twice after that. He stopped eating. Took him nine days to die after he was bedridden. My mother, sister and her husband cared for him at home. We'll go to Yosemite next month for a memorial. I haven't gone to pieces, although I started to, because I knew he would want me to carry on and I was able to do that because I see death differently as a result of my faith. I only hope that before he actually died he got a vision of the TRUTH because before that he steadfastly claimed, "I don't need redemption," and I know we all do. It was clear he didn't want to be bothered by any preachy stuff, he'd already put the social worker on notice about that, so I honored his wishes. No point in pushing something at someone, it won't work, and I had tried before.

The thing I remember the most about him is him telling me, more than once, that when he was about 10-years-old his part of helping to build a little house for the family out of cast off lumber was to pull the nails out and straighten them so they could be used again. Imagine doing that. I gave him five grandchildren and seven great-grandchildren and he was proud of that legacy. My sister told him what was happening to him was a mystery and he would soon get to know the truth of it. He also said something that made it clear he knew he was more than his physical body, because he said to her and my mom once, "Get this body off me!" They told him he had to do that himself, that they couldn't help with that.

Something else really bad happened this year. My youngest daughter lost a child. She was in her 6th month of pregnancy. What she went through was such a nightmare I couldn't write about it before now. She and her husband had to decide to do a late abortion because the baby was mal-formed. It started with an ultrasound that showed something amiss and then another one that showed the same thing. Then an amniocentesis provided a genetic sample that showed there was genetic damage that was very rare and would produce death soon. The doctors said that even if he lived to be full term he would die hours after birth. What my daughter had to go through, decide to do, and live through was unbelievably heart wrenching. Because I have to help provide morning care for my youngest son's son, I couldn't go there. The last time I left was for this daughter's marriage and without my daily support my youngest son could barely keep his situation together because his wife was in a post partum psychosis, to the point that they had to move in with me when I got back. So, my youngest daughter was supported by my eldest daughter who went there to be with her. She was there when the abortion was done. When she went home she couldn't talk about it to anyone, not even her best friends or husband. It was a mercy killing. My poor littlest girl had to kill her baby out of mercy for it.

Too bad we even have ultrasound, too bad we know how to do amniocentesis and have genetic knowledge. Without those technological advances she would never have known what was happening because there were no external signs of the problem and, although her little boy would probably have died in any event, she would never have had to make such a horrible decision. During all this I had to call my spiritual elder to ask how to think about this, how to accept this. He called it a mercy killing and reminded me the child went back to Yahweh in glory and won't suffer this physical life. My daughter has to go on living though and she's getting through it and the family has named a star in memory of Nathan.

August 29, 2005

Half my dad's ashes are under a tree near Lake Tenaya in Yosemite now. The other half goes into the ocean with Mom's ashes when she dies. Nathan's ashes were placed by my dad's in Yosemite as were some of the ashes of his very old friend who died about a year ago. Lake Tenaya is a beautiful blue jewel of a lake. I felt removed from the whole thing, watched it and took care of the baby while they all did this and that. It had little meaning for me. My father and Nathan are in the spiritual realm now, not in Yosemite. All my children showed up to honor him and Nathan and I was pleased by that. My sister and mother ran the memorial and when there was a circle for people to say things about my dad it was decided, before I had a chance to say anything, to stop and proceed with the hike to place his ashes. I would have said: "He was a good Dad to me but he was hard on me. No doubt the character his hardness built in me is what helped me to survive my somewhat difficult life and I thank him for that and I love him and will miss him."

August 30, 2005

Yesterday Hurricane Katrina hit New Orleans and other coastal areas. I'm thinking this was the second in a one two punch of "Biblical" events, the first being the earthquake and tsunami last year that claimed a quarter of a million lives. The commentators are using the "Biblical" phrase again even though the loss of lives on the gulf coast will be much fewer. This was a completely avoidable category 3 disaster in New Orleans. The levees have been known for decades to be insufficient for just what has happened and over and over Congress has refused to fund the work necessary to protect this city. New Orleans will never be the same. Was there once and although I didn't like the "Big Easy" I like even less the establishment's evident lack of compassion for all those people stuck there who have now been displaced if they were lucky enough to survive.

October 15, 2005

My son's wife tried to commit suicide and now CPS is all contrite. They wish they had done more for her. It was discovered that she turned on the gas in the apartment. They say she was almost gone when they got in after someone reported smelling gas. She's going to a mental hospital, probably for awhile. Well, at least she's safe now but they will fill her with medications that will ultimately make her worse although she'll play their game and get out as quick as she can. My son will move all the stuff out of their former apartment, some he'll sell and some he'll store. No one seems to know when or if she will pull out of it. I'm really tired but I am able to do what needs to be done to help my son with the baby who has been walking and exploring and getting on with his business of growing. Glad he doesn't know about this.

November 12, 2005

We took the baby to see her at a transitional house after she got out of the hospital. Then she returned to the area and is now seeing him weekly at the CPS offices. They have asked me to provide the supervision. This is really hard. She is calmer but still not OK. They probably put her on meds but I don't think she's taking them now.

January 2, 2006

My youngest daughter gave birth today to a healthy baby girl. She had the courage to get pregnant again soon but worried terribly throughout the entire pregnancy because of how she lost Nathan. This baby girl will be doubly loved. She lives clear across the nation so I couldn't be there for her delivery, although she didn't seem to need me because she had a dula and seemed OK with it. I really can't express how sad I am to have not been able to be there, me her mother, for the death of her first child and the birth of her second child. Honestly, for Nathan's death I probably would have been a hindrance because it devastated me too, but for the birth of a healthy baby girl I could have been a lot of help to my daughter throughout the first week but my mother and sister plan to be with her for a week. She forgives me but it seems our entire relationship has been this way, ever since her birth there have been reasons why I am not able to focus on her for long and I know she feels it. This all started with that bad saddle block. Then being one of five children meant all of them at a certain point didn't get the close focus they should have got, let alone with all the weird stuff that went on in my second marriage and with me working from then on while they were little. She was always a very easy child and never caused trouble so she obviously got less attention because she was never one of the many fires that I had to put out while my kids were growing up. I knew this too but there was never enough time to do anything about it. Later there was physical distance because she went to live with my folks which I know was much nicer for her because I was so poor and moved a lot.

One of my regrets is that I wanted to move to her town when she went to college, to be close to her. I didn't because I decided she needed to be on her own and wouldn't like me messing in her young adult life. Maybe that was true but she had a very difficult marriage soon after that. How she managed to work and complete college after the divorce I have no idea and by then I was living in a different state. She got so depressed she decided to go into a hospital for a month for intensive treatment. This daughter is now married to a pilot, has her beautiful new baby, and a challenging career with an office in New York City. She is a tenacious person, one who keeps going, one who is realistic and practical and one who can emerge whole after a devastating experience. Except for my disabled son, of all my children she has faced the most harrowing experiences in her life and almost always without me physically there to help her. I've been around during important or difficult times for my other children but somehow the timing and location is always off for my youngest daughter and me. Maybe this will change in the years to come. I hope so because I have missed her so much for so long it seems like a hole in me that needs filling. We both do what we should do and are guided by that rather than what we feel we need so we are at the mercy of the "places' we are in and our relationship seems to always take a back seat. It's not fair and I don't like it.

January 10, 2006

We haven't heard from my youngest son's wife for about three weeks. When she got out of the hospital after about a month, she moved in with a woman who wasn't a good influence, was taking all her money, hit her, and was being evicted herself. She went to a motel with that woman for about a week, then she was pushed out and she tried to stay with another woman who was the one who called CPS originally. That didn't work out. We have no means to help her get another place of her own. Can't get any but PayDay loans and we're still in a cycle of getting clear of them. I have asked again for CPS to find help for her. They and we thought the transition house was going to set her up but they didn't, not sure why. There was a visitation right after her last situation dissolved which we didn't find out about until later because she didn't tell us when we saw her, but the baby was very sad as she left and he leaned over and kissed her. Then she disappeared. So, we don't know where she is or how she is and we're very worried. She hasn't seen her son now for three weeks.

February 25, 2006

We finally heard from her in the middle of January. She was in town when she called us but is living in a tent about 10 miles out of town. We had already arranged to have flexible visitations at our house when she re-contacted us because we all knew being homeless would make it hard for her to meet appointed times and she came to the house to see the baby who was very happy to see her. CPS has softened in regard to her visitations. They clearly see she wants to be with her son, hasn't just left town, and was depressed enough to try suicide because she misses him so much. She misses us too. When she finally called she said she would be back every week to stay at a motel for a night and wanted to come over to see him then. She hitches into town. This arrangement has been going on now for several weeks. We pick her up at the motel and the baby knows where it is now and when we pass it during the week he points and says "Mom" quite urgently. We tell him she is "bye, bye" but will be back soon. Sometimes he cries a little when we take her back. I am watching close to see how he feels about her. We've extended the visitations to several hours now and that is fine. She seems very calm but depressed, with no sign of mania. She's quiet, doesn't do much but watch the baby lovingly. It's clear she's not sure she'll ever be able to live with him and is a little standoffish because of that.

March 16, 2006

She was here for his second birthday, it was a nice day and very pleasant. She hated to leave. She has begun asking my son when she can "come home." I've decided to petition CPS for her to rejoin us because it's getting really clear the baby wants her around and she seems fine now, though muted.

April 15, 2006

I created a contract about her coming back to live with us which clearly outlines what is expected of her. CPS has approved it but doesn't really have much hope she can keep it. I showed it to her and she agreed to it and signed it. One of the things it says is that I will care for the baby in the mornings and my son will care for him in the afternoons and she is only expected to just give him love. She has to smoke outside and some other provisos. She's very happy and will move back in on the 25th for a two week trial after which time we will evaluate the situation.

May 5, 2006

Things are going well and we moved into a three bedroom duplex unit about half a block away that's owned by the same landlord so that we can have more room now that she's back. Moving is getting harder for me all the time. The baby and I no longer have to share a room which is great. This unit is also very new and has a garage.

May 10, 2006

Everything is going great. She is slowly easing back into the routine of the household not doing anything but feasting her eyes on the baby and giving him love. After awhile I will ask her to cook a couple of meals a week. The baby is happy but also cautious. My son and I are continuing our attendance at some college courses. He's taking guitar, voice, math, and Tai chi. I'm taking some courses to get up to date having got my BA in 1976. I also took a children-with-special-needs class to learn how to spot any symptoms that the baby may have inherited either his father's or his mother's mental illness. However, we never leave her alone with the baby because we don't quite trust her judgment yet.

September 18, 2006

It's her birthday. Everyone is happy. When we moved we only brought into the house what we needed and everything else is stored in the garage where she smokes and my son plays the guitar. They have the master bedroom with a full bathroom, and the baby and I share the main bathroom but have our own rooms. The place has a large dining room where he plays a lot. She has begun to take more interest in being a caregiver to him. She is cooking some now. It's important she get daily naps and stress is minimal.

We go to the park a lot. It's only a block away. And we have joined a playgroup. The baby has now been on a train, in a swimming pool, on play equipment, and to the beach several times which he just loves. He calls both me and his mother "Mom". We've tried to get him to call me "Grandmom or

Granny" but so far he seldom says that. A long time ago he called me MeMa but that never happened again after he was gone those four days. His dad is still his main man and who he turns to in need. The rest of the family has been alternately really angry about how the move to California went and concerned about my health and openly skeptical about her moving back in, but they are slowly coming around to the idea that it might be OK. She is fine now, still a little quiet but no mania at all. We got a 2004 Toyota for better mileage and it's nice to have a newish car. We grew tomatoes, bell peppers, and some strawberries in the back yard this year and my son picked a bunch of blackberries and I made jam for the year. Life is good again.

November 28, 2006

All my kids and all but one of my grandkids were in town for a couple of days over Thanksgiving. Boy that was so great!! It went so fast. Everyone was happy to see the four of us doing well and seems to have resigned themselves to the idea I will probably be living with them from now on. I'm actually now the baby's legal guardian although both his mom and dad have custody. That was what CPS wanted. He's on the list for Head start, he's starting to talk more, and he now calls her Mommy. I'm still Mom but sometimes I'm DaMom because she has tried to let him know I'm his dad's mother.

Mommy and son have both relaxed and they go through the house playing and giggling. So it is now on track. I wrote a grant for the playgroup which is getting more structured and needed some gym mats and I wrote a grant the city submitted to get some play equipment that is designed for children 2 to 5 which isn't available at either park currently.

We are still keeping our Family Presents Day on the 16th of each month in lieu of Christmas which we do not celebrate for religious reasons. I'm working a little more on *www.soundingthetrumpet.com* and getting some emails about it. We study the Gospel two to three times a week. We almost bought a house! Thought it was actually going to happen but then it fell apart when the lender asked the seller to do something and he said "no". Was a shock, we didn't know about these things but now we do. We actually approached my youngest son's father to see if he'd like to move to the new area as well to a Senior complex but although he said yes he immediately went into a very strange period of time with all three personalities emerging. He's not taking his meds as directed and it would be too hard to be around him again. I had to stop talking with him even it got so bad. We may try again to buy a house in the spring or summer. All this caused a little shakeup in the household but we're past it now.

February 23, 2007

May flesh some of this journal out, about the time when she was not all right after the baby came and how it went and the fact she is all right now! But I'm also wondering, now that life is routine again, about the Iraq War which is still going on! Really a mess. Am also becoming politically active again, a little. I plan to send Congress a letter about the terrible child pornography proliferating all over the internet which will require more law and punishment than they have yet developed in order to stop it in the U.S. Wonder if they'll make the website hosts and movies ever tow the line? Or ever get out of Iraq, or what?

A friend is making his garage into a studio this summer and he's invited me to set up my easel in there so I have a place to paint. My first painting in a long time will be of a huge Madrone tree I saw last week. Wonder what figures will appear in the tree and if I'll be able to see them or if someone else will have to find them.

May 22, 2007

My eldest daughter was complemented by a children's court judge who said the annuity developed by her to protect the settlement money awarded for her son's terrible illness three years ago, was ". . . the best she'd ever seen." Now that issue has been put to rest. The main doctor in the case was on the side of the defendant and was instrumental in getting the settlement to an appropriate amount. My daughter is making sure her son is having a good life, especially in the baseball playing department lately! His sister is President of her class and doing wonderful things musically and scholastically. My daughter, however, is having a hard time adjusting to changes in her life. I think, maybe, that she just needs a real rest from enormous stress. Not sure she has totally processed almost losing her son because she is such a trooper who carries on and refuses to dwell on horrible stuff like that. Bit of my denial problem there, the Pollyanna thing.

May 26, 2007

Well I am actually depressed. Finally I am so ashamed of our country it has put me into a funk. I learned today about the island of Diego Garcia and how our leaders, in collusion with the British, forced that island's inhabitants to leave their homes so we could build a base there! That takes the ever loving cake. The very idea!

June 15, 2007

The baby, now a three-year-old little boy, and his mommy are doing great. They have a wonderful relationship. She reads him to sleep every night after his daddy gives him a bath. I am only getting up one day a week with him now because his mommy is doing it the other six days. He's talking well, he's growing well, he's happy. In short, he's a typical 3-year-old except he is still a very finicky eater which started when he got back from those four days CPS had him. One family member is pushing for us to send him to a pre-school. It's so funny to me that today all kids are thought to need pre-school! When I was in high school, there was much discussion about how the Russians had all their young kids in pre-schools and didn't let them stay with their mommies until they were five! This was considered very wrong and mean. Some of us, including my mother, think young children today are being pushed and scheduled too fast.

It all started when mommies decided to go to work and now there's this rationalization that little kids actually need pre-school. Pre-schools are actually glorified day care centers. If a little kid is able to play with other kids several times a week that's good enough because if a Mom or Dad can stay home she or he can teach school readiness stuff just as we used to do. Now little kids go to music class, to gym class, to yoga class, to all kinds of other stuff, often in addition to day care or pre-school. What about staying home and playing, feeling safe and loved, and being allowed to be stress-free about life for probably the only time they will be able to do that in their entire lifetime? What about letting them make some of their own decisions about what they want to do? Society is rushing them too fast and saying it's good for them when it's really happening because both parents want to work to maintain a certain lifestyle. There's nothing like the security of a loving parent to provide care-giving and training in the first five years of a child's life is my opinion.

Speaking of school, college is finished this year and I got an AA to go with my old BA! My disabled son took a hard algebra course this past semester and aced it along with his other three classes so he's thinking about taking chemistry next. His forte is math and science and now he is able to realize his gifts in those departments. He also plays chess at least twice a week and plans to go into competition. Another goal of his is to start teaching beginning guitar. His guitar teacher has encouraged him to do that and also wants to use him as a tutor for his college class.

On a bad note, my youngest daughter lost another child, another boy. She had a miscarriage at four months which was a total shock because she had the genetic test and he was cleared for any genetic problems. It happened about two weeks after the test and there is a suspicion the test could have caused his death but she recalls something not feeling right the first time they put the stethoscope to her belly, it hurt in a certain location. She was devastated and I hope she has the courage to try again. Thanks be to Yahweh for their darling little girl who needs them to be OK and will help them fight despair over this loss.

My oldest son has married again after four years of loneliness and deep soul searching about the end of his last marriage. He is happy like he has never been before and his wife seems to adore him. This is so good. I'm so happy he is no longer alone. Can't wait to meet her, couldn't make the wedding because gas prices are too high! They just went to a Justice of the Peace and no one was there really.

My eldest daughter is changing careers and making discoveries about herself in her continuing quest to constantly grow. I'm very proud of her ability to be honest when looking at herself and still thankful for all the help she gave me back when she was the eldest of five kids and I was overwhelmed.

My middle daughter who lives nearby is going through some stuff at work but she is happy in her private life and more secure than I've ever known her to be. We recently went to a tea for the kids club, to a play, and to a movie together. Our relationship is mending quickly now.

We're going to make a July 4th float for the parade to represent the playgroup. It's going to be a red train out of cardboard mounted on a frame over an old VW bug, I'm involved with other stuff too like trying to get a local train back into a utility status to help with transportation around town and helping to organize a fitness and nutrition fair for kids. But I am eager to continue working on *www.soundingthetrumpet.com* and to paint. It's welling up in me.

Lot's of stuff is happening outside my little life: global warming, Iraq, Iran, Korea, immigration, the coming election, 28 kids killed in Chicago this year by other kids, online Charter Schools (which is really great), a proposed Reporter Shield Law (also great—Free Flow of Information Act), and the new Continuity Plan directive put out by Bush on 5-9-07 which says he will basically declare martial law down to the tribal level if there is an extreme emergency (terrible). All of this preys on my mind. The Continuity Plan includes a phrase something like ". . . powers usually associated with a dictatorship . . ."! But I'm keeping local, keeping regional, getting ready for what seems to be coming. I'm noticing efforts to try to turn it around, but is it in time, is it enough? I'm watching democracynow.org news and C-SPAN to keep informed. We have storage food.

June 17, 2007

Yesterday was our family presents day, which we do every month instead of Christmas. I built my son a website explaining the idea, located at *www.familypresentsday.com* and that was fun.

But then I began reading *Confessions of an Economic Hitman* and *The Secret History of the American Empire* by John Perkins. The information in these books made it all fall into place, what's happening in the world, how our country is effectively dominating everything economically and that our standard of living is made possible by the slave labor of very poor people including children in poor countries whose resources are being gobbled up by our country.

I am beyond angry and wanting to scream out loud. Now I am very sad and want to cry for all the poor people of the world. The only thing I can do is to encourage my family to stop consuming, stop being addicted to oil, stop so much. We must grow our own food even, use cars seldom and only ones that have a high mileage ratio (better yet those that run on anything but gas), never buy diamonds, and refuse to buy at Wal-Mart and the like because those cheap prices come from basically slave labor in other countries. Can we do this? Can "We the People" simply refuse to participate in it? Will that change it? I don't know but I have to try. Still no move to impeach Bush and Cheney.

Lately I've also seen stranger, sometimes violent behavior in people and, sad to say, the Gentle Conspiracy seems to be breaking down as times get harder.

July 27, 2007

The float won a trophy! My son gets to keep it because he did the most work on it. We saved the float to use as a sign for the kids fair 10 days later. Had a great turnout and lots of fun on a beautiful day. There was nutritious food, a pie walk, many activities and giveaways for the kids and a lot of important information was supplied to the adults about children's activities and services in our area. There'll be another one next year.

Cindy Sheehan is back! She had stepped down from being a leader to end the Iraq War. On democracynow.org she was interviewed today about her promise to run for Nancy Pelosi's house seat in the 8th district of California if Pelosi does not start impeachment proceedings in the House of Representatives against both Bush and Cheney! There was someone on the show who also wants to see Bush and Cheney gone but wants to wait for the election and not see an impeachment, for political reasons. He's afraid there will be a backlash that will bring a Republican back into power in the coming election. How stupid that is. Whether our Constitution is being trounced on has nothing whatever to do with Republican or Democrat affiliation. It is so important it's above that completely. If Nixon had been properly impeached or found guilty in a court of law once he resigned, then we might never have got to this point we are at today! The impeachment of Clinton, though unsuccessful, was over very little and today they are unwilling to impeach Bush for starting a war on false premises that has killed perhaps hundreds of thousands of people to say nothing of making the rest of the world hate us and providing fertile ground for terrorist recruitment!

Back in the last part of May I got depressed, really depressed for over a week, about what our country has become. Somehow the straw of Diego Garcia broke my camel's back of pride in being an American. I mean the fact there is ignorance and stupidity about mental illness which was thrust onto the national stage with the Virginia Tech massacre of 32 people and the suicide of the killer himself, or the reported fact that we are paying 46,000 private mercenaries $30,000 a month for the same duty we pay our servicemen and women only a small pittance monthly in Iraq, or the fact that the bees are disappearing at alarming rates are all problems we need to fix but what on earth do you do about a government who just kicks people off their islands? Course I shouldn't be surprised because we did the same thing at Bikini Atoll now that I think about it in order to blow their Pacific island paradise up with a hydrogen bomb! What, are we crazy? If so, we are as dangerously crazy as that gunman at Virginia Tech! Time for us to get sane really, really quick. A terrorist attack is even more likely today than before it seems . . . we all hold our breath, waiting. They truly hate us and mean it when they call the United States "The Great Satan."

I'm still hoping to write an article from my journal about what happened after the birth of my seventh grandson to hopefully show that when a family sticks together and keeps trying to support a mentally ill member things can miraculously change. It is so much better that my grandson have both of his parents and now he also gets the positive of having a Grandmom, which he now calls me, around too. He would have missed her all his life if she weren't able to come back to him and be his Mommy.

But! I am so worked up about the state of our country and the world that the next thing I write is going to be a retrospective about our country. What it was like, what events happened, how it's changed, and where we are today. To get that AA I had to take an English course called Critical Thinking and it helped me remember how to write an essay and I'm going to do it.

August 8, 2007

Well, today I am 67 years old! Two husbands, five children and eight grandchildren with another one on the way. Not too shabby.

I want to see the film "The Eleventh Hour" with narrator Leonardo DiCaprio which I understand is an attempt to go further than "An Inconvenient Truth" in getting people to see the reality of global warming and exactly what it means: destruction of our home. It also purports to give hope and remedies to effect changes. It is such a big topic that few want to look very hard at it, too scary. Another thing hard to really look at is the fast approaching pandemic of Bird Flu which authorities say will hit us as hard as the 1918 Spanish flu did. Watched a show that advised staying inside once it's reported to be in our country and to wear surgical masks to decrease exposure. Plan to get some masks and already have storage food. I stopped filling my bird feeder over a year ago and that hurt because I love to watch them. My dad and I used to feed birds on the ocean, one of the few pleasant things we ever did together, so not having bird feeders around is sad to me. Seems they don't doubt this plague is coming but they're not sure when and its almost impossible to be completely ready: no vaccine, not enough respirators in the U.S. to deal with it, anti-virals might help but create flu-like symptoms themselves so they will confuse the issue, and global air flights make it a disease that could jump into a country literally over night. Once here it might be two weeks before it's really diagnosed properly and reported. That only leaves about one week to really implement deterrents according to a World Health Organization official.

Being in denial was easier but got us where we are so I will persist in seeing this stuff and sharing the information in hopes of helping to be part of the remedy rather than part of the problem. Lots to keep aware of and still enjoy life. Am working on my essay. Hope my kids read it. Need to add something about the sad state of psychology today in view of the fact that the American Psychological Association seems to be having a hard time simply stating, "We do not condone or want any part of torture." They've been in bed with the military for a long time and now the cat is out of the bag and the pressure is mounting. Wonder what Bob would have to say about that whole thing?

That Jehovah's Witness guy who made an appointment to come again to debate me about using the true name of Yahweh instead of Jehovah never showed up. They know the true name but refuse to use it. There are other big issues with their doctrine among which is going door to door like they do. When Yahweh wants someone to know something He'll set it up, no need to pound on doors. Sadly, most people don't want to know the truth of our times let alone the TRUTH of all time but if someone inquires I'm ready.

August 21, 2007

Yesterday was my oldest son's birthday, he's 41 now. I'm very proud of him. He's a man with ethics, a man who stands tall even through enormous pressure to fold. When he makes a mistake, he works through it and owns up to it. He is committed to his children. They are his top priority. He looks whatever comes his way straight in the face and never runs away.

Today on democracynow.org news show they interviewed a man who had the most basic understanding of the Mideast I've yet to hear. He knows those countries, their history, how they operate, what the people there want, what has been and will be foolish in regard to dealing with them. About Iraq he simply said, "It's too late." He said we should have left already and he called our troops "hostages". He had no hope really but felt we should leave the region alone to work it out. He talked about the Sunnis, the Shi'aa, and others. He made it clear that Syria has been the best neighbor of all to Iraq but their ability to take in refugees is fast being depleted. He talked about how Jordan and the Saudi's only took refugees who had money and now not those. He admitted that our administration is probably going to attack Iran who he noted was actually our best ally in the beginning of this Iraq war because they hated Sadam. The fact that this war has ripened many Muslims into terrorists is the direct result of our occupation of Iraq, he said, beyond a doubt. He had nothing, really, to offer in the way of a strategy to end this.

Also on the show were two teenagers who are walking from San Francisco to Washington D.C. in support of peace, peace anywhere any time. When asked who was giving the most support to them in their travels they answered, "People who are in their 50's and 60's." I knew elders like me were screaming in their souls. That's why they are coming out to help these brave young people. These kids said this elder support was amazing but they wanted more support from young people because they noted, "We are the future." Yes they are but there are only seven of them today who have decided to demonstrate in this manner to show a commitment to the idea of peace everywhere.

RETROSPECTIVE

RETROSPECTIVE

*An Essay Respectfully Submitted for the Citizens of
the United States to Consider*

In 1940, the year I was born, the U.S. started drafting men while still officially considered to be at peace and the Lend Lease program began helping Russia in particular in its fight against Germany. Although the draft was finally ended in 1973 there is talk of reviving it again in 2007.

At the secret Atlantic conference in 1941 that was convened after the U.S. froze German assets and closed its counsel offices in the U.S., Franklin Roosevelt and Winston Churchill met to outline objectives for a combined war effort. In August Japanese assets in the U.S. were frozen and an embargo went into effect, especially on the exportation of oil to Japan. Then on December 7, 1941, Pearl Harbor was suddenly bombed by Japan in retaliation and that put the war on two fronts for the U.S. and its allies. Today in retaliation mode from 9/11 we are in the Iraq War and oil is still creating problems. Other fronts appear to be looming, such as an Iran and Russian alliance.

The Warsaw Ghetto was sealed off in 1941, followed by the murder of 33,000 men, women and children near Kiev, and the holocaust was in full swing. Finally, after three years of fighting, the allies stormed the Normandy Beaches on June 6, 1944, ultimately winning the war in Europe. Then on August 6, 1945, President Truman ordered the Manhattan Project progeny, Little Boy and Fat Man, to be used. Little Boy (uranium bomb) was dropped on Hiroshima first and then three days later Fat Man (plutonium bomb) was dropped on Nagasaki. World War II was over and the nuclear age had begun. Even though the Soviet Union fell apart in 1989 nuclear war is still threatening us today.

The post war years were full of hope, energy and technological revolution. During this time the traditional American values had full sway: the flag, home, mother, apple pie, pursuit of the American dream, and an abhorrence of divorce. In the early 50's the Korean War was fought as a new type of military involvement: a police action. This effort was a direct result of the fact that the U.S. feared the Soviet Union, an ally in WWII, and its aggressive attempts to spread its brand of Communism which had reared its head in China which borders Korea. Along the way Russia got the atomic bomb too. Julius and Ethel Rosenberg were executed for giving them information on how to make it. This period of time was known as the Eisenhower era. It's also when the military-industrial complex began and about which Eisenhower himself warned us as he left office. Today what he feared has happened: the U.S. is pretty much controlled by that very military-industrial complex which now has global interests.

The first television I saw was at my aunt's in the late 40's. Mostly it had a test pattern on it with evening shows like wrestling of all things. Not like today's entertainment wrestling with hype, colorful costumes, and scantily clad women. It was two burly men in woolen shorts and tops actually wrestling. They also showed boxing, puppet shows, and variety shows like Ed Sullivan eventually.

At first not everyone could get a TV and it was broadcast live in black and white only. When we actually got one in 1952 I watched the "Kukla, Fran and Olli" puppet show after school at the age of 10! I loved the Caboose Goose who was always asking, "Where is my Muddo?!" Seems so stupid now. Families would get together to watch "I Love Lucy" and "Liberace" in the evenings every week. These first shows were all live. Then came color TV, and eventually video tape. As for news shows, Edgar R. Murrow comes to mind who in the early 50's went after the Commie witch-hunt called McCarthyism in which Nixon played a huge role and over which he sprang into national fame.

Few realized the enormous power this medium would bring to bear on our lives. Consumerism began in earnest as people saw ads on TV that whetted their appetites to have stuff, at first stuff they needed but very quickly stuff they just wanted. The first suggestion of crime I remember on TV was in "Dragnet". The first actual violence I remember in a movie was in "Rebel Without a Cause". These were probably not the first, just the ones I saw first. It was many years, though, before blood was seen and graphic sex became a topic in these entertainment mediums. Everyone knows what we have now: horrible, bloody violence and naked sexual encounters.

By 1953 there was an uneasy truce in Korea and we were in a heated arms race with the Soviets with both sides escalating from atomic to hydrogen bombs that they set off in the atmosphere for awhile. The so-called "cold war" was being waged. Both sides finally realized that setting hydrogen bombs off in the atmosphere was not a good idea and took to underground tests. Could the ones in Nevada, I've often wondered, have destabilized an already geophysically active West Coast and/or Yellowstone National Park? Any way you look at it, testing those things is bad. Oh, and about Korea, we have apparently had a presence at the 38th parallel de-militarized zone separating North and South Korea for 46 years now. North Korea is vying for emergence as a nuclear power and South Korea is very nervous because the North has the now fully awakened giant of China backing them while there is American backing for the South.

In 1958 I graduated from a high school that included the children of German rocket scientists recently given citizenship status by an Act of Congress. I was never taught in high school what the Nazi's had attempted and nearly accomplished: the annihilation of European Jews. I was 20 and married before I read Leon Uris' *Exodus* and found out what had happened. My mother verified that it was true—by the time I knew this horrific information it was 1960! Why weren't we taught about the holocaust in history classes? Perhaps it was because my high school was so sensitive to its new German students it omitted this vital information. This is the first "management" of information I recall. Today a spin mentality is the norm and some people are actually trying to claim there was no holocaust at all despite all the horrible pictorial and written evidence.

On October 4, 1957, the Russians had put up Sputnik showing they were ahead of us technologically. When President Kennedy came to office one of his primary goals was to outdistance the Soviets in technology, hence the pressure to "put a man on the moon" by the end of the 60's. Today we want to dominant space for itself, not just to prove technological superiority and we are going to the moon "again".

With the 60's came two major revolutions: Civil Rights and the youthful fight against hypocrisy loosely known as the Hippie Movement or Flower Power. The civil rights movement started in earnest when Rosa Parks decided she would not go to the back of the bus and Southern blacks followed suit everywhere. At the urging of Robert Kennedy in particular, the Supreme Court finally came out for civil rights and ordered desegregation of schools as well as public facilities. Today we see some changes but still discrimination persists and now it's aimed more and more at Latinos.

Just recently I read the "Letter from Eight Clergymen" and Martin Luther King, Junior's response. He was a brilliant scholar and hit the nail on the head beautifully in that letter he sent them back from jail. At the time I never truly realized how very intelligent and educated he was as well as being a minister. The Latinos need a leader of this quality but quite possibly it will put whoever that is on a fast track to assassination. Cesar Chavez came close, at least in California.

In the 60's Hippies took over Haight-Ashbury in San Francisco and also migrated to Taos New Mexico, among other places. They practiced "free" love (really, promiscuous sex) not war, communal living and began experimenting with drugs or as it was known then, "mind expansion". The culmination and epitome of this era was the Woodstock Music Festival in '69. Today Hippydom has re-emerged with the Gen-Xer's but they fall back into society in a low-profile manner when they have kids, which is good, but they are ill prepared to deal in the high-powered, fast-paced marketplace of today.

Because I was married in '59 and had four children by '69, I wasn't involved in the hippie movement or civil rights activism. I would have been if I hadn't had children, I'm sure. Within 10 years many hippies spread out especially in Northern California to live independent of the establishment with some then later rejoining it to become "Yuppies" who basically sold out some of their ideals in order to have and get all the stuff pandered on TV as necessary for a happy life but they also supported save-the-environment or mother earth movements. Now we have more and more people getting on the Green side because of information about global warming and what that could mean: possible extinction of *Homo sapiens*.

About 1962 the general public became aware, finally, that the U.S. was involved in another "police action" in which we were officially stated to be in an advisory capacity. This time it was in Southeast Asia: Vietnam, Laos, and Cambodia. Our involvement started secretly and was an extension of the Indochinese conflicts that started after World War II. The logic behind the U.S. decision to train indigenous troops in South Vietnam was a belief in the "Domino Theory" which maintained that all communist incursions were ultimately inspired and supported by the Soviet Union. Then on March 8, 1965, 3500 Marines were sent in to begin the ground war in Vietnam and by December that year 200,000 U.S. forces were "in country". By 1969 U.S. troops totaled 553,000 according to the online encyclopedia *Wikipedia*. The European nations, Canada, and Britain declined to fight this war with the U.S. although some other nations like Australia, the Republic of Korea, Thailand, and the Philippines sent in troops. There were major anti-war demonstrations against this war for more than a decade, most of the country wanting out of it. Finally, on January 27, 1973 the Paris Peace Accord was signed which called for the withdrawal of U.S. troops within 60 days. We admitted we had lost this war which the Vietnamese continued to fight for another two years. Before the conflict ended completely, 5.1 million people died according to documents released in 1995 by the Vietnamese government. Approximately 50,000 U.S. citizens were killed as a result of this 15 year conflict.

Now 30 years later we have openly gone into a country in continuation of the "Carter Doctrine" to unseat its dictator for our national interests, in this case to insure we have oil, with the help of a few other countries and we are staying around to make sure the government develops like we want it to do. However, the Iraqis have fomented, with outside help no doubt, a religious civil war about which we have no idea what to do but our people are dying because of it. In the meantime an immediate and clear result from our occupation of Iraq is the major recruitment opportunity it has created for Muslim terrorist groups. Not as many of our people have died yet as in Vietnam but the ramifications of this new war bode ill for our freedom from terrorist attack with weapons of mass destruction which was the tenant under which the war erroneously began. Moreover, the war is causing the destabilization of the Mideast. Maybe destabilization is what we want because it wasn't until the early 20th Century that the Ottoman Empire fell which had united Muslim forces for centuries and I suspect only Muslims want to see such a unification again. What we are without a doubt after is control of the Iraqi oil reserves which are said to be the third largest in the world. Saudi Arabia has the first largest oil reserves so that's why they are our buddies. Oil, often called "black gold", is the top natural resource today and there are other countries too where we insist on having an impact in order to assure ourselves the continuation of our current lifestyle which, oddly enough, must logically stop anyway because of the impact the use of oil is having on our planet. The entire scenario appears a little insane with no magic pill to fix it.

Continuing the walk down memory lane which included the nuclear threat and the growth of Russian style communism, in 1961 we were treated to the infamous "Bay of Pigs" debacle when the U.S. mounted an operation to overthrow Fidel Castro which failed miserably. This eventually led to the "Cuban Missile Crisis" with Russia supporting Cuba by putting missiles there just 90 miles off U.S. soil. The U.S. response was to blockade Soviet ships that were bringing more missiles into Cuba, an action which brought the world to the brink of nuclear war. I can remember listening to the news at my workplace that day we were poised for war until such a catastrophe was avoided when the Soviets backed off. Over twenty years later I listened privately to the story of a Navy retiree who was on a ship that actually boarded a Russian vessel during this confrontation and he made it very clear to me how really close we had been to a nuclear war. Now, everyone is pretty careful, taking into consideration alignments such as Russia's with Iran but we could misstep again so easily and then it could all go up in radiated smoke. This is the domino effect I fear.

During the 60's there were assassinations and murders in America. On November 22, 1963, President John F. Kennedy was assassinated with the suspect murdered later on live TV. While there was a report given to the country by the Warren Commission, they also sealed until 2039 secret files about the assassination!

In addition to Medger Evers and Reverend Martin Luther King, Jr. being murdered, I remember three young men who disappeared and were finally found dead and buried. More than three decades later some justice was finally meted out for these murders. After King was killed, Presidential Contender Robert Kennedy, well on his way to winning the Democratic Presidential nomination, was murdered at the Ambassador Hotel in Los Angeles right after the California primary. I was still politically active but concentrating more on my family and I still voted. Today people fear their votes really don't count because of the Supreme Court's decision that Bush would be president and the voting irregularities that were documented during his second election. Just recently computerized voting programs have been found to be easy to hack so that's troubling too. Then in Bush's second election there were concerns about voter fraud especially in Ohio and electoral materials from that state were ordered saved but have recently been found to have "disappeared".

During the 60's the youth of the nation experimented, flagrantly, with drugs and LSD was legal then. A university professor, Timothy Leary, supported its use and was ultimately fired by Harvard. A marijuana economy developed in several areas of the nation and became entrenched. Today we have terrible damages to our families and the whole society from illegal drugs like methamphetamine, heroin and various forms of cocaine while the relatively harmless marijuana is lumped by the feds into this category when it should no doubt be legalized for many reasons. If it were so bad why would pharmaceutical companies be trying to synthesize THC right now? To make a lot of money that's why.

At the end of the 60's one of the worst examples of an alternative "free" lifestyle was the deeply sick Manson Family commune on Spahn Ranch whose activities ended in the Tate-LaBianca murders in August of 1969 with references to the Beatles' White Album, especially the song "Helter Skelter". This startled the nation which was fascinated by the Manson Family trials in much the same way we watched the O.J. Simpson trial 25 years later. The only difference being that Manson and his cohorts were found guilty. The Manson Family murders, the killing of eight nurses by Richard Speck and the murder of an entire rural family on November 14, 1959 which was immortalized in the Truman Capote book "In Cold Blood", are the beginnings of my memories of the escalation of mass and serial murders which are now plaguing the U.S. Prior to these events in our country I only remember the Black Dahlia murder of the 40's. I am sure there were more murders than I remember, not publicized and/or not known by me, but I am equally sure there were far fewer such acts of diabolical evil when I was young. Today a lot people even collect mass murder trivia!

Unbelievably, the 1970s were ushered in with four protesting college students being killed and nine wounded by the National Guard at Kent State University on May 4, 1970. The Kent State demonstrations against the invasion of Cambodia had started on Friday, May 1st. The "Riot Act" was read twice over the weekend and on Monday the students assembled anyway with National Guardsmen shooting tear gas, advancing with fixed bayonets and finally firing their weapons on the crowd. The students were hurling rocks and verbal abuse. After this happened, U.S. students everywhere got the message and settled down. They got quieter about their divergent views from the establishment—the "free speech movement" on college campuses was over. Today students are being even more careful because of Homeland Security.

During the 70's the war in Vietnam was unpopular to the point of demonstrations by a cross section of the entire populace. Jane Fonda even visited the enemy in North Vietnam and is vilified to this day for doing that. Then, in the early 70's Nixon ended the Vietnam War two weeks before the election which he went on to win for his second term in office. I have now heard reported on TV it has been discovered from audio taped conversations that Nixon had considered ending that war more than a year previously but on the advice of Henry Kissinger he waited until just before the election, for political advantage, to stop the war. Today we have demonstrations all over the world against our invasion of Iraq which has no effect at all.

On August 8, 1973, Nixon resigned when faced with three articles of impeachment for accusations of perjury stemming from the Watergate matter. Many thought that legal action should have been taken against him after Nixon's resignation to avoid impeachment. Instead he was "pardoned" by President Ford who had become Vice President by Nixon's appointment after the elected VP Spiro Agnew resigned in disgrace! We have seen an impeachment action in the 90's, all over a blue dress and Clinton's "parsing" of the English language. Many are calling for impeachment of Bush the Second because of the invasion of Iraq on false premises but it's clearly not to be.

The 70's were also marked by a continuation of the "sexual freedom" movement that started in the 60's. Homosexuals "came out of the closet" by droves and protested for equal rights. Women declared they also wanted equal rights and began to have babies out of wedlock deliberately. Books were written about the merits of "open marriage" and "wife swapping". Feminism reached ugly levels with men reacting in various ways including being violent toward strong women and refusing to accept traditional male responsibilities like supporting their children. An equal-rights constitutional amendment for women took years to put forth, but it failed. Today women still make less than men and recently the Supreme Court ruled an effort to challenge pay discrimination has to happen within 180 days of employment and yet it's almost impossible to know another employee's salary which usually is only discovered accidentally or after years of service.

It was in the 70's when I learned about the corruption in bureaucracies with federal funding being operated at a local level. The amount of wasted social action dollars just in the agency I worked for was staggering, in the millions. We also often hear of huge amounts of money being distributed by the government for vague studies while spending for social services has been rapidly decreased since the Clinton Administration. In 2007, hobbling of justice by the politicization of the Department of Justice is being investigated by Congress which finally occasioned the resignation of Bush-appointee and old crony Attorney General Alberto Gonzales for either allowing the hiring and firing of attorneys for political reasons, for supporting particular prosecutions or lack of prosecutions for the same reasons, and for supporting the Bush administration's insistence on using torture methods opposed by the Geneva Convention and surveillance without warrants. According to Gonzales' testimony in hearings, he generally states he does not know or remember anything of value regarding these matters even though he was the head of this national department which, at the least, suggests malfeasance of office.

Domestic violence started being discussed openly by the late 70's and shelters were established over time for abused women and children. Today domestic violence is rising with especially children being the victims more and more while social services efforts to help them have failed miserably. There are now some specialized police programs to handle the situation better but it's such a problem that an underground network has sprung up to help women and children start a new life with new identities to escape violence.

The first inkling the populace really had of a big problem came in the 70's when OPEC took shape and then flexed its muscles resulting in us having to wait in line for gas. The Carter Doctrine was framed which basically said any effort to keep oil from our shores would be met with force if necessary. Anyone today can see where that got us. We should have started getting free of our oil addiction right then. Then in 1979 the Iran hostage crisis began with 52 of our citizens held by Iran for 444 days!

A big national scare came when on March 28, 1979 there was a nuclear accident in one of the reactors at Three Mile Island nuclear power plant. This accident was nothing compared to the Chernobyl accident in the Ukraine on April 27, 1986 that killed and is still killing thousands of people and perhaps started a process called the China Syndrome explained in a movie by the same name starring Jane Fonda and Jack Lemon that hit the screens a couple of months after the Three Mile Island accident. Seems the demonstrators of the past were wise to be worried. What will happen when it gets there if that radioactive matter is on its way to the center of the earth?

During the 80's, while the country tried to recover from the national trauma of the Vietnam War as well as the civil rights violence and assassinations, our culture continued with "free" sex attitudes, and government corruption grew along with increasing violence in both the adult and youth populations. Then we began to see mankind's huge impact on the entire planet and its systems when in 1985 the British discovered a hole in the ozone layer over Antarctica. Also early in this decade the knowledge spread about the deadly AIDS virus (HIV) and sexual revolutionaries were jolted into becoming circumspect in their sexual activities. Condoms became the device of choice to keep sex free to the point, ultimately, of their distribution in our public schools. The sexual revolution made AIDS possible and now we have the HIV virus along with sexual promiscuity to deal with in our families.

There were also several very unpopular military skirmishes in South America during this period. Additionally, the late 80's and all through the 90's saw major destruction in the spiritual beliefs of the "baby boomer" generation. On November 18, 1978 the Jonestown cult massacre stunned the nation. Over 900 people were killed, some in suicide and many murdered, which included Congressman Leo J. Ryan. Then corruption gave the religious a one two punch by virtue of the Jim and Tammie Bakker and Jimmy Swaggart TV ministries scandals. This was topped off by the slow revelation of an overabundance of pedophiles among the priesthood of the Catholic Church. Many well-meaning people lost their faith and had no where to go for hope or absolution anymore. I was fortunate because after searching for 15 years, in 1994 I was taught a body of knowledge that comforts me while explaining what is actually going on in this mad world. If you are interested please go to *www.soundingthetrumpet.com* for an education that will stop you in your tracks. There is a seeming rush to give up faith when this is the time we will need it the most, but only the TRUTH will help us, not man-made traditions and lies to gain power and money.

The late 80s saw a ray of hope with the fall of the Berlin Wall typifying the fall of Communism in the Soviet Union which country crumbled into diverse and often fighting smaller "nations". Glasnost was in style and the threat of nuclear war between the U.S. and Russia seemed to disappear over night. By '96 the U.S. was involved with bailing out the economy of the devastated new Russian state whose citizens were alternatively starving and freezing. A Mafia type economy began to take over Russia as American freedom of enterprise, better known as capitalism, tried to replace communism. We also got involved in trying to bring peace to some Slavic countries which began mass murdering their religious minorities while trying to grab power in the political vacuum created by the collapse of the Soviet Union. The rest of the world also took a stand against these actions. The U.N. became very involved in "police actions" with heavy support from the United States military might. We were giving lip service to taking problems to the U.N. but when they didn't agree with us and it came time to invade Iraq we formed a sort of coalition and just did it.

Soviet technology was on the black market during the 90's and emerging countries began to try buying nuclear bombs outright along with the materials and technology to make more. Quite correctly Hillary Clinton dubbed the world a "global village" so the U.S. obviously had much at stake in helping to stop these former Soviet Union geopolitical upheavals. Previously, during the early 90s a "surgical" war with Iraq was fought because it had tried to move in on its neighbors, Saudi Arabia and Kuwait. In the Mideast the problems were about oil AND religion. This hotbed of problems began to be our biggest nemesis and now we have the problem of the Iraq War. There is also the fact that Iraq is basically a country of tribes and our government has never understood tribes nor has it dealt with them well here at home.

In the U.S., on the cultural level, the 90's geared up in a diverse polarity of the deep institutionalization of selfishness as a "good" value on the one hand and on the other hand the slow development of Generation X in a swing back to Hippie values and lifestyles. Alternative spiritual doctrines and medicines grew rapidly along with communications technology which made the World Wide Web possible for the common man, the internet having only been used by scientists and the military before this time. Today the internet is widely used but oftentimes for pornography which has become a plague in regards to abuse of children. While users must be diligent to evaluate sources, the internet provides tons of free information now made available to anyone in the world with access to a computer and an internet connection which can be had at cyber-cafes. Citizen journalism has grown into a business by the emergence of blog sites that have proven to be valuable and have documented situations while also attempting to put forth ideas. They are actually citizen editorials.

Our President, Hillary's husband Bill, was our brilliant but sexually amoral President in the 90's who admitted he had smoked pot but said he "didn't inhale" and he pandered openly to people of color who loved him deeply. As the 90s wore on, the poor got poorer, welfare was cut, Medicaid was cut, and Social Security and its viability was challenged just as the baby boomers began to be in line for retirement. On a more positive note, in some circles the 90's were called the Decade of the Brain because of the great advances in understanding how it worked and medicines were created to assist the mentally ill with their symptoms. Today people with brain disease have the medicine they need but there is little public understanding about mental illness and there is still major discrimination against those suffering from it.

In the late 90's things in the world continued in the same vein: Saddam Hussein continued his wily efforts to outfox the U.N. weapons inspectors (so we have been told), North Korea launched a ballistic missile, Israel suffered the assassination of a leader and continued alternately to make war and peace with the PLO, famine continued in African countries, El Nino and now La Nina disrupted weather patterns causing worldwide flooding, the hole in the ozone layer got bigger, the greenhouse effect was mentioned more and thought to be happening partly because the Amazon Forest was going up in smoke (a treaty was introduced to address environmental problems but not accepted by some of the major violators), volcanoes were beginning to erupt with greater regularity, the drug culture was disabling-killing-imprisoning hundreds of thousands of our people, the water everywhere in the U.S. (and probably the world) was compromised, and because the Soviet Union had been dissolved, America's defenses were trimmed and there was talk of a New World Order.

We arrived in the 21st Century still falling apart morally and disunified. The common people who were raised with time honored American values were getting old and tired. Those of all ages who were in power were apparently hell-bent on world domination. This powerful country of great promise was in chaos. The election of 2000 was a farce with former Vice President Gore (who was an advocate for environmental protection for decades) receiving more of the popular vote than the winning candidate, George W. Bush (Junior or The Second or "W" by which he later became imperialistically known). The fantasy of the "chads" was played out with the Supreme Court deciding who would be President. This confirmed my suspicion that voting was a nonsensical action.

As the century changed from 20th to 21st, the computerization of power grids, weaponry, information systems, communications, financial institutions, and much more were threatened by one simple little computer problem nicknamed Y2K that theorists thought might devastate the world. That was overcome easily and the dire predictions were not realized but now we have computer viruses attacking regularly to the point we have to have virus insurance for computers. I've heard more than one person speculate that the companies who have the anti-virus software might have something to do with the proliferation of those very viruses! Who knows!?

Then came 9/11 or 911 or September 11th, 2001, when the North and South Towers of the World Trade Center in the financial district of Manhattan were attacked by terrorists for the second time in a decade. The Pentagon was also attacked and a hijacked plane was brought down preventing another attack. More than 3,000 of our citizens were killed. The War on Terror began. Our world had changed dramatically and, apparently, irrevocably just as the planet itself was in extremis as proved by the 2004 earthquake and tsunamis, hurricane Katrina, and the melting of polar icecaps and glaciers to name some symptoms that come most readily to mind.

We now know we are threatened by chemical and biological weapons of mass destruction in addition to our fears about nuclear weapons. To ease our fears we have allowed the establishment of a secret agency with broad powers including, it appears, the suspension of *habeas corpus* and the erosion of our cherished freedoms of privacy and speech.

As we undertook this new, different, war, the U.S. went to Afghanistan to find the 9/11 culprit, Osama bin Laden, who by the way hails from Saudi Arabia. We never found bin Laden but freed the Afghanis from his friends called the Taliban for now at least. The stage was set for the next war known as "Iraqi Freedom" to overthrow Saddam Hussein's brutal regime that supposedly had weapons of mass destruction. If they did, they got rid of them really quick because we have never found them. Little is said about the fact the good 'ole USA has biological and chemical and nuclear weapons of mass destruction or that we put Saddam in power to begin with. But apparently we are the kingpin on the planet, the power that "knows" when and how to use such weapons and that knows who should be in power when and where. It appears to the rest of the world, it is quite clear, that we think we are the benevolent dictator of the world while espousing that we are a democracy and want that for all mankind. Maybe we do or maybe we just want their oil, etc.

We invaded Iraq, we overthrew Hussein's government, finally found him, and made sure he was tried and executed (or was it one of his doubles?) by the new democratic government which on other levels is barely functioning. As a result of our intercession now Iraq has a religious civil war going on with our soldiers in the middle of it. Iran has apparently sent insurgents into Iraq to further destabilize it hoping, no doubt, to annex it, with our soldiers in the middle of this as well. Additionally there is a resurgence of both the Taliban and Osama bin Laden's group. To state it simply, we are in a really, really big mess.

We are hard pressed to figure this all out while Iran sits there defiant and steadily building into a nuclear power. Well, why not? We stopped Hitler from getting it then we got his scientists and made it ourselves and used it. Then we let India and Pakistan, not to mention, Russia, France, England, and Israel develop this abomination without much conflict. The big wild card, though, is The People's Republic of North Korea which has apparently set off a small nuclear device after being warned over and over and over by our government not to do that. The latest on that seems to indicate they are trading their nuclear power ambitions for goodies from us, not sure though.

Meanwhile China, which has loaned the U.S. massive amounts of money for a war only about 20% of our country is in favor of continuing, is emerging as one of the world's greatest powers. It was always called the sleeping giant and now that giant has awakened. While industrializing it is spewing tons and tons and tons of carbon into the atmosphere. I read recently that the U.S. West Coast gets smog from China! So now we come to global warming which is a short phrase for a host of climatic problems that threatens our very existence although there are people who think this is a hoax, perpetrated just to make more money from efforts to fight a fearsome catastrophe in the making.

These are some highlights of what has gone on this past 67 years with many more topics of interest falling by the wayside of time and sensibility. Some current facts are: recently there was a "wild storm in Europe" shortly after which there were truly amazing multiple snow and ice storms in the U.S. Midwest; more of our troops are apparently heading for Iraq even though the Democrats took over power in the Senate and House and other countries are decreasing their troops; people are still driving gas guzzling SUV's; child kidnapping and molestation as well as child pornography on the internet is at epidemic proportions in the U.S.; the most popular news shows are the comedy ones like *The Daily Show* (it's either laugh or cry I guess); celebrities are adopting infants from poor countries whose families give them up thinking they have done something good for their children, and so on and so on, *ad infinitum.*

Who knows how long this can continue? I certainly don't. It is far too complicated and totally, totally out of my hands. But I can comment on what I see and hear because we do still have the 1st Amendment power of free speech. I think.

Seeing the handwriting on the wall, many communities in the U.S. are economically localizing as fast as they can. Our country is in the midst of a vast de-centralization process, quietly. I don't think the current administration is even aware of what is going on throughout the country even with all its expanded powers. The real America, the one we all know and love is still working as it always has with the people taking control of their country if not by election then by the simple process of attending to the business of survival. A good website to visit for information about that is *www.willitseco nomiclocalization.org.*

Families are beginning to come back together, people who lived to work to buy stuff are beginning to simplify their life and focus more on home and hearth, and towns and cities are coping with their developing needs in the face of what appears to be coming. We are opting out of the mess that exists, one we never made and don't support, going back to tried and true values in an effort to stem a tide. Unfortunately only the moon leaving its orbit and slamming into the earth can stop the tides so one must ask oneself, "What is going to happen next?"

Or to Put it All Another Way

It is true that what actors call sense memory psychologists call Post Traumatic Stress Disorder. Everyone calls it life. We only have now but we constantly remember and relate to what we remember of then. Today this phenomena produces a very unpleasant feeling in those who recall a time when our young were not captured by drugs, were not incarcerated in "schools", and when we had a feeling we could have an impact on our world, that certain tenants were unassailable, that mad terrorism can't touch us, and that the future would bring a better and more wonderful world, maybe even a utopia.

In the late 50's, something big happened. It was so big it took decades to understand how it would impact everything. It had a name: Sputnik. We walked the halls at recess, getting into our lockers as the announcement came over the PA system. The Russians had just put up a space machine and it was circling the world! Everyone was amazed and afraid they might send down an A-bomb aimed at the U.S. Sure we knew about Hiroshima and Nagasaki but that was different, that was all out war and we knew about Pearl Harbor, or thought we did.

From then on THE BOMB fear literally hung over the world. As the arsenals grew, everyone knew the fear of the possible, maybe even probable annihilation, of mankind. Bomb shelters were built and the fear was so deep it was seldom mentioned. You had to live with it along with the knowledge that Russia was ahead of the U.S. in technology.

Overkill went into effect. Bigger, better bombs and intercontinental ballistics missiles were built that could cross oceans carrying those bombs.

Soon, hundreds (maybe thousands) of their bombs were aimed at us and ours at them. Total insanity took over and we knew it but did not know how this situation would manifest changes in our country.

Simply put, this fear and insanity might have been why people began to focus on wanting and getting. TV helped of course. All that wonderful stuff to have. Besides it was good for the economy, put people to work. It led us from thinking about what life was about, what was really right and wrong, into concerning ourselves almost primarily with getting, having, and experiencing NOW—before it was too late. Of course, this had all been prophesied in the Bible and all of Christianity took great pride in chronicling the fall of morality and decency even among blood relatives. The sheer numbers of homeless people, a majority of whom are mentally ill, make it clear that people were not looking at family in the same way they once did. TV did one thing unusual and probably needed: it showed the Vietnam War in all its colorful gory detail. That no doubt is why there were so many demonstrations. The war couldn't be forgotten about, it was right there in your face at night.

Kennedy declared a technological war when he announced that the U.S. would put a man on the moon by the end of the 60's and it did (or did it? ever see an unsettling film called *Capricorn 3?*). Now there is talk of going back there and establishing a station, but first we put into orbit a satellite that could assess the Van Allen radiation belts that are the really big problem with going anywhere but just outside our atmosphere.

There was no Cold War, though it was called that. The real war was technology. Now if you could see a map showing the amount of satellites circling the globe you would be amazed. There are thousands of them! A technological triumph happened just before the Soviet Union collapsed. We put into orbit the Hubbell "telescope." I have also wondered if it is a laser weapon. See how paranoid everyone is, even me?

It is easy to see how we got where we are now, in retrospect—hindsight always being better. But while it evolved there were signposts, esoteric ones and obvious ones. When my friend Mary said to me in about 1962, "I think that if I ever stopped wanting, I would be better off dead, that's what it's all about," I was amazed. It was a stunning statement. Must just be her I thought, something wrong in her. After all she went on to buy a Corvette and left her husband and two small children without any remorse or guilt!! Forty-eight years later it is clear to me that all too many people were thinking this way for decades.

It seems to be changing now though. Our government has made it so that we have to start our own process of providing safety for our loved ones and some of us are doing it despite what they do in Iraq or elsewhere. When it gets tough, the tough get going. That has always been a U.S. credo and our elected officials forgot that. We don't need them. We will go on and secure ourselves, peacefully too. I'm glad for this direction because the other would have been very bad.

There are others who say they want peace, environmental protection, and so forth but they are still manifesting "I want" in their daily lives of acquisition. There is a global consciousness in place and serious fear of annihilation by means of environmental death has suddenly jumped to center stage. Officialdom is very slow to catch up, much too little, much too late, simply because the corporations were protecting their moneyed interests through what we now call "lobbying" which as it is practiced today was once called "bribing".

The United States is no doubt one of the best countries to live in but fundamentally big government and the "I want" syndrome have undermined what this nation stood for at its establishment. Liberty is a big word. This liberty, defined by the populace now, has become a cancer which eats up, especially, the young of our nation, a peculiarly nihilistic proposition (fated to cause annihilation). Moreover, this current *status quo* strikes at the very heart of a once treasured honesty (did you see "Wag the Dog?" which will probably make you physically ill—I saw it three weeks before Clinton testified before the Grand Jury and three days later he bombed terrorists). One output of this so-called liberty nowadays in the U.S. means the common person must put up with a Kafkaesque and dehumanizing trek (read *The Trial*" by Kafka if you haven't and weep) through bureaucracy to start a little business, to get mandated help in time of need, to secure quality medical care, to right any wrong, and sometimes to just get the proper change from a purchase in a store.

It all appears to be beyond treatment, to be terminal. Surgery is too inhumane (can't just have a revolution and kill all the bad guys, there are too many anyway, including ourselves), chemo is too hard and distasteful for the rebellious pleasure seekers being bred now (they could not take the heat, couldn't do without), and the people who know something is terribly wrong, the ones with the sense memories or PTSD symptoms are too old to stop it now and they are riddled with guilt because they coddled, spoiled and accepted the moral changes that fed their own lusts—they are guilty of creating it. We all forgot that attention and love and the proverbial rod made good citizens. Instead many got the money and threw it at their kids in the form of whatever popular material goods TV was advertising as necessary for happiness. And almost no one is happy. Not really.

It's based on a lie now, the American Dream. Can't be taken seriously. Nothing said, reported, quoted or rumored can be trusted because of the current "spin" mentality. It would be better to call "spin" what it is: a way to make a more clever lie by incorporating truthful elements that are engineered logically to wrong conclusions which is then "leaked" to the masses. The basic tenant of logic is that if the premise is a lie, the whole thing is a lie.

We've recently found out that hundreds of thousands, maybe a million families are going to lose their homes to lenders who made them loans that had interest changes the buyers didn't understand. This is what the so-called sub-prime market has done. The key element of the American Dream was to own one's home and that's very hard to do by any but pretty well off families now.

So, what do we do? Some of us are trying to simplify our life, to still live "properly" under the threat of annihilation, being careful not to speak out too much, and in many cases some of us are buying into the lies because we want, first of all, TO LIVE and secondly TO HAVE as much as we can get of the "good" life before its over (individual death, annihilation, The End). The survival instinct is an essential ingredient in human nature and it wills a person to conform his/her behavior to survive. It takes an inbred intellectualism or a spiritual revelation to defy the survival instinct. Understanding that successful acquisition is not what makes a person happy is the only antidote for the "I want" syndrome.

Just 30 years ago people were leaving small communities for the opportunities of the big cities. Today people are trying desperately to get back to small towns where there has classically been less crime, a slower pace of life, and an appreciation of life's grander values. So desperate are they that people with strong educational credentials, such as a doctorate or master's degree, will accept part time jobs out of their field and for a pittance of the salary they command in a big city in order to get their family to a small community.

Life is harder but nicer in a small town. The icon of "culture", meaning opera, theatre, and music, can be produced and experienced on video and DVD now so live, big city performances are no longer required to enjoy anyone's idea of "culture". The computer has allowed many innovative souls to work from their home, traveling when necessary to the centers of commerce, only as required. This is all well and good, but what of the people who can't get out, the people in the ghettos of those big cities? What of the impact on the smaller cities which then become a conglomerate of dissimilar persons all striving for the feeling of a "home town" and yet driving real estate values up with the impact of their big city money upon entry?

One only has to look at the supermarket to realize how vulnerable we all are. If the food stores shut down for some reason, most people would not have a clue how to survive. Growing one's own food or store housing is not that popular a past time except among Mormons and among the tough survivalists who are facing reality now and setting up self-sufficient homesteads. Most people, hard working people, are living paycheck to paycheck and if their company is downsized or roboticized they and their families could be on the street within a few months.

The complexity of living in the U.S. now, the economic realities of the majority of people living beyond their means, the lack of morals and devaluing of one human life, the abandonment of child rearing, the massive impact of drugs on young and old, the helplessness of people to feed themselves, the incredible scandals at high levels where role models dwell, and at the bottom of it all the fear of global nuclear war (still possible because even though the U.S. and Russia are now friendly those bombs are still there and could proliferate quickly into irresponsible and even insane hands) has many of us silently screaming at the core of our beings. Such a lovely promise of a country with freedom for all, governed by all, and so horrible to watch it start to die slowly of an assortment of societal cancers which no one seems capable of looking at clearly or impacting.

In retrospect, what has happened over the last 67 years is apparent but it's very alarming to realize a requisite requirement for this state of affairs was desensitization of the common man and woman and that it only took about that long to achieve. The idea of taking a life, murder, was a powerful taboo in the 1940's. Now, there are parents killing their own children at alarming rates. Sometimes they just forget the kids are in the car and leave them locked in there all day to die!

Life is becoming cheap and more and more ruthless here in the Land of the Free. We expect such traits in "third world" countries and in the barbaric nations throughout history, but we see it now in the most powerful nation that ever existed on the earth, the United States of America, where once it was touted a person could achieve his or her dream because of protected rights. Sure, we all know that some people had more rights than others and despite the civil rights movement that inequity is still the case but more and more minorities were becoming able to get the dream for their families, but now people of all colors are having a harder time actualizing that dream.

Is this similar to the proverbial fall of Rome? But we have a President and they had a Dictator, an Emperor who thought he was God! The reality is that it feels more and more like we have a dictator too now. You might also say well, they did not have the "bomb" as an underlying threat to hope and decency. That's definitely true. This situation has caused a new progression of events to an inevitable end: corruption in high places, abominable crimes increasing, primary family dissolution, the "gimme" value structure, and deep abiding unhappiness even in the so-called "silent majority" who see it and feel guilty but who are too old and glutted by their lusts to respond. In short, it is overwhelming and very scary. Our young people today don't even know how it once was. What they see is the norm for them.

And now we add to all this the loss of freedoms and the gain of fear, fear of terrorism. Never before have we confronted the specter of mass murder striking suddenly in our nation by people who apparently hate us. For what do they hate us? Probably for our power and excellent life style they see on TV. They also hate our economic imperialism. Even though the terrorism is couched in religious terms it is the same ole "gimme" in operation—the haves and the have nots. Sounds a lot like Marx's Dialectic Materialism doesn't it? Odd, just as Marxism has been dying out we see the societal operation Marx explained rise upward to blackened skies, now on a worldwide level.

In fact the U.S. is beginning to develop space weapons and declaring itself the pre-eminent power in space as well as on the earth. We recently refused an invitation by the Chinese to talk about a space treaty regarding uses of space and territorial rights in space. Since then China has sent a missile into space and destroyed one of its own satellites just to deliver a message to us! They have joined in a race that never should have begun. We have something like 400+ operational satellites which if shot apart would have the effect of making us and especially our military unable to talk with each other or to go on with business as usual. The military-industrial complex has now geared up to make enormous profits from this space race and we are left to look over our heads and wonder what might rain down onto us from above.

It's true the minimum wage is being slowly raised to over $7 per hour but that is still a pittance because of inflation which no one talks about. There are calls to impeach President Bush and Vice President Cheney but the Democrats have said they won't do that. Our infrastructure now includes something like 180,000 bridges that are structurally deficient or not functionally appropriate any more (translation: they were built for 30,000 cars a day and now have 150,000 cars a day go over them for instance) and one that bridged the mighty Mississippi and joined our famous Twin Cities collapsed killing or maiming over 80 people! So the reality is that we are now fighting a war to get oil, the use of which is killing our planet, to fuel our already too many cars for our insufficient bridges! What tomorrow holds is anyone's guess but by the time you read this there will be more, much more.

The American Dream has become An American Scream. In a scream there is sometimes hope for change but how could that possibly happen in time to prevent all the disasters that we are facing, to say nothing of the irrevocable, underlying terror of nuclear annihilation? "The sword of Damocles," Jack called it and it's still hanging over all of us oh these many years after he was killed in Dallas.

The cost to the world of our greed is enormous. Anyone wanting to understand how we have gobbled up the resources of emerging countries, used their poor as slave labor, and have polluted their environment and culture legally, and sometimes illegally, should read *Confessions of an Economic Hitman* and *A Secret History of the American Empire* by John Perkins which ties it all together and makes one face the reality that we have let this happen. We the People have let this happen because we wanted the "Good Life" so much and didn't pay close enough attention to where all this was going.

Perkins carefully shows that corporations are running not only the U.S. but the entire world. He proposes that in order to stop what is happening we need to take personal responsibility. He points out that people run corporations and he thinks they are feeling guilty (like he felt for his involvement in it) and just need to be given permission to change their goal to a unifying principal such as "creating a stable, sustainable and peaceful world for all people." In a recent appearance I heard him say he's not worried about being assassinated because of his disclosure about economic hitmen and worse because his books are singing to the choir basically. He did note that more and more people are reading his first book, the media is giving it more attention, and while this might seem to put him in danger he has concluded that it won't simply because if he died even more books of his would sell. Additionally, he cites examples of where people like Rosa Parks and Rachel Carson for instance have made a big difference in starting movements and he is clearly trying to start one. He talks about a group called the Rainforest Action which has been successful he says in all its battles against corporations.

He is hopeful it can be changed simply by putting pressure on corporations, by talking with their leadership because he says they are caught in the same trap he was in and that they would really like to do the right thing. Perkins also stated, though, that whether he dies in 20 minutes, 2 years, or 20 years is irrelevant because he is doing what he feels is right finally and he would die a happy man with a clear conscience. He also noted that the only thing to fear is doing nothing. This man is clearly trying to empower people to believe it can change. That it must change in fact and he recommends they go forth to make that a reality by mounting non-violent actions against corporations. Clearly he says in his new book that the political realm will follow with better laws and more moral goals if the corporations change because they are running everything anyway all over the world. Getting corporations to be accountable, if we can, will help everywhere and in more matters than just global warming including in Darfur and the rest of Africa where there is horrible mayhem and bloody murder as the result of the wealth not being distributed to all indigenous peoples instead of to a few corrupt rulers who play the game with corporations to let them literally steal the resources of country after country.

He mentions Amy Goodman and the DemocracyNow.org news show and the internet as great instruments of change. The regular media he notes is, again, controlled by corporations but other news sources are emerging which are not. In October of 2007 a one week opening for non-profits to obtain radio licenses was declared by the FCC, a once in a generation opportunity said Amy Goodman. Many licenses awarded means more real news will go out throughout regions of the U.S. over the radio.

Right after I saw Mr. Perkins talk about his new book on C-Span, I saw a discovery channel show that featured the flight of birds migrating. All kinds of beautiful birds. In one instance a group landed in an ancestral migratory area to seek food and shelter before continuing and it was befouled by an industrial operation. Then a bird floundered in the goop and the rest suddenly left in fear. How different from the place where a group of cranes stopped to rest and an old woman walked out to them and hand fed them grain. They came right up to her to eat out of her hand. It comes down to which of those scenarios do we want to see continue?

It will be more than interesting to see if the current local sustainability efforts in different regions in the U.S. along with activism to get corporations to make their goals consistent with what humanity needs will succeed to bring about a change in the planet and its peoples. However, an important change that needs to happen now is to get Bush/Cheney out of the White House ASAP and get someone in there who will actually refuse to trample on the Constitution of the United States of America or to rattle sabers at Iran. If we don't get Bush/Cheney out then the next administration, Republican or Democrat, will most certainly try to keep the imperial powers exercised by the Bush/Cheney administration and allowed by the Republican Congress. Like that Brit Lord Acton once said, "Power corrupts, and absolute power corrupts absolutely." That's why they put those checks and balances in the Constitution, to prevent exactly what we have seen happen during the last six years in the most powerful country in the world, our country. Under immense pressure many people in the Bush inner circle have left including political mastermind Karl Rove who is now, no doubt, fiendishly working to get another Republican slate elected in 2008.

Although a lady President is tempting to support, I must conclude that in reality such an eventuality would worsen our relations with Islamic countries and terrorists who do not have the ability to deal with a woman on such a level. This may not be the time for feminists to propel a woman into the Oval Office just because they can. This might be the time to let a man take the helm, one who is not afraid and who will do what is necessary while presenting strength and mercy at the same time to our current enemies with a hope of making them our future friends before it is too late. Maybe it has already gone too far but someone has to try, someone our adversaries will talk with and respect. The United States of America is at a gigantic crossroads with many ghost paths bisecting it. Dare we to believe that the slow but massive turn-around underway throughout the country is in time to prevent nuclear holocaust, massive climate change, and more?

I have to put this continuing story to bed sometime so here it stops for this essay but I hope by the time you read it we are not at war with Iran. For those who might read this and understand what I say now, I have always striven to be a fair witness.

ACKNOWLEDGEMENTS

Thanks to the people in my life who have taught me, as hard as it may have been at times, what I needed to know to be able to perceive the heart of a matter rather than to be naive, to conceive of how to present information by use of the written word, and to more than survive what life has dealt to me. You know who you are.

Special thanks to Fred, Tony and Mona, Debbie, Renay and Donald, Dr. Gill, Dennis and others who taught me to know and to be able to prove the TRUTH thus saving me from despair and instead making me humble enough to receive correction and comfort in the face of anything.

Appreciation and love go to my children who lived a life with me that is hard to understand and even harder to appreciate. To my grandchildren I leave this thought: love is all that matters in the end.

Thanks to Jason for coincidentally sharing my vision and saying in a few words what I took an entire book to say. Thanks to Ginny for her invaluable help with this project.

Laird Smith